HOW TO
START YOUR
OWN BUSINESS

HOW TO
START YOUR
OWN BUSINESS
...AND MAKE IT WORK

Consultant editor Cheryl Rickman

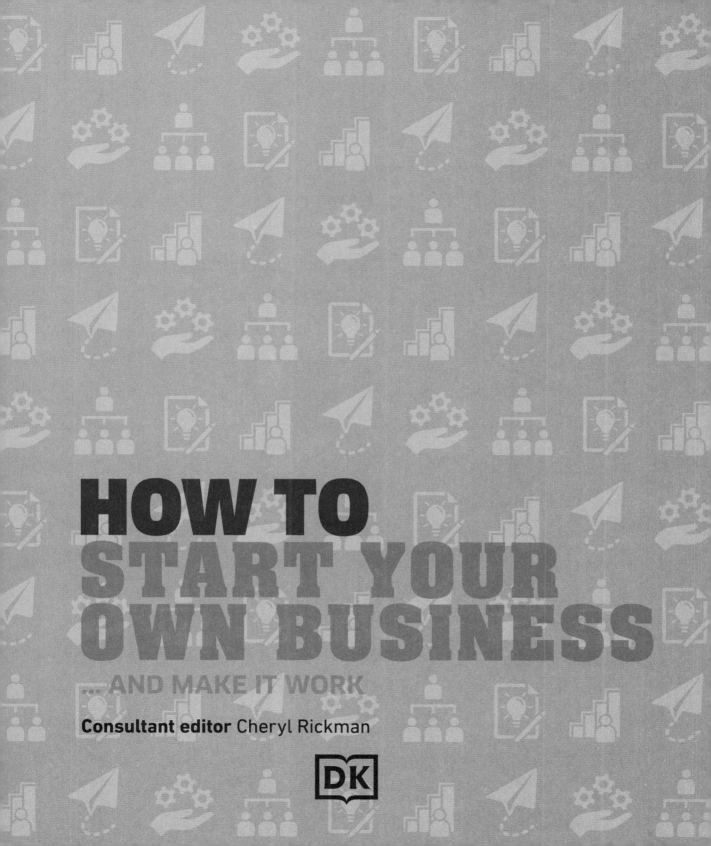

Senior Editors Chauney Dunford,
Scarlett O'Hara, Alison Sturgeon
Art Editor Mark Cavanagh
Editors John Andrews, Daniel Byrne, Sharon Lucas,
Fiona Plowman, Steve Setford, Lucy Sienkowska,
Andy Szudek, Rachel Warren Chadd
Designers Vanessa Hamilton, Clare Joyce,
Mark Lloyd, Daksheeta Pattni
Managing Editor Gareth Jones
Managing Art Editor Lee Griffiths
Senior Production Editor Andy Hillard
Senior Production Controller Rachel Ng
Jacket Designer Tanya Mehrotra, Surabhi Wadhwa Gandhi
Publisher Liz Wheeler
Publishing Director Jonathan Metcalf
Art Director Karen Self
Jacket Design Development Manager Sophia MTT

First published in Great Britain in 2021 by
Dorling Kindersley Limited
One Embassy Gardens, 8 Viaduct Gardens,
London, SW11 7BW

A CIP catalogue record for this book
is available from the British Library.
ISBN: 978-0-2414-3745-2

Printed and bound in China

For the curious
www.dk.com

This book was made with Forest
Stewardship Council ™ certified
paper – one small step in DK's
commitment to a sustainable future.
For more information go to
www.dk.com/our-green-pledge

CONTENTS

GETTING GOING

RUNNING YOUR BUSINESS

GROWING YOUR BUSINESS

CONTRIBUTORS

Cheryl Rickman (consultant editor) is a *Sunday Times* best-selling author and ghostwriter of 19 business and self-help books – and a qualified Positive Psychology practitioner. Her first book, *The Small Business Start-Up Workbook* was published in 2005. She has since started and sold her own businesses, and now specializes in writing practical books to help people flourish.

Philippa Anderson has a business degree, and is a writer and communications consultant, who has advised multinationals including 3M, Anglo American, and Coca-Cola. She has written a number of business books and was a contributor to DK's *The Business Book*, *How Business Works*, and *How Management Works*.

Alexandra Black graduated with a degree in business communications before moving to Tokyo to write for financial newspaper group, Nikkei Inc. and investment bank, J.P. Morgan. She has written widely on cultural and economic history, and has contributed to many books on money, medicine, management, architecture, and design.

Pippa Bourne is director of Bourne Performance, which helps organizations and individuals to succeed. She is a Visiting Fellow at Cranfield University, where she supports the work of the Centre for Business Performance. Pippa has an MBA and is a business coach. She has many years experience of managing small businesses within universities and professional bodies.

INTRODUCTION

All businesses start as someone's dream. This book has been written to help make your dream of starting your own business a reality.

With more and more people starting their own businesses each year, and with technological advances offering unprecedented access to information, talent, materials, and products, there has never been a better time to start your own business. At the same time, there has also never been more competition.

Being your own boss can be as challenging as it is rewarding, so equip yourself with as much knowledge as possible on the issues you may face and the options available before you start. *How To Start Your Own Business* aims to provide you with a toolkit to help you build a successful enterprise.

Chapter 1 covers everything you need to know before you start, from coming up with your business idea and finding a gap in the market, to choosing a business structure, model, and strategy. Chapter 2 looks at the steps you need to take to start your business, including how to choose a name and develop your brand, and how to sell online, take payments, and fulfil orders. Chapter 3 shows you what you need to do to get going, including planning and building a website, sourcing and recruiting staff, and generating interest in your business. Chapter 4 tells you everything you need to know about how to run your business, including: how to encourage customer loyalty and build strategic alliances; how to analyse performance and finance growth; how to manage a supply chain; and how to retain talent and look after your employees in the workplace. Finally, Chapter 5 shows you how to grow your business, how to manage change, how to retain customers and license products, and how to sell your business when it is time to move on.

BEFORE YOU START

Making the big leap

If you are thinking about starting your own business, developing your idea in your spare time is a good way to start. Then weigh up the pros and cons, and understand your motivation for making the change.

Working for yourself or others?

It is crucial not to underestimate the hard work involved in running a business. Rather than having one role, business owners often take on multiple responsibilities – from producing a product or performing a service to carrying out all the administrative tasks as well as going out and selling the idea. Although you may no longer have a boss to answer to, your working hours may be much longer, especially at the start.

As a business owner, you have more responsibilities and need to invest more in your future. You will take more risks and feel more pressure running your own business, but the potential for success is often greater than working for an existing company. Running your own business will mean you have more control and flexibility.

Be clear about your motivations for starting up a

Considering your options

Remember that paid employment brings many benefits, whereas being your own boss can be stressful and financially risky. Weigh up your options carefully before you reach a balanced decision.

THEIR COMPANY

Pros

> **Financial security** comes from a regular weekly or monthly pay cheque.
> **Sickness and holiday pay** bring more consistent income.
> **Sense of belonging** comes from working with others towards a common cause.
> **Investment in your development** and training is paid for by employers.
> **Opportunities to build** experience and develop new skills are available.

Cons

> **Earnings are limited** depending on the company's pay policy.
> **Your hard work** helps to achieve another person's dreams rather than your own.
> **Office politics** can be frustrating.
> **Time and money** is spent on commuting to a workplace chosen by the company.
> **Lack of flexibility** in work hours and conditions can be problematic.

business. Perhaps you want to run a business from home doing what you love. Maybe you are driven by wanting to make a positive impact on society. Think about how you see your business in the future. You might want to grow your company and employ staff, building a family firm for future generations; or perhaps you want to make enough money to sell up and move on. Maybe you want to generate wealth to buy your dream home or travel; or you may simply want enough income to replace what you earned as an employee.

SIDE HUSTLES

Rather than give up your paid employment straightaway, you may want to start your new business venture in your spare time. A start-up that begins in this way is known as a "side hustle". You keep the benefits of being employed, while testing the viability of a new business. It is a compromise, but it can also be a springboard, allowing you to develop your business idea with less personal and financial risk.

"**I knew that if I failed** I wouldn't **regret that, but** I knew the one thing I might **regret** was not trying."

Jeff Bezos, founder and CEO of Amazon

MY COMPANY

Pros

> **Potential for higher earnings**, without the limits put in place by an employer.
> **Greater control**, independence, and flexibility to work round family/personal commitments.
> **Ability to choose** your hours and work at your own pace.
> **Potential for greater** job satisfaction – all your efforts go towards achieving your goals.
> **Opportunity to pursue** your dream.

Cons

> **Greater financial risk** with less security as a business owner.
> **Sense of isolation** from working independently with less human interaction.
> **Responsiblity for mistakes** and failures, as well as successes, rests with you.
> **Potential strain** on family/social life from working long hours.
> **No income** if sick or on holiday.
> **Inability to switch off** at the end of the working day.

THE BOSS

Why you? Why now?

When contemplating starting your own business, it is wise to do some self assessment first. Take time to weigh up your strengths and weaknesses, and consider if you are ready to be your own boss.

Why you?

Starting your own business is an exciting opportunity but it is essential to be practical from the beginning. Before making any decisions, ask yourself some key questions. First and foremost, do you have a realistic business idea, and do you have the drive and energy to bring it to fruition? Also, do you have the necessary skills to develop your idea, and if not, could you acquire them? If the answer to these questions is "no" that does not mean you will never start your own business, just not the one you are thinking of now.

Assessing yourself

Being your own boss requires a wide range of abilities, many of which you will need at the outset. Take time to identify the transferable skills you know you have – plus other talents you could develop – that would be useful for the business. Ask friends and family to give you fresh insight by listing your strengths. Conversely, scrutinize yourself, looking for areas of weakness, and think of ways you can overcome them.

Running a business is a long-term commitment, so trading in a field that interests you is important. However, you need to be confident that your interest is strong enough to last the duration of the business.

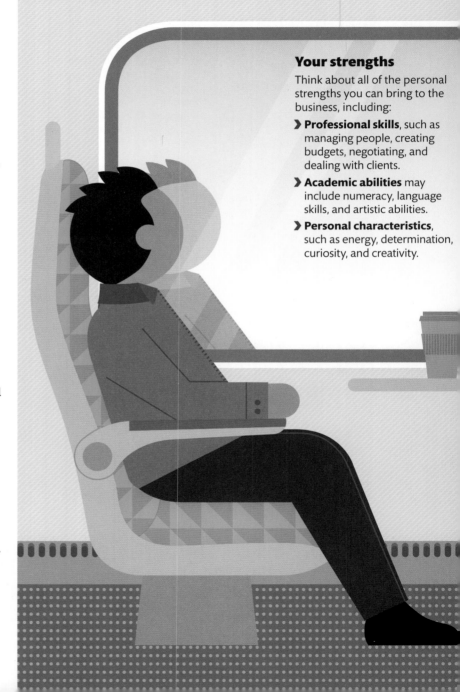

Your strengths

Think about all of the personal strengths you can bring to the business, including:

> **Professional skills**, such as managing people, creating budgets, negotiating, and dealing with clients.

> **Academic abilities** may include numeracy, language skills, and artistic abilities.

> **Personal characteristics**, such as energy, determination, curiosity, and creativity.

> ## "The only way to do great work is to love what you do."

Steve Jobs, co-founder Apple Inc, 2005

Why now?

Timing is essential in business, and offering the right product at the right time can set you on the path to success. As such, spend time researching your potential market (see pp.20–21), look at what rivals are doing, and seek professional advice. The timing also has to be right for you, of course, but are you ready?

Starting a business requires time and money, and also involves pressure and risk, which you need to be prepared for. Unless you are fully confident, look for ways to start trading slowly and gauge demand. If you are currently employed, consider starting the business in your spare time as a side hustle, (see p.13), perhaps reducing your employed hours as the business grows.

Your weaknesses

Identify aspects about yourself that could hinder the business. These might include:

> **Inexperience** in setting up IT systems, recruiting staff, and managing accounts.
> **Lack of knowledge** in areas such as using social media and software packages.
> **Personal traits** can include a lack of confidence, untidiness, and impulsiveness.
> **Personal circumstances**, such as the need to care for children or living in a remote location.

Your interests

Think about what interests you and how you might incorporate this into your business.

> **What do** you enjoy doing in your spare time?
> **What sort** of people do you like spending time with, other than your family?
> **Have you gained** particular skills and knowledge through your interests and hobbies?
> **What issues** are you most passionate about?

✓ NEED TO KNOW

> **Hard skills** are formally acquired indicators of ability, such as a qualification or certificate.
> **Soft skills** are personal abilities that have developed naturally, such as creative thinking and problem-solving.
> **Transferable skills** are the capabilities and areas of expertise that can be easily transferred from one role to another. Examples include time management, communication, and leadership.

Coming up with your idea

Every business begins with an idea, whether to solve a problem or improve an existing product or service. It is an exciting first step, although you must also ensure that your idea is viable.

Finding a good idea

A business idea does not have to be new, but it must satisfy a need in order to succeed. Start by thinking about problems you have encountered yourself, such as not being able to buy a certain product or access a useful service. This may be a gap in the market (see pp.20–21) that you could fill. Alternatively, where products and services are available – but are unsatisfactory – this could be an opportunity for you to improve them and offer something better.

When looking for a good idea, consider what existing businesses currently offer and what they do not – which could pose an opportunity. Also look out for niche or specialist markets, where you could meet the demands of a small but dedicated group of customers (see pp.38–39).

Researching markets

Markets are made up of people with common demands, so learning what interests and concerns them is valuable information. Pay close attention to the media, especially online, and look out for growing trends that you could tap into. Depending on the market that interests you, joining relevant internet forums can give you a useful insight into members' needs, desires, and problems. Ask questions and seek opinions, and discuss your idea with those who may become your customers one day.

Another source of useful information are online trade journals, which most industries publish. Here, you can learn about developments, trends, and how well potential rivals are performing, and gain essential knowledge that can help shape your ideas.

Will your idea work?

In order for your idea to succeed, it needs to be achievable and viable. Scrutinize it from all angles and question every aspect of it, as well as your ability to make it happen. Consider how it might be affected by market changes. Identify its strengths and how you could build on them, while also resolving any weaknesses. Also, try to predict any threats and how you might overcome them, while making the most of any new opportunities.

CASE STUDY

Honest Tea

Seth Goldman first had the idea for a low-calorie beverage while working on a case study of the drinks industry at Yale, noting there were sugary drinks and bottled water on the market, but nothing in between. After a run in New York's Central Park, he could not find a suitable drink to buy. Goldman saw a problem and came up with a solution: in 1998 he co-founded Honest Tea, making organic, not-too-sweet, bottled teas, which went on to become a market leader.

Using a checklist

A "good idea checklist" is a widely used tool to help assess the merits of a new business idea. Good ideas usually meet most of these criteria (see right). Once you have your idea, be sure to keep it safe (see pp.96–97).

THE GOOD IDEA CHECKLIST

1. Fills a gap in the market
The idea fills an untapped market by offering a product or service that is not currently available.

2. Innovates
The idea should solve a problem or meet a need in a way that is better than available alternatives.

3. Challenges existing alternatives
The idea offers a new, better way of doing things, and challenges existing approaches.

4. Stands out
The new product or service will stand out from existing ones by being clearly better or different in some way.

5. Meets customer expectations
The product or service offered will be provided at a level of quality expected by the customer.

6. Offers good value
The product or service will benefit the customer in some way, and create a sense of money well spent.

7. Has a purpose
The idea will give customers a sense of pleasure or of having helped an important cause.

8. Harnesses your strengths
The idea builds on your skills, experience, market knowledge, and/or contacts in an industry.

9. Is in a growing market
The idea serves an expanding market, with sufficient potential demand for a sustained period.

10. Can be scaled up
The product or service can be delivered at an increasing scale without costs growing at the same rate.

"**Always think outside the box and embrace opportunities that appear.**"
Lakshmi Mittal, CEO ArcelorMittal

Offering products or services

Most businesses typically sell either products or services to their customers. When starting up your business, deciding what you will offer is essential, and there are many factors to consider.

Considering the options

An important consideration when deciding between creating a product- or service-based business, is the time and costs involved – and how soon it will generate income. With a product-based business, it takes time to source or create, then test, the goods being sold. The goods then need to sell in sufficient numbers to cover their cost before any profit is made, which may also take time. When the goods are sold, however, they are usually paid for immediately by the customer.

In contrast, services can be offered immediately and with minimal set-up costs, if it is you providing them yourself. However, if you require training or need specific equipment, this will take time and money. Also, customers typically expect to be invoiced for certain services, which can mean waiting several weeks to be paid.

Some businesses offer products and services. A motor mechanic, for example, might repair and sell cars, enjoying the benefits of both types of business. However, when starting out for the first time, it is advisable to concentrate on one type first before trying the other.

Selling products

> **Customers can see** what they are buying, helping them decide to make a purchase or not.

> **Stock needs** to be replenished, which is an ongoing cost. It may also be perishable, so will mean a direct loss to the business if it is not sold.

> **Products need** to be stored, which means having access to suitable storage facilities, which may be costly.

Selling products and services

In addition to the differing amounts of time and money required to set up a business selling products or services, you should also consider longer term factors.

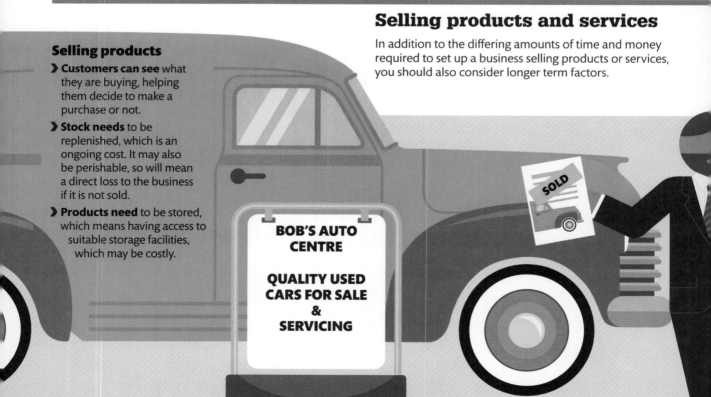

BOB'S AUTO CENTRE

QUALITY USED CARS FOR SALE & SERVICING

SOLD

SCOPE FOR GROWTH

Scalability is the ability of the business to increase sales without costs rising in proportion. It is an area where product- and service-based businesses differ.

› **Certain products** can be highly scalable. For example, once created, online courses, apps, or software, can be sold in unlimited numbers with little further cost.

› **All services** take time to deliver, which makes them less scalable, especially if more people need to be recruited to deliver them, raising costs. However, extra services can be added to the offering, giving scope for growth.

! BE AWARE

› **Avoid running out** of stock, which will frustrate customers and might encourage them to shop with your competitors.

› **Do not expect** a good product or service to sell itself. The business must be set up to distribute and sell the product effectively.

› **Regularly compare** your prices, products, and the quality of your services, against those of your competitors.

› **Ensure the products** and services you offer are fully compliant with all regulations. Check this regularly.

> "Quality in a service or product is not what you put into it. It is what the customer gets out of it."
>
> Peter Drucker, US management consultant

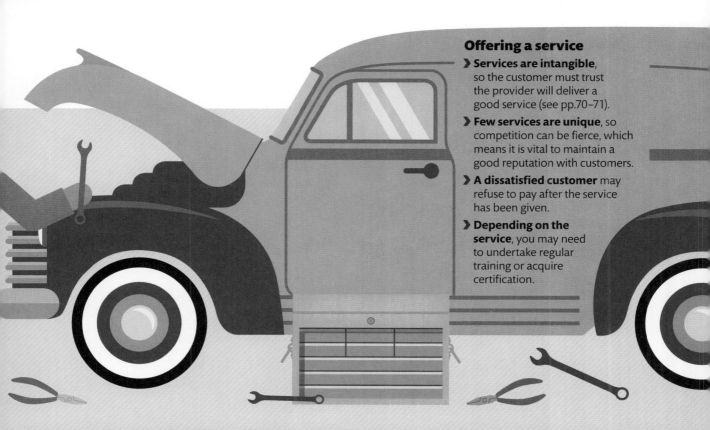

Offering a service

› **Services are intangible**, so the customer must trust the provider will deliver a good service (see pp.70–71).

› **Few services are unique**, so competition can be fierce, which means it is vital to maintain a good reputation with customers.

› **A dissatisfied customer** may refuse to pay after the service has been given.

› **Depending on the service**, you may need to undertake regular training or acquire certification.

Finding a gap in the market

For your business to succeed there must be a market – or potential to create one – for what you plan to offer. This means either selling something entirely new that people will want or providing a better alternative to what is available.

Identifying gaps

A gap in the market is simply a need that is not currently met. This is either because the product or service to meet that need does not yet exist, because existing businesses fail to meet it adequately, or because the need has not yet been identified. For example, while a town may have several restaurants, it may lack one serving Mexican cuisine, which is a need you could address. Alternatively, the town may have a French restaurant that fails to meet customer needs by not catering for children, which is also a potential gap.

Finally, while the town's residents may feel content with the existing restaurants, they may still eagerly adopt a completely new alternative approach that meets a need they did not know they had. For instance, a food delivery service that allows them to order any cuisine, at any time, to enjoy at home.

In order to find a gap, research the market you are planning to enter, and think about your own experiences (see pp.16–17). Look for products and services that are not currently available, which you could offer. Also look at those that are available to

HIGH PRICE, HIGH QUALITY
> Stylish product crafted from quality leather
> A look older, wealthy customers will pay for
> Well-made and hard-wearing

YOUR NEW OFFERING
> Trendy new look with wide age-range appeal
> Medium price
> Durable product of quality

Filling the gap

A gap in the market is a chance to reach an untapped group of customers. There may be a portion of an existing market that is underserved or a new opportunity within an existing industry. In this example, the newcomer to the market has identified a gap for mid-priced, fashionable shoes of decent quality.

see if you could provide something better – that customers would value more highly. If you are planning to open a local business, speak to people about what is available nearby, and what is not. Also try out existing products and services yourself to learn what you could improve upon. Think laterally and look for needs that others have not yet identified.

Assessing your options

When considering potential gaps, research why they might exist. While it may be that no one has thought of a suitable product or service yet, it could also be because there is insufficient demand to justify filling it (see pp.42–43). For example, the town without a Mexican restaurant may once have had one that closed through lack of demand.

Be flexible when looking for your potential market, and willing to adapt your ideas. Research your options thoroughly before committing yourself.

NEED TO KNOW

> **Competitive markets** are those in which there is a large number of buyers and sellers, meaning no one can control the market price.
> **Demand** refers to the amount of a product or service that customers and clients will buy at a given price.
> **Market disrupters** create new products, services, or approaches that transform existing markets, and often become a new market leader in the process.

> "High expectations are the key to everything."

Sam Walton, founder of Wal-Mart Stores Inc.

LOW PRICE, LOW QUALITY
> Attractive but clearly affordable
> Targets young with fast-changing wardrobes
> No claim to be a durable product

MEDIUM PRICE, LOW QUALITY
> Key selling point is its trendy, new look
> Stylish and appeals to all ages
> Disappointing quality; soon wears out

Standing out from the crowd

In a crowded marketplace, your business needs to stand out amongst rivals in order to attract customers and clients. This involves building and maintaining a unique competitive advantage.

Creating advantage

When starting a business, you need to quickly identify what will make your product or service stand out, giving you a competitive advantage. Gaining and sustaining this advantage by offering greater value or better benefits than competitors is especially crucial when you first enter a crowded market.

You can create this greater value in several ways. You can offer a product or service that is unique or new, one of higher quality or with superior customer service, or give guarantees. These are your unique selling points (USPs). Whichever you choose, it is important to make sure that customers perceive their value, as these are what gives you a competitive advantage.

Providing better benefits than the competition (a differentiation advantage) or offering the same benefits at a competitive price (a cost advantage) are possibilities, but beware of making price your USP. Low prices can be interpreted as low quality, and since you can be undercut by rivals, you will not attract a loyal customer base.

Identifying your customers and understanding their needs (see pp.40–41) is central to building a competitive advantage. However, to retain their custom, you will need to pay attention to what is happening in the marketplace, and constantly monitor what existing and new competitors are offering.

The value your business offers to its customers must be commercially viable. There would be no point in increasing business costs in order to attract customers if your profits become minimal. It is crucial to strike the right balance between the value offered and profit.

What sets you apart

Promoting what makes your business better than the competition tells potential customers why they should choose you, and will help to attract your target market. This uniqueness should form part of your "value proposition" – the promise you make to customers about the qualities and benefits they can expect from you and your business.

> "You should learn from your competitor, but never copy. Copy and you die."
>
> Jack Ma, co-founder of Alibaba.com, 2007

Go above and beyond

In order to attract and retain customers, your business must offer value and benefits they cannot get elsewhere. These are your USPs.

⚙ MAKING IT WORK

› **Constantly learn** about your customers to ensure you meet their needs, which can change over time.

› **Review your USPs** regularly to ensure they are unique and are valued by your customers.

› **Regularly assess** your rival's USPs and find ways to ensure that yours surpass theirs.

› **Monitor the costs** and benefits of your USPs to the business to ensure profit margins are healthy.

› **Keep watching** for new market entrants and what they offer.

CREATING USPs

How to differentiate your product or service will depend on what you are offering, the market, and your competition.

› **Offer products** that provide something different from those of rivals, for example, better quality, safer, or unique designs.

› **Provide services** that customers cannot find anywhere else or that are distinctive and more appealing.

› **Attractive prices** can set a business apart from competitors, but quality cannot be ignored. Customers assess both when deciding if something is value for money.

Defining your goals

One of the first steps in starting a business is to define what it is you want to do, and why you want to do it. This will help you to focus your ideas more clearly and allow you to start making specific plans.

Defining your purpose

When starting a business, first decide what you want to achieve. Known as your business "vision", this is a long-term view of what your business will become. To then help make that vision become a reality, identify why you want to start *this* business and not *another*. For example, you may want to open a travel agency, but why is this?

It may be because you want to offer exciting trips, to serve a particular market, or because you simply see it as a way to make money. This is the "purpose" behind your business vision. Use this to inform your decisions and to focus your plans. For instance, an agency offering bespoke holidays would be planned differently from one aimed at only making money.

Your vision and purpose embody your business, which you can use when deciding your strategies, and planning your working procedures and practices. Share them with other people involved in your business from the start, including investors, customers, clients, and staff by encapsulating them in a "mission statement" (see right) that sums up you and your business.

Setting out your values

While deciding the vision and purpose of your business, also consider the values you want to uphold, such as honesty, integrity, value for money, and passion. These provide a map and compass to guide your decision-making, and should be reflected in how the business operates. Incorporate these values throughout the business, and communicate them with others, so that everyone dealing with you knows what you stand for. For example, a travel agency catering for older travellers may choose "commitment, quality, adventure, and luxury" as its business values.

"People don't buy what you do; they buy why you did it."

Simon Sinek, author and motivational speaker, 2009

Creating a mission statement

A mission statement is a written declaration that clarifies the purpose of your business – what it does, who it does it for, and how it does it. It should be concise, and give clear answers to three key questions:

What? Define the products or services that your business provides.
Who for? Say who your products or services are designed for.
How? Explain how your customers' aspirations will be met.

To support your mission statement, you can also write a vision statement, outlining where the business aspires to be in the future, having achieved its mission. You can also write a values statement, explaining the values your business will maintain in pursuit of its mission. Together, the three statements form a pledge between your business and those who deal with it.

CASE STUDY

Microsoft

In 1975, Bill Gates founded the software company Microsoft. Its initial vision was simple, but ambitious: "to put a computer on every desk and in every home". The company aligned its strategy, communications, and culture to make that vision a reality. Since then, computers have become commonplace, and so the company has a new vision: "to empower every person and every organization on the planet to achieve more".

MOTIVATING OTHERS

Your mission statement (see above) not only provides focus for you, it also serves as inspiration for others. It can be used to help attract and motivate staff, giving them a clear set of values to follow, and a keen sense of what the business does and why. It can also be an important marketing tool, projecting a precise image of your business's unique identity – its brand – to the outside world, helping to attract customers and clients. However, it is essential to demonstrate the values you portray, as failure to do so can undermine the message.

Choosing a structure

You may be starting out on your own, with family, or with a business partner. There are other options, too. The structure can change as the business grows, but begin with a form that is a good fit for where you are now.

Considering your options

The business structure you choose depends on the nature of your business (its complexity and growth potential) and the level of risk you are willing to take. Your choice will be influenced by whether you are starting out alone, or with one or more business partners, and by the purpose of your venture – whether this is ethical or charitable as opposed to financial.

Most people start out as a sole trader or in an informal partnership, and are responsible for all business debts. As the business grows, it may eventually become necessary to register it legally (see pp.212–215) as a limited liability, or a limited, company. This protects your personal assets from any business debts, and also enables you, and your business partner, to more easily secure loans and other finance.

 Sole trader

Run by the owner under a business name; larger businesses may need to register as limited companies.

Pros

❯ Set up is simple
❯ Profits can be retained after tax
❯ Capital required is minimal
❯ No annual business accounts to file, only a personal income tax return

Cons

❯ Debt liability unlimited: no distinction between your business and private assets
❯ Capacity to raise additional capital is low
❯ Decision-making rests on your shoulders

 Contractor

Tends to work for one client at a time for the duration of a contract; can operate as a limited company.

Pros

❯ Security of income from long-term contracts
❯ Control over which contracts to accept, and when to take a break
❯ Pay is typically at a lucrative "day rate"

Cons

❯ Contracts can end without warning, depending on terms
❯ Working hours may be long and away from home
❯ Time required to establish credibility

 Freelancer

Self-employed sole trader who typically works on multiple projects for more than one client.

Pros

❯ Start-up costs are minimal, with the ability to work anywhere – including from home
❯ Workload and schedule chosen by you
❯ Flexibility around your working hours

Cons

❯ Work can be sporadic, causing cash flow issues
❯ Sense of isolation if you work alone
❯ Financial management is your responsibility alone
❯ Work–life balance may be difficult to achieve

 Partnership

Enterprise where two or more people share the ownership, control, and profits of the business.

Pros

❯ Partners bring their expertise, knowledge, and contacts to the business, along with their capital and other resources
❯ No need to file any annual accounts

Cons

❯ Issues can arise if one partner leaves or feels they are doing more than their pre-agreed fair share of the workload
❯ Partners expected to pay tax on their own portion of profit

BUYING A BUSINESS

If you have the funds, buying an existing business that is already trading may be a tempting option, since it removes the need to start from scratch. However, there are many reasons why businesses are sold, including poor performance, so research the business thoroughly to find out why it is on the market. Seek professional advice, review the financial records, check online reviews, and ask around locally. Be aware that buying a business involves upfront investment, which will be at risk until the venture proves successful.

59%

of the UK's private sector **businesses were** sole traders **in 2019**

UK Government, Department for Business, Energy & Industrial Strategy

Family business

Commercial entity owned and run by members of the same family, often across multiple generations.

Pros
> Stability and continuity in the long term
> Trust, loyalty, and understanding
> Commitment and values shared
> Profits remain within the wider family

Cons
> Nepotism – a preference for hiring family members, even if they lack skills or experience
> Potential for conflict, and conflicts that arise may be more difficult to resolve

Limited liability

Legally registered business, whose assets and debts belong to the company itself, not the owners.

Pros
> Risk is lower because the owner(s) are not personally liable for business debts
> Ability to go public to attract inward investment if rapid, high growth is anticipated

Cons
> Owners invest their own money and assume legal responsibility
> Company distributes part of profit to shareholders
> Corporation tax and tax return must be filed and paid annually

Franchise

Independent branch of another business; franchisee pays a fee for the right to represent the parent business.

Pros
> No need to develop an original business idea
> Franchisor gives training, support, and knowledge
> Risk is low, as business model is already proven
> Amount of capital required is minimal

Cons
> The business must still answer to the franchisor
> Creative control lacking in brand, training, or culture
> Franchisor could go bust
> Payments to the franchisor are ongoing

Not-for-profit

Cooperative, social enterprise, or charity that is committed to a cause rather than to making a profit.

Pros
> Profits can be reinvested into beneficial causes
> Eligiblity for grants and tax exemptions
> Opportunity to "make a difference"
> Organization is self-governing

Cons
> Profits cannot be dispersed – personal financial reward may be lower
> Competition for funding, making finance uncertain
> Reliance on the public's generosity and empathy for donations

Starting a family business

Creating a family business is an opportunity to work with those you most trust and care about. It can be very successful as long as it is set up and run correctly – as a professional business.

Working together

Creating a family business can be highly rewarding, and it offers many advantages, such as a shared desire to succeed and the benefit of mutual support. However, there are also disadvantages. Where most roles are performed by family members, the business can lack the breadth of skills and experience found in more diverse companies. Also, family relationships are not the same as working ones, which can result in conflicts that could harm the business (see pp.54–55).

To help ensure the business succeeds, it is essential to make some early decisions, such as who owns it, how it will be financed, and how profits and liabilities will be shared. You also need to decide the roles of everyone involved, when and how they work, and how they will be rewarded. To do this, draw up a written family charter together (see right) so that everyone knows what to expect from the business.

Is it right for you?

Setting up a family business is not always straightforward. Before you take the plunge, you – and everyone involved – need to weigh up the pros and cons to decide objectively whether this is the right choice. A new business requires full commitment and a mutual determination to make things succeed. Families working together can be a potent force. However, if there are any areas of conflict, these will need to be settled at an early stage to prevent them jeopardizing future success.

PROS

> **Familiarity** Knowing each other well, you communicate easily and effectively.

> **Strong commitment** You all share common goals.

> **Speed** You can launch your business quickly and cheaply, with minimal need to recruit.

> **Support** As you understand each other's personal and financial issues, you can accommodate different needs.

FREDA'S

"Family businesses make up more than 60% of all companies in Europe."

European Commission, ec.europa.eu, 2020

FAMILY CHARTERS

Establishing clear roles and responsibilities is particularly important in family-run businesses. Conflict can lead to long-term divisions. To avoid this, create an informal agreement or charter.

All family members involved will need to decide what the charter should cover. Such documents typically outline how the company will be run, its short- and long-term objectives, areas of accountability and authority and, sometimes, how it might be passed on to the next generation. You may need to consult a lawyer or business mentor to help you agree on difficult issues, such as sharing control and potential wealth.

A business charter is not legally binding. Once you have started trading, it will need to be reviewed regularly to ensure it remains relevant to the business.

CONS

> **Familiarity** Knowing each other well can lead to unprofessional attitudes.

> **Narrow thinking** A family workforce may not be open to helpful, external ideas.

> **Personal resentments** These can affect the business and damage family relationships.

> **Assumptions** If there is no charter, senior family members may assume they are in charge.

Setting up a franchise

If you want to start off with a ready-made business model and a recognizable brand, you might consider taking on a franchise. Careful research, thorough planning, and available funds are all essential.

Understanding franchises

A franchise is an agreement that authorizes you to start a business selling the products or services of an established brand. You become the franchisee, the established company is the franchisor. Not all arrangements are the same, but they always involve the franchisee paying an initial fee and a percentage on sales (called a royalty) in return for the right to sell a branded product or service.

Fast-food chains – for example, McDonald's – are examples of the most common type of franchise, a "business format franchise". In these cases, franchisees pay for the right to establish independent outlets under the franchisor's brand. New outlets will have the same design, menu, and operating systems as all other franchised outlets across a particular region.

Weighing up the costs

There are some clear advantages to this type of business. You can benefit from a brand with a loyal customer base, a market-tested product or service, and established logistics. In return for this, you will be expected to make a substantial initial investment and accept that you will be tied to the brand's offerings and infrastructure.

Becoming a franchisee

Before deciding whether to take on a franchise, ask yourself how involved you want to be in the day-to-day running of the business. If you want the franchise to provide you with an income but you want to limit the hours you work or your involvement in the business, then it is important to find a franchisor that will permit this.

Franchisors will have their own expectations, so you need to assess these and make sure you are willing and able to meet them. Careful research, negotiation, planning, and developing good relations with your franchisor are all key to success.

TYPES OF FRANCHISE

There are three main types of franchise, each with a different level of rights and varying business models. All involve a firm financial commitment.

Business format

As a franchisee, you get not only the right to sell an established brand, but also a full business system to follow and a support network. This type of franchise is used in mass-consumer areas, such as hair salons, and in car repair, plumbing, and cleaning services.

Product

The franchisor grants you the right to sell or distribute a branded product, such as a computer or car, using the manufacturer's trade names, but you do not benefit from the franchisor's business systems. The products you can distribute or sell will be restricted.

Manufacturing

In return for a fee, you acquire the right to manufacture a product and to use associated brand names and trademarks. The product could, for example, be a soft drink, with the drink flavouring ingredients provided by the franchisor.

! BE AWARE

> **Start-up costs can be high**, often significantly higher than if you were launching an independent business.

> **Your reputation** will depend on that of the franchisor, so research your franchisor thoroughly. Note that you will be bound by the franchisor's rules and regulations.

> **Consider** your motivations. If your driving force is to create a business in your image and achieve personal goals, then a franchise may not be the answer.

1 Research possible franchisors

Search for information online, but if possible, also attend franchise seminars and trade shows, where you can meet potential franchisors and ask questions. Compare types of franchise formats and fees.

2 Look for a proven formula

Assess the tried-and-tested business models of brands that are already established in the marketplace. Look for examples of thriving franchise networks, and analyse the reasons for their success.

3 Match your skills

Consider how compatible you are with potential franchisors. What can you offer them, and what will you get in return in terms of business know-how and talent development?

4 Negotiate

Choose a location, and discuss the potential for being the only franchisee in the locality. Talk about what will you get and what is expected of you. Agree on product pricing and the percentage royalty on revenue you will pay.

5 Check financing and legal issues

Prepare a business plan and cash flow projection. Find the most cost-effective financing options, possibly through the franchisor itself. Seek legal advice, and read the fine print before signing anything.

6 Prepare the business

Pay any initial fees due to the franchisor, according to the contract. Find a site for your business, and set up the appropriate accounting and software operating systems agreed with the franchisor. Make sure you take full advantage of any other resources or services that the franchisor offers as part of the deal, including marketing, quality control regimes, staff recruitment and training facilities, payroll systems, customer service support, and assistance and advice regarding relevant health and safety measures.

7 Get up and running

You will usually need to report to the franchisor and pay royalties on a monthly basis. Do this in a timely fashion to secure the ongoing support of the franchisor. Be prepared for quality control inspections.

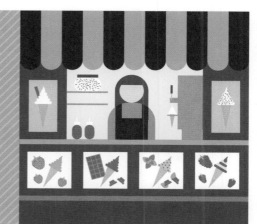

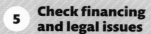

Alternative types of business

Your new business can be more than simply a money-making venture. By adopting a less conventional structure, your start-up can gather support to help those in need, or fund causes and projects that you care about.

Looking at your options

If you are starting your business in order to pursue specific social, charitable, or other objectives, a conventional commercial business type might not suit your needs. Other business types include cooperatives, social enterprises, or charities (see below). Enterprises like this are often lumped together under the catch-all description of non-profit organizations, but this is a little misleading, since many do attempt to make money. The key difference is that instead of giving out profits to shareholders or withdrawing them yourself, you put the money back into the business to keep it running and to fund any charitable or social cause that it supports. If you follow this route, earning profit for profit's sake will not be your focus. Rather, the business will be run for the benefit of its members, a community, social, or environmental cause, or to fund charitable activities.

Non-profit organizations are self-governing entities. If you set one up, you will be a founder rather than an owner (although cooperatives, by definition, will have multiple founders). Being a

Find the right fit for your business

A cooperative belongs to its members, and is controlled and run by and for them. Since it is not owned by shareholders, all monies stay within the cooperative, to be used as members decide. Clearly, if you wish to set one up, you will need to find like-minded individuals and be happy with democratic decision-making.

A social enterprise might appeal if you seek more control but want to combine commercial activity with "doing good". Social enterprises buy and sell on the open market but aim to create employment and reinvest profits in the business, and local or wider community.

If supporting a cause close to your heart is your prime business objective, a charity may be the best option, but strict laws govern how charities operate; these vary between countries and sometimes states.

"Be greedy for social change, and your life will be endlessly enriched. The only failure lies in not trying, or in giving up."

Ann Cotton, founder and chief executive of Camfed,
The Guardian, 2007

Cooperatives

Cooperatives can take many forms, including farm, retail, or housing, and can also be banking providers (such as credit unions) and workshops.

The business would be jointly and equally owned by you and the rest of the members, with business decisions made collectively.

❯ **Goal** You must have a clear economic, social, or cultural objective that the business's revenue helps to fund.

❯ **Membership** This will tend to be open and voluntary, with each member having one vote on business decisions.

❯ **Profits** Surplus profits can be given to members who have a financial stake in the business.

founder means that you cannot profit directly from the net earnings of the business, although you will be entitled to a salary for your work. While the business's income can come from selling goods or services, you may also be able to fund-raise via donations, sponsorships, and grants. Some non-profit enterprises, especially charities, may also be able to apply for tax benefits.

Businesses that profess to have ethical dimensions are likely to face scrutiny from both the public and official bodies, so you will need a clear mission statement (see pp.24–25). You must be transparent and accountable, exercise good governance, and keep accurate records. You will also need to develop excellent PR (public relations) to help sustain funding.

Different... but similar

Although its focus is different, a non-profit organization will often use similar business strategies and management techniques to those found in "for-profit" businesses. Even those that rely heavily on volunteers will usually need to hire some paid staff and employ similar promotional techniques to those used by commercial enterprises. Like them, the aim of your business is still to make money, but your objective is to channel it into your chosen charitable or social cause.

NEED TO KNOW

> **Governance** is how a governing body oversees and manages the way an organization functions.

> **Mission statement** refers to the formal expression of the aims and values of a business.

> **Non-profit or not-for-profit** are terms denoting enterprises not primarily focused on profit. The two are often synonymous, but in the US are distinct in terms of tax, governance, and functions.

> **Social entrepreneurs** are people who set up businesses in order to help solve social problems or bring about social change.

Social enterprises

If you set up a social enterprise, your main aim will be to promote social change. This could involve tackling social problems, improving people's life chances, providing training and employment opportunities, supporting communities, and helping to protect the environment. Your business will do this using the profits earned by trading.

Examples of social enterpises could include a magazine whose profits go to help the homeless, a café that provides work opportunities for the long-term unemployed, a business promoting recycling, or a gardening service that improves green spaces in the neighbourhood.

Although the exact definition differs between countries, here are some key aspects likely to mark your business as a social enterprise:

> **Mission** Whether social or environmental, your mission must be clearly set out in your governing documents.

> **Independence** Your business is independently owned.

> **Income** Your business earns the majority of its income through trading – or is clearly working towards this aim.

> **Operation** Your business is run entirely in the interests of your social mission.

> **Profits** You reinvest or give away the majority of your profits or surpluses to support your mission.

> **Transparency** You are open about how the business operates and the impact it has.

Charities

To be granted charity status to raise funds for your chosen cause, your business will have to meet strict criteria. It can be set up as a trust, corporation, or association, but all resources must be geared towards its charitable goals.

> **Your cause** You will typically be required by law to devote a specific percentage of income to your charitable cause.

> **Remaining funds** Anything left over can be used to pay for administrative costs.

> **Associated ventures** Any charity shops and other activities that support your business may have to be part of a separate trading entity, such as a social enterprise.

Choosing a model

One of the first decisions to take when planning a business is how it will operate and make money – its business model. Examining the choices available will help you decide what will work best.

Understanding the options

To be successful, all start-ups need a sound way of operating that generates profit. This may involve adopting a single business model, such as retail, or a combination of models. For example, a magazine publisher could use a subscription model, charging its readers a regular fee, and an advertising model to earn money from companies who want to promote their brands to those readers. Alternatively, the publisher might give away the magazine for free to increase its audience, then charge more for advertising.

As you shape your business model, seek the opinions of potential customers, take expert advice, then trial the model in a pilot – adapting it as necessary (see pp.132–133). The following are common examples of business models, but there are many more.

Offline retail
Customers buy goods directly from a shop or outlet. The retailer makes or buys the products from a wholesaler or distributor, then adds to (or "marks up") the price to make a profit, and sells directly to customers, face-to-face.

Online/e-commerce retail
Businesses may sell online from their own websites or on "third-party" sites that act as virtual marketplaces, and charge a fee. Leading European third-party websites include Allegro, Fnac, and Otto (see pp.68–69).

"Bricks and clicks"
Businesses with a traditional offline store and an online presence use this. Customers can order online and/or collect and buy from physical stores. Helps retailers offer a larger range of products than a physical store can hold.

Manufacturing
Manufacturers, such as furniture makers) use raw materials to make products, which they sell to a wholesaler (such as a dealer or outlet), who sells them on at a marked-up price to the customer.

Wholesale
Wholesalers generally buy products from manufacturers and producers, then resell to retailers, who sell to customers. Wholesalers may sell direct to customers, or first to a specific distributor, who sells on to a general wholesaler.

Direct sales
Individuals sell products directly to customers – either via product parties or one-to-one sales. Some companies, such as Avon cosmetics, sell products to individual agents, who take a share of the profits on each item they sell.

"Familiarity with different [business] models is key."

Abdo Riani, www.forbes.com, 2019

Franchise

Big successful companies (franchisors) allow private individuals (franchisees) to buy the right to trade under their brand, use their systems, and sell their products or services. It is a way of buying into an established business (see pp.30–31).

Licensing

This model allows companies (licensors) to commercialize their intellectual property by licensing their designs, products, or services to others (licensees) in return for a fee, while retaining ownership (see pp.206-207).

"Freemium"

Some companies attract customers by offering a free product or service, and the option of a paid-for superior version. LinkedIn, for instance, offers a free networking platform or a paid-for version with advanced features.

Subscription

Customers pay a regular fee (membership fee) to access content, products, or services. Many gyms, dating agencies, online classes, and software and media companies, such as Netflix and Sky TV, use this model.

"Bait and hook"

Also known as the razor blade model, this works by selling a basic durable product, such as a printer, at a low price to encourage ongoing sales of essential components, such as ink cartridges, sold at premium prices.

Advertisement

To sell advertising space, a company creates entertaining copy, music, video, or other content, to attract a large targeted audience to a publication or platform, where other businesses will then pay to advertise their products.

Agency/brokerage

Agencies connect buyers with sellers and earn a transaction fee from one or the other, or both. Users of this model include estate agents and financial advisors, who earn a commission based on the value of the transaction.

Affiliate

Most website owners use this model to make money. They invite retailers to promote their products on the website and receive a commission from the retailer when a customer buys a promoted product.

Creating a strategy

The process of creating a business strategy will help you identify what is possible and what is not. It is a map setting out your goals and how to reach them.

Defining your business

Every new company needs a business strategy that is well thought-out, communicates its long-term goals to everyone involved, and sets out broadly how these aims will be achieved. Creating a strategy takes research and thought, and should include the input of others with an interest in your business. When complete, you can then use it as a guide to help decide courses of action.

Start by clarifying the purpose of your business, what it stands for, and what you want it to achieve. Also consider the nature of your business – its target audience, and how it will operate and compete. For example, offering a community service requires a totally different strategy from selling luxury goods.

Once you fully understand the aims and nature of your business in more detail, encapsulate this in a simple statement that tells everyone involved why the business exists – its mission statement (see pp.24–25).

Fighting your corner

A vital aspect of your strategy is to take into account the business's strengths and weaknesses, as well as the opportunities and threats it may face. Conduct a SWOT analysis (see p.155) in order to make full use of your (S) strengths, such as expert knowledge, while also addressing (W) weaknesses, like having limited funds. Include ways to seek and benefit from new (O) opportunities, as well as how to deal with (T) threats.

Your strategy must include how you plan to compete, which, for a new business, is essential. While you may not be able to compete on price against established rivals, there are other approaches, such as value, uniqueness, quality, and customer service. Deciding the best way to compete is central to the success of your business.

MAKING IT WORK

> **A strategy must be** kept under constant review, since the environment in which the business operates will change.

> **Check in particular** if there are impending changes in the external environment that will have a negative (or positive) impact on the business.

> **New legislation**, new technology or even changing economic forecasts can have a significant effect. Keep abreast of current affairs and all new developments in your field of operation.

COMPETING ON PERCEIVED VALUE

What is worth more?

As a small business, we cannot compete on price, but can we offer greater value to our customers? For example:

> **Stay local**, which is more convenient for customers and means the business can offer a more personal service.

> **Provide a personalized service**, where competitors do not, which better meets customers' needs and makes them feel special.

> **Offer convenient** business hours, such as remaining open after office hours.

Evaluating your options

When developing a strategy, every aspect must align, so that what you want your business to achieve is realistic. Similarly, the customers you want to reach must be those that best meet the needs of the business. Take time to carefully compare and contrast each idea against the overall aims of your strategy.

COMPETING WITH A UNIQUE OFFERING

What is not readily available?

Can we create a product or service that is hard to find and that competitors cannot easily copy? For example:

> **Create unique products** that cannot be found elsewhere, such as bespoke goods.

> **Build a website** devoted entirely to local needs, based on local knowledge.

> **Find a niche** that is too small for bigger companies to be interested in.

> **Select additional services** that will appeal to our customers.

COMPETING ON CUSTOMER SERVICE

What do customers really want?

Can we give customers a level of service better than our rivals so they stay loyal? For example:

> **Provide a personal service**, and know our customers by name.

> **Make buying an enjoyable** experience for our customers, so they come again.

> **Develop a follow-up** service to encourage repeat purchases once a first purchase has been made.

> **Offer flexible terms**, such as allowing customers to pay by instalment or offering an extended returns policy.

"To be strategic is to concentrate on [...] those few objectives that can give us a comparative advantage."

Richard Koch, UK management consultant

Knowing your market

When planning a business, you must decide whether to offer products and services with broad appeal or to target a niche. You also need to choose your market – to sell directly to consumers, to other businesses, or both.

Mass or niche markets

Deciding the best market for your product or service – your target market – is critical to the success of any business, and should form part of your business strategy (see pp.36–37). In broad terms, you have two options – mass market or niche – though you may be able to combine the two. Mass-market offerings require a broad appeal to attract the widest possible customer base, whereas niche products should appeal directly and specifically to a small but dedicated customer base.

Selling to the mass market can produce a high sales volume but a relatively low profit. While there is greater security in the wider market, it is harder and more expensive to reach customers in that large, disparate group.

Once you achieve a high sales volume, however, your product or service becomes cheaper to produce, due to economies of scale.

A niche market may have a low sales volume but can generate a high profit, if goods or services are tailored to a particular group willing to pay a premium price. There is more risk in a niche market, but it is easier and cheaper to target a smaller, defined group of customers.

Some businesses can successfully combine both approaches by initially launching a specialist product or service to a niche market, before eventually expanding their offering to cater for the mass market.

BUSINESS TO CONSUMER

In this model, the business sells products and services directly to consumers, who are the end users.

> **Examples include** retail shops, online outlets, market stalls, and service providers, such as plumbers, and childminders.

> **B2C sales** are governed by customer emotions. May be impulsive, often involves brand recognition and loyalty. Amount per sale generally lower than B2B transactions.

Understanding business models

There are three main ways in which businesses trade according to the markets they serve. Business-to-consumer (B2C) sales are conducted directly between a business and consumers. Examples include traditional retail shops and service providers, such as hairdressers and plumbers. Business-to-business (B2B) is where one business sells directly to another. B2B examples include manufacturers selling to wholesalers, and wholesalers supplying goods and equipment to service providers.

However, the line between B2C and B2B can be blurred, as some businesses sell to other businesses, as well as to consumers. Examples of this include DIY suppliers and food wholesalers. Some service providers may also cater to both markets as an offshoot of their main business.

The final way in which businesses commonly trade is business-to-business-to-consumer (B2B2C), where companies sell consumer goods or services to businesses, who then distribute them. Consumers recognize the initial business as the product or service provider, even though they do not buy directly from them. The food industry is an example: products are marketed to consumers, but are sold by food manufacturers (B) to wholesalers and retailers (B), who sell to consumers (C). Similarly, in financial services, one company may create a product, then partner with major banks or others, to sell their product to consumers.

MASS MARKET

❯ **Large, disparate group**, so the product or service should have a broad appeal.

❯ **High marketing spend** to make an impact when targeting a wide, general audience, resulting in lower profit margins.

❯ **High sales volume** giving economy-of-scale benefits; can produce/sell high quantities at a low cost.

> "Nearly 40% of UK companies derive all or the majority of their income from B2B activity."

www.thebusinessintelligence.group, 2019

BUSINESS TO BUSINESS TO CONSUMER

Here, one business sells products and services to another business, which sells them on to consumers.

❯ **Examples include** manufacturers and suppliers who sell products to a retail outlet.

❯ **B2B2C sales** are promoted to the consumer by both the initial supplier/manufacturer and the retail outlet.

BUSINESS TO BUSINESS

In this model, a business sells its products or services directly to another business, which is the end user.

❯ **Examples include** companies in a supply chain network, where one sells materials to another or provides a service, such as equipment maintenance or IT support.

❯ **B2B sales** are typically planned and well researched, with customers likely to shop around before buying. Purchases driven by logic. Transactions usually larger than those in B2C sales.

NICHE MARKET

❯ **A small and select group** with specific wants and needs, which the product or service must accurately address.

❯ **Lower marketing spend** for a targeted campaign when there are relatively few competitors.

❯ **Higher profit** potential if target customers will pay a premium price for a specialized product or service.

❯ **Low, steady sales volume** reduces potential to produce benefits of economies of scale.

Identifying your customers

Understanding who your potential customers are enables you to develop products and services to meet their needs. It also allows you to promote your business using the most effective means in order to attract sales.

Targeting customers

Different people have different needs, interests, and desires, which is reflected in the products and services they buy. As only certain people will be interested in what your business offers, these are the ones to target.

Identifying this group, or segment, allows you to develop your products and services to specifically meet their needs and expectations. It will also enable you to promote your business in a targeted way, using messages, techniques, and channels that will appeal to them. Alternatively, you can also use your own knowledge and experience of a particular segment, and plan your business accordingly.

One of the most widely used tools to help identify your customers is market segmentation. This involves breaking the whole market down into four groups with shared characteristics, then to pinpoint potential customers within those groups (see below).

Segmenting the market

There are several ways to group your customers based on who they are and how they behave. One way is to use four broad segments – demographic, geographic, psychographic, and behavioural – which relate to how and where people live, what they think, and how they behave. These segments can be further divided into narrower subgroups.

DEMOGRAPHIC FACTORS

These are the fundamental factors that define a customer profile, including age, gender, marital status, ethnicity, income, and occupation. Some age groups are identified by specific names, such as Millennials (those born between the early 1980s and mid-1990s) or Generation X (those born in the 1960s and 1970s).

GEOGRAPHIC FACTORS

Products and services can be targeted based on where a customer lives – from continent and country, down to neighbourhood and street. Factors considered might be as broad as climate and population density, or as local as types of housing, seasonal foods, and community groups and clubs.

Targeting or segmenting customers can increase revenues by as much as

760%

Data & Marketing Association, 2014

BRINGING CUSTOMERS TO LIFE

To understand potential customers, it helps to picture them as characters or "avatars". Some simple research techniques can be used to compile detailed customer habits and interests.

> **Study competitors'** social media pages for insights into customer opinions and behaviours. Compile any customer contact details.

> **Read trade or industry blogs** and articles and note customer-related comments and insights.

> **Identify key influencers** who have a connection to your product or service area, and note the views of those who follow them.

> **Make a template** for your avatars, giving them an identity and filling in personal details based on the four main areas (see below).

> **Consider the characters** who are unlikely to be your customers. That way, you avoid wasting time on marketing to the wrong people.

PSYCHOGRAPHIC FACTORS

This area of segmentation targets customers' interests, values, opinions, personality traits, attitudes, and preferences. Psychographic factors might include customers' preferred mode of contact, whether they buy mainly organic produce, how often they give to charity, and which kinds of social media they use.

BEHAVIOURAL FACTORS

Customers can be further segmented based on their shopping and purchasing behaviour. For example, some may prefer direct contact with certain stores and services, while others may buy everything online. Customers may prefer to pay more for particular brands or shop around for special offers and discounts.

Assessing demand for your business

Being enthusiastic about your business is essential, but it is a mistake to assume that everyone else shares that enthusiasm. Be objective and carry out research to establish what kind of demand there is for your product or service.

Understanding demand

In order to sell your product or service, there must be a demand for it. In other words, there must be enough people willing to buy from you at a price that will generate a profit. You must also consider the number of existing suppliers of your product (your competitors), since over-supplying a market can force down prices, which would then reduce your potential profits.

In addition to the size of the market, also consider where and when demand exists. For example, although people may want your product, they will need to be able to access it. How will you make this happen? Similarly, if people only want your product at certain times of the year, or in response to a current trend, your idea may not be viable in its current form. If you are unable to answer

Developing your idea

To identify and assess the demand for your business idea, carry out some careful research. This is not expensive but will take time. Start with a full understanding of your current idea, who it is for, and why people want it. Research potential markets, seek advice, and try out your ideas. Take time to review each stage and be willing to adapt your idea. Be prepared to walk away from ideas that will not work, but do not give up. Even if you find little demand for one idea, you may uncover a much better alternative during the process.

Clarify your idea

To assess the viability of your product or service, find out how much demand there is for it. To do this, begin by asking yourself the following questions:

> **Who are your customers?**
Are they local, national, or global? Are there enough of them, and can you reach them?

> **Who are your competitors?**
What do they offer, and what do they charge? Are they a threat to your business?

> **What are customers looking for?**
Would they buy your product? What else could you offer instead?

> **How are potential competitors performing?** Are they growing, stagnating, or failing?

Conduct desk research

Look online to see what rivals offer and read customer reviews. Search for statistical data, customer profiles, market research reports, and industry journals, much of which is available at little or no cost.

Refine your idea

Take time to refine your idea based on what you have learned. Consider rethinking your product or service if the market for it is small or already well catered for.

these questions about demand, you will need to modify your ideas, if not rethink your business entirely.

Assessing demand

There are many ways of assessing the demand for your business, ranging from doing research into your competitors to speaking to people in your chosen industry (see below). All of this should be done at the business planning stage, giving you plenty of time to refine your ideas if necessary. Only then should you think of committing resources to your business.

However, it is worth keeping notes on all of your ideas, and to continue to monitor the market even after you have estimated the demand for your business. This is because markets can change quickly, and you will need to respond swiftly to fluctuations in demand, or to changes to the ways in which you are expected to deliver your product or service. The more ideas you have the better placed you will be for facing the future – but remember not to be blinded by your enthusiasm, and to listen to what your research tells you.

42%
of businesses fail due to poor demand for their services or products

Georgia McIntyre,
www.fundera.com, 2020

Know the level of demand

You should now know what kind of demand there is for your product or service. To establish whether it is sufficient to support your business, think of the following questions:

❯ **Will you have enough customers?** Will you be able to develop a stable customer base?

❯ **How much are customers willing to pay?** How much can you charge to make a profit?

❯ **Will you have too many competitors?** What can you do to keep your customers loyal?

❯ **What does your competitors' performance mean for you?** What can you learn from them?

Refine your idea

Use the feedback from testing your product or service to refine it, or even to rethink your idea if it was poorly received. Do not commit resources to your business until you are sure it is viable.

Approach people

Speak to people in the industry, visit trade shows, and join internet forums. Create simple online questionnaires and surveys using tools, such as Google Forms or SurveyMonkey, or try a Twitter poll. Seek the opinions of friends and family.

Refine your idea

Use the information you have learned from other people to refine your idea if necessary. Does your product or service meet the demands of the people you have spoken to?

Test your idea

If possible, test your product or service on potential customers or clients for free. For example, if you are offering coaching services, offer short sessions to gauge their response.

Where to base your business

Selecting the right kind of workspace for your business is an important decision. There are a number of options to choose from, with pros and cons to each.

Setting up a workspace

Deciding where you will work from is a key step in the start-up process. Most businesses start life in some part of the home – including a garage or shed – and may stay there, especially since Covid-19 has changed the business landscape, encouraging more flexible working. As things get busier, however, you may want to establish a clearly defined working environment, such as an office, studio, or workshop. Having a dedicated workspace offers many advantages: it helps free you from outside distractions and interruptions; it can be tailored to your type of work, with sufficient space for equipment; and it can provide, if necessary, a suitable environment for meeting customers or clients.

WORKING FROM HOME

Basing yourself at home is an attractive and cost-saving option, but you will need to find a dedicated workspace.

PROS

> **No commute** saves you the time, stress, and cost of travelling.

> **Flexible working hours** enable you to start work early and to work during the evenings if necessary, helping you to navigate your other commitments.

> **Lower costs** are possible as you have no rental or parking fees or other transport costs to pay, and your refreshments are prepared at home.

CONS

> **Switching off** from work can be more difficult when you can take your laptop into any room and your office space is so easily accessible.

> **Working in isolation** can be stressful and lonely, and other household members may be distracting.

> **A home address** may seem less professional to clients than a separate business address.

SHARED SPACES

A shared space can be an affordable choice, but working alongside others can be helpful or a hindrance.

PROS

> **Shared resources**, rented on a flexible basis, offer you affordable office space that you do not need to equip.

> **Working alongside** other business people provides the opportunity to network.

> **Some co-working** spaces provide breakout areas and communal kitchens, which can give sole traders a valuable sense of community.

CONS

> **The commute** to the office may take time, cause stress, and cost you petrol or fares.

> **Lack of privacy** in an open office space may not be appropriate for some businesses.

> **Working in close** proximity to others can prove a distraction.

> **Higher costs** than home-working, due to rental fees and transport costs.

It also provides a formal setting for your business, giving it a physical base from which to operate. Such spaces come at a cost, but there are options.

Using shared spaces

Shared workspaces, where basic equipment and services (such as internet access), are part of the rental package, are now widely available. These provide professional settings, where you rent space – sometimes a single desk and computer – for as long as required. They offer many of the benefits of a private office, without the maintenance and set-up costs.

For some businesses, creating the impression of having a dedicated workspace is more important than having an actual physical space (see box, below right).

Storing and warehousing

Some businesses will need storage space on their premises to keep stock safe, dry, and secure, and may need to rent additional storage space or warehousing. Self-storage is one option, but if products have to be shipped out to customers, you will have to find premises with sufficient room to accommodate inventory or hire warehouse storage space.

Warehousing can offer both storage and logistics (the inbound and outbound flow of goods, plus transportation and inventory control), but the costs may be high. Some distribution and fulfilment companies now provide flexible, cost-effective storage options, depending on how much you trade each season, where you pay only for the storage you use.

PRIVATE WORKSPACES

A private office outside your home puts you in control and gives your prestige, but it comes at a cost.

PROS

> **Private office space**, whether furnished and fully equipped or unfurnished, can be tailored to your needs.

> **You have privacy** and can control the work environment with fewer distractions than if you were home-based or worked in a shared space.

> **An office address** can offer more professional credibility, and a place to meet clients.

CONS

> **The cost of overheads** when renting a private office space are much higher than for a virtual office or a home-based working space.

> **The commute** may again take time out of your day, and may add to your stress and costs.

> **Networking is not** as easy as when you operate from an open, community-based, co-working space.

VIRTUAL WORKSPACES

The cost of business premises can be one of the largest overheads for a small business, and start-ups may find renting office space unaffordable. One possible solution is a virtual office – a service that can offer start-ups credibility and many of the benefits of a physical office for a fraction of the cost. Entrepreneurs can work from home, but use a telephone-answering service to manage calls, as well as reception services, and the option to book real meeting rooms when required. A virtual office can also offer a business address and mail-handling services to give a home-based company greater prestige.

66%
of companies begin in a spare bedroom, garage, or other part of the home

Entrepreneur Europe, 2020

Choosing where to locate your start-up

Finding a good location for your business can be vital. It will affect your costs and may influence the number and type of customers or clients you attract. Making the best choice relies on careful analysis.

Assessing what you need

Your line of business will determine the sort of location you need and how important a role location plays. If planning to open a restaurant or shop, for example, you need to be where you can maximize trade, but location is less critical if you work largely online, manufacture goods, or sell to trade buyers. Even so, you may need to consider costs, such as rent, storage, and transport, and what sort of working environment will make you feel comfortable.

Unless you work from home, you will need safe, secure premises in a neighbourhood that you and any employees and clients can travel to easily. Parking spaces and easy access may also be essential.

Researching the area

First, decide your key criteria such as "on a main shopping street" for a retail outlet, or "near a station" if your business relies on client visits. Look online and in newspapers, for information about an area and its available business premises, and visit commercial property agents. Try to single out areas where

Questions to ask yourself

Before starting your search for business premises, work through this list of questions. Be as honest as you can about the answers, as commitments can be difficult to undo once you make a decision. Also, think about your future needs. Working from home may initially save costs, but it could leave you without the space to expand your business. Once your business is up and running, and you can assess, forecast, and monitor its growth and development, it may be worth setting out a plan for finding the right location for expansion when it reaches a certain size.

Do I really need physical premises?

Many businesses can simply be run from home, such as those trading online. If you need to make alterations to your home in order to trade, make sure you follow local planning rules. If you intend to prepare or sell food from your own kitchen, adhere to health and safety regulations (see pp.212–215).

What type of premises?

Most people setting up a business will rent or lease their premises. Think about the space you will require. How much storage is necessary? Do you need an area for preparing food? Can the existing premises be adapted to create more space and facilities?

Who are my customers or clients?

If customers or clients will be visiting your premises, you will need to consider facilities for them, such as parking spaces and possibly toilets. If your business provides a service to the public, you will also need to ensure that you can make adjustments to provide for disabled people.

What sort of building and area will best suit my business?

Think about the type of space you need to accommodate employees, customers, or clients. Consider the feel of the surrounding neighbourhood, the look of the premises from the outside, and whether its internal layout and design match your business's needs.

special deals, such as cash grants or reductions in local taxes, are offered to new businesses. Get a feel for an area by visiting potential locations. If possible, chat to local business owners and ask them about the area. If enterprises like yours have failed there in the past, try to discover why, as the reasons may be linked to the location.

Check if there are any restrictive local regulations that might affect your business, or any planned developments that could have a detrimental impact on the area. Also consider your space and service needs, and any permissions or licences you may require.

Does it suit your business?

Make sure the area you choose is right for your style of business. For example, siting an upmarket beauty salon in a rundown area is unlikely to work. Try to view the location from the perspective of customers in your target market.

Assess the level of competition you will face in a particular area and whether this will impede the selling of your goods or services. Having competitors nearby is not always a bad thing. If you run an antiques shop, for example, your potential customers are likely to be browsers, so a similar shop nearby may actually increase your footfall.

 NEED TO KNOW

> **Lease term** is the minimum period covered by the lease.

> **Lessee** is the person taking out a lease on a premises from the lessor, the property owner.

> **Renewal options** define when and under what terms the lessee can extend the lease.

> **Security deposit** is the amount paid by the lessee at the beginning of the agreement. This sum is returned by the lessor at the end of the lease.

Can I rely on people booking my service in advance?

If you offer a service such as hairdressing or beauty treatments, you can choose whether people need to book ahead or can just turn up. If you think you can rely entirely on appointments, then a tucked-away location for your salon, such as a quiet side street, should not be a problem.

Is my business seasonal?

 Most rental or lease agreements can last at least one year, or longer. If your business is seasonal or dependent on changing tastes and trends, you may want to explore a short-term lease or consider alternatives, such as setting up a "pop-up" facility.

What can I afford?

This is a critical question because the cost of premises is fixed, whether you are trading well or not. Make sure you are aware of all the costs involved and work out what you can afford over the term of your rental or lease, based on realistic trading estimates.

Do I need passing trade to make my business work?

 Attractive premises on a popular street is important for a business that relies on drawing in passers-by. However, this usually comes at a cost. If you are starting a bookkeeping or accounting business, for example, an accessible office in a professional-looking building may be enough.

What is available?

 You will be lucky to find ideal premises in the perfect location at the right price, so you will probably have to compromise on at least some features. Make a list of "must-haves" and a list of "nice-to-haves" and be prepared to make sacrifices.

Are there any other options?

 Instead of having premises on the high street, could you trade from a mobile van or bus? Perhaps you could rent space from another small business? Locating a small craft shop within a café could be an advantage for both businesses.

Sourcing products and supplies

Consider how and where to find the supplies you need to produce your product. Look for stock that is both safe and ethically produced, and weigh up whether to source it locally or internationally.

Choosing suppliers

There are various factors to consider when deciding on a supplier, including price, safety, quality, and durability of your product, along with the (proven) reliability of your supplier. Ask who else they supply and if they have industry-standard documentation.

It is cheaper to buy direct from a manufacturer or factory, but it might not be possible to buy your supplies in small enough quantities, and you may be asked to put down a deposit on initial orders.

A distributor (a firm that distributes goods on behalf of manufacturers) will probably sell smaller amounts, though most likely at a higher price. Small producers offer a personal service, but they may not be able to guarantee continuity of supply, fast turnaround, or all relevant ethical and safety standards.

Research suppliers by visiting trade shows and networking with people in your industry via LinkedIn or similar websites. Visit possible suppliers to see how they operate and ensure they grasp the needs of your business. If buying from abroad, be mindful of potential language barriers and keep your communications simple.

Make, reuse, or buy?

In some cases, it might be better to make the product yourself rather than buy it in. But always consider if this time would be better spent enhancing or running other aspects of the business. Sourcing recycled, reused, or repurposed items and materials could be a cheap and ethical option.

Reused or repurposed
Reused or vintage items have environmental benefits and may be cheaper, but maintaining consistent quality, quantity, and safety may be a problem.

Small, local suppliers
Buying from producers nearby supports the local community and reduces delivery miles. However, local producers often carry a limited range of goods and can be more expensive.

IMPORTING GOODS

Importing (see pp.212–215) may offer the widest choice of suppliers and products, but expect some issues with speed and reliability of supply: some countries, such as China, can change import/export terms at very short notice. It can also be harder to build a relationship with a supplier who is far away.

> **Check whether any** special licences are needed: for example, some countries prohibit the export or import of antiques without a licence.

> **Assess how much** tax or import duty is to be paid, and agree trading terms with your supplier.

> **Set a delivery date** with the supplier and agree the means of delivery.

> **Discuss potential problems** in advance; agree what will happen, if, for example, goods do not arrive on time.

> **Work out how** potentially longer shipping times might affect your business processes or impact on customers.

> **Investigate ethical standards**: are factory conditions acceptable? Is the supplier environmentally friendly?

> **Make sure you understand** every link of your supply chain (see pp.180–181).

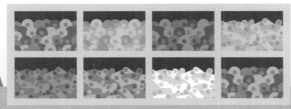

Major national suppliers
Items that you need to order regularly and in bulk may be easier to source from major national suppliers. While cheaper, your competitors may be able to buy the same stock.

Sourced internationally
Items produced overseas may be cheaper. However, you will have to factor in a longer lead-time and may need to outsource checking of your items before they are shipped.

Outsourcing tasks

Finding professionals to help with specific operational tasks costs money, but can save you time and may increase your chances of commercial success.

Identifying your needs

Getting your business up and running can seem overwhelming, with many aspects to coordinate, such as dealing with customers, handling your accounts, and other legal requirements, plus the need to provide your goods or services. However, this can be made simpler by looking at each function, and deciding if making use of external help would be a good option.

Utilizing friends and family with specific skills is one possibility, while another is to seek out small business services that may be available from government or civic organizations. You could also consider paying a professional for their services. This could be a one-off commission, such as a web designer creating a website, or it may be an ongoing arrangement, such as using a logistics company to store and ship your products.

These decisions will depend on the type of business you are setting up: a home-based, graphic design studio might only need outside help for end-of-year accounting, whereas a restaurateur may need a wider range of services.

✓ NEED TO KNOW

> **Inventory** describes the goods produced, or in production, that will be sold by a business.

> **Logistics** manages how things are moved between the point of production to the consumer, including packaging, distribution, and transportation.

> **SLA** (service level agreement) is a contract that lists the type and value of outsourced services, along with any conditions, such as annual maintenance.

> **Warehousing** is the storage and management of goods waiting to be sent out to distributors and consumers.

Using third parties

Although keeping outgoings to a minimum is crucial for any new business, paying for outsourced services from a specialist can save money in the long run. There are a wide variety of services you may need. An independent professional can provide a fresh perspective, pointing out problems or suggesting solutions. However, before enlisting external services it is important to be clear about the specific needs of your business, and have an idea of budget. Ask for quotes before making a decision, and research the outsourcers thoroughly. If there are no reviews online, ask for examples of their work and references from previous clients, and never pay for anything upfront.

Marketing
If your business needs specialist marketing expertise, a particular form of marketing, such as social media, or you want to launch a bigger campaign than you can handle in-house, you will need to go to professional marketers.
> Creating content
> Managing social media
> Running email marketing

Website design and maintenance
Regular website maintenance is crucial for an e-commerce business, and can be outsourced to an IT specialist, who may also offer website design. Occasional maintenance will suffice for less website-dependent businesses.
> Managing updates
> Hosting website
> Search engine optimization

IT
For occasional or longer term IT needs, freelance or agency experts can improve computer networks and operating systems, as well as maximize the performance of your website.
> Developing apps
> Implementing new technology
> Troubleshooting

Customer care
A customer relationship specialist can respond, on your behalf, to your customer calls or emails in a timely manner, as well as provide after-sales follow-up, if required, and data management.

❯ Handling sales
❯ Dealing with complaints
❯ Customer service training

Logistics
Outsourcing logistics means that when orders come in, someone else handles their fulfilment and distribution, along with warehousing, product inventory, and insurance.

❯ Warehousing
❯ Managing inventory
❯ Packing and shipping

Manufacturing
Unless your product is unique, few small businesses will invest in building a manufacturing plant; the most viable alternative is to use an existing manufacturer. They can also produce prototypes or samples of your product.

❯ Designing products for manufacture
❯ Producing components
❯ Assembling products

Payroll
A payroll provider charges a monthly fee in return for handling the payment of staff wages, automatically deducting amounts owing for tax and insurance. Using a bookkeeper is another, cheaper way to run payroll and monthly sales data.

❯ Managing payroll
❯ Data entry and processing
❯ Distributing payslips

Recruitment
Finding just the right person for a position can be a struggle. A recruitment agency may help, producing a shortlist of candidates, and charging a one-off fee or a percentage of the new recruit's salary.

❯ Headhunting for senior roles
❯ Providing contract staff
❯ Workforce planning

Accounting
Accountants can help with the initial business set-up, submit annual tax returns, or provide monthly or quarterly services. Fees are tax-deductible, and it is one of the most commonly outsourced services.

❯ Preparing tax returns
❯ Running monthly sales data
❯ Ensuring payment of sales tax

Legal and HR
A solicitor can help you draft business contracts and legal agreements, as well as guide you on the latest regulations. An HR advisor can assist you with staffing issues and contracts.

❯ Drafting licensing contracts
❯ Drawing up business partner and rental agreements
❯ Preparing employee contracts

Striking a balance

Running your own business can be exciting, challenging, and highly rewarding, but it is important not to ignore other aspects of your life. Striking a healthy work–life balance is essential.

Setting boundaries

Starting your new business is both exciting and highly demanding. You have to put in time and effort, but long hours can take their toll, affecting your relationships and your health. Try to draw clear boundaries between work and leisure. To create a good work–life balance, aim for routine working hours, starting and finishing at the same times each day, and make sure you take a lunch break. If you are based at home, try to mark the transition from work to leisure with an end-of-work ritual, such as going for a swim, walk, or jog.

Set boundaries around physical spaces to separate work and home areas. You might want to establish a dedicated workspace at home, ideally a separate room or another area reserved solely for work. If you have sufficient resources, you could consider building a garden room to work in, or renting an office, studio, or business space elsewhere.

If you have employees, consider how you can help maintain their work–life balance, too. It may mean a flexible approach that focuses more on their productivity than on being present for a set number of hours per day. This approach also helps to build a happy, dynamic team.

Work–life balance

While your business may suffer if you are distracted by personal worries, your partner or family may also feel neglected if you are always working. It is possible to get the balance right. Agreed routines and good communication can ensure that your work life and home life complement each other, rather than clash head-on.

MANAGING STRESS

> **Take regular breaks** throughout the day.
> **Exercise** to clear your head, relieve stress, and open your mind to new ideas.
> **Do not neglect your diet**. Junk food causes sugar spikes, which can leave you feeling hungry and tired.
> **Practise meditation** or mindfulness, together with deep-breathing exercises to relax your body and mind.
> **Stick to a sleep routine**, based on your natural sleep-wake cycle, to ensure you get the rest you need.

WORK LIFE

> Plan out each day; carefully time–manage meetings and set specific times for tasks like checking emails.
> Try different ways to improve productivity.
> Delegate when it makes sense to do so.

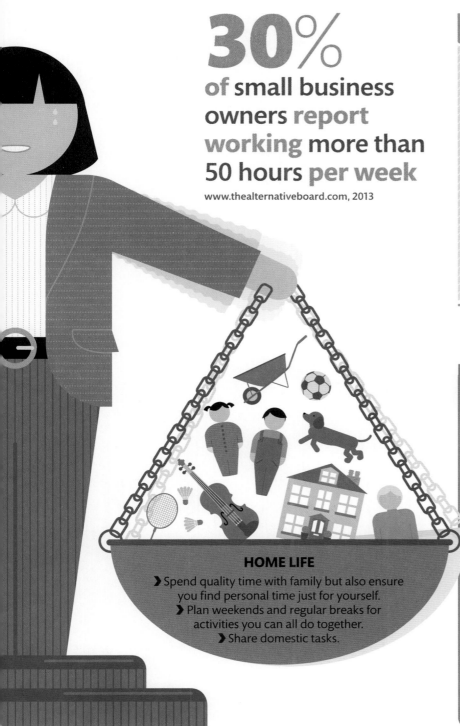

30%
of small business owners report working more than 50 hours per week

www.thealternativeboard.com, 2013

MAKING IT WORK

> **Find a mentor** to bounce ideas off. Local chambers and members groups associated with your industry can offer peer mentoring or networking events, and it can be helpful to talk to others who understand the pressures of running a business.

> **Stay social** and meet up with friends to keep you grounded and put work concerns in perspective.

> **Draw up a schedule** to block out work and leisure time, and maintain it to monitor balance.

JUGGLING PARENTHOOD

Childcare is a challenge for all working parents and especially for those who run their own business. Organizing work around childcare responsibilities can help and is why parents often choose to start a home-based business.

> **Rather than working** traditional 9–5 hours, parents may choose to work from 9am until 3pm, stopping work to collect children from childcare or school, then spending time as a family before resuming work once children are in bed.

> **Parents can share the load** by taking it in turns with co-parents or friends to do the school run when they have time-sensitive tasks, such as urgent emails to send or presentations to finish.

HOME LIFE

> Spend quality time with family but also ensure you find personal time just for yourself.
> Plan weekends and regular breaks for activities you can all do together.
> Share domestic tasks.

Working with family and friends

You can make a success of your business by working with family and friends who share your vision. However, it is advisable to set rules and boundaries that keep your working relationships professional.

Working together

There are many advantages to working with family and friends. You know and trust each other and can be more relaxed. You all have a vested interest in the business, shared values, and a shared desire to succeed, which often means that team members are more flexible and more willing to make sacrifices than other employees might be. Yet, to avoid misunderstandings that could damage that bond and lead to resentment or disappointment, it is important to set guidelines and put processes in place early on.

Facing issues

Start by gathering your team together and asking everyone to write down their hopes for the new business – and their concerns. Discussing these points, which are likely to vary, leads to a greater awareness of everyone's perpective.

Agreeing the rules

The bonds you share with family and friends are intensely personal, so working with them is both a pleasure and a challenge. Agreeing roles and setting job descriptions is an important first step. You must also decide practical details, such as holiday allowances and how expenses will be claimed. Discussing your goals can help cement the team, but you will need to be able to address disputes, too.

Agree roles

Try to be objective and think about what value each friend or family member is adding. They may be providing finance, or perhaps they came up with the idea for a new product or service, or have useful access to contacts. Knowing the strengths of each team member will help you and others plan what they should do. Agree roles with them and create job descriptions as you would for any other employee.

Create formal processes

Consult your team members and agree guidelines on how the business will run. These may include voting rights, rewards, holiday allowances, and how expenses will be claimed. They should also cover what will happen in the event of a dispute, such as two people wanting to take their holiday at the same time, which is not uncommon in family businesses. Once decided, put the agreement in writing.

You should also create a charter (see pp.28–29) to establish team members' roles and responsibilities. It is also important to draw up a legal agreement that sets down any investments in the company that individual members have made and establishes how assets and investments would be divided if the business does not work out.

While the bonds of friendship and family can create a supportive workplace environment, there must be boundaries in place that prevent special treatment. If a friend or family member does something wrong or illegal that could damage the enterprise, you need to respond as if they were any other employee in the company. Failing to act, could set a terrible example to other members of the team.

Working with friends and family can be fun, but the team must operate professionally. Good communication is key to settling disputes and misunderstandings, and dealing with the changes that every business experiences as it grows. Your strength is the stake you all have in the business and the shared goal of making it a success.

✓ NEED TO KNOW

> **Buy-sell agreement** sets out how shareholders can sell stock, who can buy it, and under what circumstances it can be sold.

> **Owners' council** is when the business owners gather to discuss their goals and direction, and relay their thoughts to its board.

> **Succession planning** involves deciding who will lead your new business if you are unable to work for any reason. Without such a plan, the business could fail.

"...for me, building the family business and being with family, was worth it."

Baba Kalyani, Bharat Forge

Create shared goals

Discuss the goals of the business and the strategy and tactics you believe will achieve them. Ensure that everyone has a chance to contribute their ideas and that all team members understand what needs to be done. When working with friends and family, it is easy to assume that they are thinking the same thing as you, but it could be the case that each person has a slightly different picture in their head.

Avoid and resolve conflict

Good communication is essential to avoid conflict. If a problem arises, try to talk it through. Do not rush to judgement, but listen to your friend or family member. Create a process, if possible, for resolving serious disputes. Overwork can make people impatient and irritable; remember that it is just as important for those involved in family businesses as it is for others to have time for leisure and relaxation.

FIRST STEPS

Choosing a name

First impressions count, so consider carefully when deciding on a name for your business. Think about how to make it descriptive, catchy, unique, and, above all, memorable, so you stand out from the competition.

Getting it right

Since your company's name is likely to be the first thing customers note about your business, it is crucial to get it right. Decide whether it should personify what your start-up offers, reflect your values, or capture your brand's personality (see pp.60–61).

Sole traders looking to build a personal brand might include their own name and a description of what the business does. Businesses targeting local clients might include their location in the company's name.

Formal names can convey ideas of reliability and trust but may lack youthful appeal. Your name should be simple, easy to say, and easy to remember. A name that is fun, clever, or humorous may grab attention, but be careful as wordplay may not translate, and you risk your start-up not being taken seriously.

Research your business field to ensure that your preferred name is not already in use. If it is similar to another company's name or trademark (see pp.96–97), you may have to change it – or face a costly lawsuit.

What makes a good name?

The best names are memorable for the right reasons – they are accessible and have positive associations. They should be easy to say, write, and spell, and should be an asset to your business. If you plan to trade internationally, check how your name translates in other languages.

Unique

Your company's name needs to be unique to avoid legal issues or confusion with other brands. Consider making up a new word. IKEA, for instance, is an acronym of the name of the founder, his family's farm, and his home town.

Simple

A simple name with fewer syllables is easier to recall, say, and search for – Skype or Twitter, for example. Customers might abbreviate longer names to a less favourable version. Unusual spellings can also backfire, so take care.

???

REGISTERING YOUR NAME

Once you have chosen your name and you are satisfied that you can use it (see right), then you should register it as a trademark to prevent others from operating under the same or a confusingly similar title. This is a separate step from legally incorporating the company that will trade under the chosen name, which is generally handled by a different government agency (see pp.212–215), and perhaps at local or state level too, depending on the country.

Usually the name will end with a suffix such as Limited (Ltd) in the UK and Incorporated (Inc.) in the US. Whether sole trader or a company, try to secure a top-level domain for your chosen name – .com; .co.uk; or .au (see pp.114–115), which is the web address you will use for your website. This does not have to be the same as your chosen name, but it helps if the two are as close as possible. While a fee is payable, registering will give you sole use of that address.

! BE AWARE

> **Search national business registers** to see whether your prospective name has already been taken (see pp.212–215). Sole traders can consult local website listings.

> **Check trademark registers** and intellectual property office sites (see pp.212–215).

> **Look at domain names**, as you cannot register one that is taken, as well as social media, too.

Descriptive

You might decide on a name for your company after compiling a list of brief descriptors of what your business does. Facebook, WeChat, and Netflix all have names that convey their purpose or function.

Meaningful

A name that has meaning behind it makes for a more compelling brand story. LEGO, for instance, comes from the Danish term *leg god*, to "play well". The name Hotmail arose from HTML, the language used to write web pages.

Unusual

Company names that seem unrelated to the nature of the business may also be highly successful, as they can capture attention. Good examples include online retailer, Amazon, and IT and media giant, Apple.

Alliterative

Using alliteration – starting words with the same sound or letter – makes names fun to say and is another way to make them memorable. Brand names such as Coca-Cola or TikTok, for instance, stand out through their alliteration.

Developing your brand

A brand is a tool for helping a business to stand out from the crowd. Creating and refining your own brand will enable you to inform customers what your business is about – and what sets it apart.

Creating a brand

Your brand is more than just a logo or design used for advertising. It is a means of communicating your company's purpose and values to your customers.

Imagine, for example, that a start-up develops a new fruit drink made only from organic ingredients.

In order to attract sales, the owners might promote the idea that the product is sustainable, ethical, and healthy. By building these values into their brand, the start-up owners can convey the benefits of their product to their customers. In addition to its values, the brand might also embody a particular personality, such as a spirited or youthful outlook (see below).

You must be consistent and authentic, however. For instance, if customers discover that the drink contains artificial ingredients or is sourced unethically, they may lose faith in your brand.

Deciding on your brand

Consider what your customers are looking for, what you are offering, and what your company stands for. Ensure that these align. Your brand is about conveying your values, such as being ethical, along with your "personality", which is the public perception of your company's character.

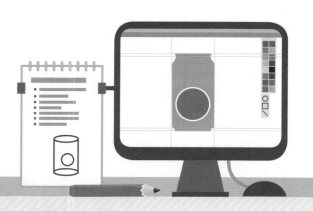

BRAND PERSONALITY

Traditional
Reliable, comforting, familiar

Bold
Carefree, spirited, youthful ✓

Sophisticated
Exclusive, romantic, elegant

Rugged
Tough, strong, outward-bound, masculine

Developing the concept

Consider the benefits that your customers derive from your products or services. Then decide what ideas you would like customers to associate with your brand. This could be notions such as "traditional and reliable", "sophisticated and exclusive", "rugged", or "bold".

Choosing your brand personality

Your brand's personality is the human characteristics that you would like to be linked to your brand. So, if your target audience is involved with sport, for example, you might want your brand's personality to embody energy and vibrancy.

It is wise to register your brand as your trademark (see pp.212–215), so that rivals cannot imitate it and undermine your business.

Personal branding

Developing a personal brand can also be highly beneficial for freelancers and contractors. It is a reflection of how you present yourself to colleagues and clients. Like a business brand, a personal brand encompasses outward appearance, but is also about your behaviour: if people are to trust you, your actions must be genuine and consistent.

DEFINING BRAND IDENTITY

French professor of marketing strategy Jean-Noël Kapferer created the Brand Identity Prism in 1996, with six aspects he considered vital to brand identity.

Physique The brand's physical appearance, materials, and qualities, including its packaging and colour.

Relationship The bond between the brand and the consumer, which is particularly important for retailers and the service sector.

Reflection The outward mirror: the type of person the consumer perceives the brand to be aimed at.

Personality The type of person the brand would be if it were human.

Culture The building of a cult following, closely allied to the brand's country of origin.

Self-image The inward mirror: how the company perceives its own brand.

Audio-visual elements
Use memorable symbols, phrases, and sounds that resonate with customers.

Brand name
Choose a name that reflects your brand concept; make it both different and memorable (see pp.58–59).

Design and packaging
Pick a style that reflects your image and values. If you are a green business, choose recyclable material.

Strapline
Use a few words to encapsulate what your business is about. Keep it short and snappy.

Communicating your brand identity

Brainstorm how you can best convey your brand to potential customers, perhaps through eye-catching design, a distinctive logo, and an unforgettable slogan. Remember that you may need to communicate your brand across more than one media platform.

Nurturing the relationship

Branding is really about creating a lasting relationship with the customer, (see (pp.62–63). People will remain loyal and be preferential to your brand if they can empathize with its concept, personality, and values. Ensure everything you do reinforces this relationship and does nothing to harm it.

Telling your story

People like to buy from businesses they feel reflect their own beliefs. Creating a story around your brand will encourage your customers and clients to feel a connection with you, leading to a sense of commitment and loyalty.

Boosting your brand

More than just a description of how you began your business, a brand story reveals your personal reasons and motivations for doing so, and underlines what it stands for.

When people choose a product or service, their decision can be based as much on emotion as it is on logic.

While customers and clients consider price, quality, and availability when making a choice, many prefer to buy from people and companies they like and respect.

If you can convey the personality of your business to your customers and clients in the form of a story, it will help you to differentiate your product or service from that of competitors, and encourage trust, loyalty, and repeat business. A powerful story also makes your business more memorable – much more effectively than logos and slogans do. Putting people at the heart of your story will attract potential employees, too.

How to tell the story

Your brand story must attract the attention of your audience and maintain their interest throughout. If you sell ethically sourced goods, explain why, what you have seen, and what motivated you. Keep it concise and compelling, but also authentic and unique to your business, so that it appeals to your target audience.

DEVELOP YOUR STORY

At its heart, your story must encapsulate your business's origin and core values. Think about the problem or personal goal that drove you, and the insight that inspired you to solve that problem or achieve that goal. Describe the ways in which your business meets those expectations today, and tie this in with your vision for its future (see pp.24–25).

> "If people love a brand story, 55% are more likely to buy the product in future."

The Brand Storytelling Report, Headstream, 2015

Shaping your story

It takes time and planning to create an effective brand story. Begin by asking yourself what motivated you to start your business. Perhaps it was because you could not find something you wanted to buy, so decided to make it yourself, or because you were passionate about a particular product or service, and keen to make it more widely available. Look beyond the potential financial rewards and consider what makes you excited about your business, and jot down some words that express your emotional responses.

Think about your customers and clients. How would you like them to feel when they trade with you? What would you like them to say about your business? Note the answers to these questions and keep reviewing them. You can then weave the elements you have compiled into a positive and convincing brand story.

! BE AWARE

> **Do not** make false claims. If your story is not genuine, when the truth emerges, your customers will no longer trust you, and your brand will be damaged.

> **Focus on** what makes your business different. Your story must be unique and stand apart from that of your competitors.

> **Make sure** that daily operations live up to the story you tell your clients, and reflect the message behind your brand.

> **Encourage colleagues** to understand and embrace your business's core message and the values you want to convey to your customers and clients.

TARGET YOUR AUDIENCE

Not everyone will be your customer or client, and not everyone will share your values, so tailor your story to those who will, and do. Use the information you have gained about your market, and potential customers and clients (see pp.38–39), to target your brand story accordingly. For example, if you have identified that your customers or clients are likely to have families, weave a family element into your story.

SPREAD THE WORD

Share your brand story on the social media sites most used by your customers (see pp.140–141). If you have a website, post messages, images, and videos relating to your story on it. As you gain more customers and clients, actively engage with them to build closer relationships. Try to gain the support of online "influencers", who may share your story with their followers (see pp.198–199).

A marketing mix

When planning a product launch or marketing campaign, you need to consider four key elements that together make up the "marketing mix": the product or service itself, its price, how it is promoted, and where it is sold.

Using the mix

The success of your product or service – however brilliant or innovative – relies on sales. To achieve good sales you need a well-targeted marketing approach, using a mix of four ingredients. The first is your product or service itself and what it offers the customer.

The next is the price structure, reflecting what your target market will accept. You must then decide how to promote your offering, and where and how to distribute it. Each of these ingredients is a powerful tool you can use to persuade target customers that your product or service is what they want and need.

4Ps – business-oriented

The product, price, promotion, and place marketing mix is an approach that is business-led rather than customer-oriented.

PRODUCT

> **Will the product design**, size, features, colour, and packaging appeal to customers?
> **What unique benefits** and solutions does the product offer?
> **How does it compare** with competing products?

PRICE

> **What is the usual price point** for this type of product?
> **How much** is the customer willing to pay based on their perception of the product's value?
> **How might minor tweaks** to the price affect sales volume and profit?

4Cs – consumer-oriented

Commodity, cost, communication, and convenience emphasize that customers are influencing the ingredients in the marketing mix.

COMMODITY

> **Has the product** been designed, developed, and possibly even modified to meet and exceed customer expectations?
> **How and why** will the design, size, features, colour, and packaging appeal to a specific niche market?

COST

> **What will attract** the customer? Premium quality? Low cost?
> **Do customers make** buying decisions for this kind of product based on quality or on budget?
> **Will target customers** think it represents good value?

Product, price, promotion, and place make up the "4Ps", the traditional marketing mix. Today, many businesses use the newer "4C" mix that combines commodity, cost, communication, and convenience. This approach shows the increasing importance of focusing on your customers and their experience, and of seeking out niche rather than mass markets. To get it right, you must define and analyse your target market, then examine each element in the marketing mix to ensure that it will attract customers and meet their expectations.

> "The 4P's was about 'What does the marketer want to say?' while the 4C's asks 'What does the customer need to hear that the marketer can say?'"
>
> Robert F. Lauterborn, originator of the 4Cs

PROMOTION

> **Which combination** of marketing channels and materials will be most effective?
> **What type** of promotions do customers generally prefer?
> **When are customers** most likely to respond to promotional calls to purchase?

PLACE

> **Where do customers** prefer to shop for products such as this?
> **Which distribution channel** is preferred? Is it online, shops, or catalogues?
> **How can this offering** stand out from competitors' products sold in the same place?

7Ps

In addition to the original 4Ps, some companies use a model that adds these extra 3Ps:

> **People** Are they the ideal mix to create a team that exceeds customer expectations with the best level of service?
> **Process** Are order-processing, and customer complaint and query systems in place and sufficiently effective?
> **Physical environment** Is the place or website from which the product is sold attractive enough?

COMMUNICATION

> **What type of messages** get the best customer response?
> **What marketing** information will interest your customers?
> **How do customers prefer** to receive marketing messages? Are the messages relevant to them?

CONVENIENCE

> **How convenient** is it for busy customers to find, buy, and get the product into their hands?
> **What can be done** to make this process as simple and straightforward as possible?

7Cs

To the original 4Cs, some businesses add an extra 3Cs. These are:

> **Corporation** Does the company structure, its competitors, or stakeholders unduly influence the marketing drive and results?
> **Consumer** Do you know what the customer needs and wants, and do the marketing materials and product itself address this?
> **Circumstances** Can the business cope with adverse external factors that might impact sales?

The selling process

You may have great products or services, but you still have to sell them. To do this, you will need to understand the selling process, and know how to build relationships with customers to generate further sales.

Understanding sales channels

There are many routes, or channels, to bring goods and services to market so that consumers can buy them. These sales channels range from online and retail, to selling direct to the customer and selling through a third party. Before deciding what channel is right for your business, reflect on what makes people buy your type of product or service and where they buy them from. Consider the qualities of your product or service. Are customers more likely to buy your product if they can see and feel it? Is yours the type of service people can buy online, such as producing illustrations?

Whatever the approach, there are basic principles to follow when you are selling. Know your audience and speak to them in a way that they can relate to. If you are selling a piece of technology to people who are not technically proficient, use words they will understand. If you are selling face-to-face, do not describe at length why your offering is so good. Listen to your customer and let them know that their opinions matter.

Fulfilling orders

Once you have made a sale you need to fulfil the order. Think about your customers' expectations, such as when they will expect to receive their order, and make the process straightforward. You may decide to take orders and despatch the goods yourself. However, as your business grows, you may want to outsource this task to a third party, such as an e-fulfilment company (see pp.74–75).

The sales funnel

A good way of thinking about the selling process is imagining it as a funnel – one that shows the stages prospective customers go through before making a purchase, each step bringing them closer to becoming a customer. At the top of the funnel there is a large number of prospective customers, but these become fewer and fewer as you descend through the funnel to the people who actually buy your goods. Your job is to ensure that there are enough customers in the funnel to generate sufficient sales for your business.

! BE AWARE

> **Thinking about price** is one of the most important factors when selling. Find out what your customers really value, and be prepared to adjust your price.

> **Pay attention to your existing customers** for they are your best prospects for future sales.

> **Tailor what you say** to different types of customer, based on their individual buying behaviour. Do not use the same message for everyone.

> **Beware of not listening enough** to your customers. Your business will benefit from what they tell you.

"We exist as businesses to serve our customers and they are always right."

Manish Chopra, CEO of Little

1 Awareness

This is the stage at which prospective customers become aware of your product or service. Promote awareness through activities such as writing blogs, being active on social media, advertising, and putting your products on display. The key is to focus their attention on your business and away from others.

2 Interest

Once you have gained attention, you need to keep it by creating interest. Consider how you can persuade someone to spend more time looking at what you have to offer. A good way to do this is to think what problem you are helping the prospective customer to solve, and to focus on that.

3 Decision

At this stage, your prospect is seriously thinking about making a purchase and is probably weighing up alternatives. Use supporting material to remove any doubts and help them reach their decision. Provide testimonials from satisfied customers or helpful comparisons with other products.

4 Action

Once your prospective customer has made a decision, you will need to encourage them to act on it. Make it obvious how they complete their purchase and make it as easy as possible.

Online selling

Selling online gives you access to a much wider market, while also saving on the cost of a "bricks-and-mortar" shop. There are several platforms you can use to sell to customers.

Identifying online opportunities

There are obvious advantages to selling your products online, such as avoiding the ongoing expense of maintaining a physical shop, being able to trade at any time of day or night, and reaching a much wider market. On the other hand, you face the challenges of customers being able to find you when searching online (see pp.118–119), and having to compete with all the other thousands of offerings on the internet.

To sell online you have a number of options: to set up your own website; to use an e-commerce site-builder; or to host your products through an online marketplace.

Using third-party sites

While creating your own site gives you complete control over how it looks and functions, (see pp.114–117), it takes time, money, and expertise. In contrast,

Choosing your platform

There are several ways you can sell online, with advantages and disadvantages to each approach. The platform you choose will depend on your product. If selling a personal service, then your own website may be preferable. If your product is very expensive you may want to choose an online marketplace that charges a smaller commission on your sale – or even use a range of platforms for your various products.

In 2018, online global e-retail sales amounted to

$2.8tn

Statista, 2018

Your own website

Building your own website allows you to create a virtual shopping experience that reflects your brand. You can also use additional software, allowing your site to take secure payments, and process invoices and shipments.

PROS

> **Website promotes** your unique brand
> **Easy to change** when necessary and according to how shoppers use it
> **No concerns** about changing internal algorithms, as found on online marketplaces, such as Amazon
> **Easy to tailor your structure** to improve searchability using search engine optimization

CONS

> **Takes time and money** to maintain, market, and host online
> **Requires technical knowledge** to create and maintain
> **Payment and data security** are essential and your responsibility: you will be liable for any breaches
> **Larger competitors' websites** are easy to find and may offer customers a better shopping experience

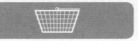

e-commerce site builders, such as Shopify or Wix, offer ready-made website templates onto which you simply drag and drop your content. They also provide secure payment systems, customer data protection, and elements such as shopping baskets, search bars, wish list functions, and review options.

Alternatively, you can also sell your products on large online marketplaces, such as Amazon, eBay, Etsy, or Facebook Marketplace, which also have the necessary infrastructure. Whichever option you choose, your customers will only buy your products if they like what they see and read. Be sure to describe them clearly and accurately, and include attractive, but honest, images.

SEARCH ENGINE OPTIMIZATION (SEO)

If you are selling on your own website, rather than an online marketplace, it will be up to you to make your site visible to potential customers. Most people search the internet using a search engine, such as Google, which creates a list of sites related to your search term. As most users only view the first few options listed, website owners compete to be as close to the top of these lists as possible. There are various ways you can optimise your website for search engines and improve your ranking (pp.118–119).

E-commerce site builders

These website builders specialize in e-commerce and offer software services for free or on subscription. You can choose from a template and fill in information fields to create your site, and use the shopping cart systems to sell, ship, and manage your products.

PROS

❯ **Easy to set up**, requiring little technical knowledge and no ongoing maintenance

❯ **Commonly multilingual**, so more likely to appeal to a global audience

❯ **Provides secure** payment and data systems, and other e-commerce tools, with some guarantees and insurance

CONS

❯ **Fees are payable**, either as a subscription or as commission charged on sales – typically 2–5 per cent or more

❯ **Customer service terms** and conditions are set by the site builder, with no flexibility

❯ **Site structure** is fixed by the site builder, which might not be optimized for search engines

❯ **Design is limited** to the site's available templates

Online marketplaces

These sites are like huge, online supermarkets, where thousands of products are listed internationally. To sell on these sites, you just need to create an account, choose a selling plan (in some cases), and then list your items.

PROS

❯ **No need to create** or market a website

❯ **Easier to market** your product

❯ **Massive marketplace** with international reach

❯ **Multilingual** and can deal with different currencies

❯ **E-commerce tools** are all supplied

CONS

❯ **Thousands of traders** make it hard to stand out

❯ **Referral fees** (the commission the sites take when items are sold) can be high – up to 45 per cent depending on the site and product sold

❯ **Site structure and trading terms** are fixed, and may not suit your business

Providing a service

When clients sign up to a service, they do so on trust: unlike buying a product, there is nothing to handle or see before they part with money. Every aspect of your service must meet, or exceed, their expectations.

Making promises

Providing services involves using your skills and knowledge to satisfy the needs of your clients – it is you and what you do that must meet their expectations. Because of this, the relationship between you and your clients is closer – and more important – than it is for a business that sells a product. By offering a service, you are making a promise to do something for your client, and satisfy their needs.

In order to run a successful service-based business, you must thoroughly understand your clients' requirements and do everything you can to make their experience of buying from you a positive one. You must also convey a sense of trustworthiness – that you will at least deliver on your promise, and hopefully even exceed it. Examine and analyse all the various stages your client will have to go through as part of their experience with you: from seeing your marketing material, to using your service, and their satisfaction with it afterwards.

Identifying expectations

When planning your business, always consider the services you intend to offer from your clients' perspective. For example, if you are planning a dog-grooming service, think about the level of service you would expect yourself from such a business, the kind you would be happy to receive, and what would encourage you to return there. If you intend to target a particular clientele with your service, such as older or more affluent people, research their requirements carefully, as their needs are likely to be very specific.

It is important that you are clear about exactly what your clients will receive when they sign up to, and pay for, your service. To ensure clarity, write an SLA (Service-Level Agreement), which defines and agrees the commitment between you and your client in terms of service quality, responsibilities, and availability.

How to create a successful service

Maintaining a strong relationship with your clients is central to running a successful service business. Treat relationship-building as an ongoing process – one that is essential to growing a loyal client base. Take time to understand your clients' needs. Be prepared for those needs to change, and look for ways to adapt, enhance, or add to the services you offer in order to keep clients interested. Most importantly, always be honest, as the relationship relies on trust, which is easily lost.

 MAKING IT WORK

> **Stay in touch** with your clients after the initial service; for example, by sending newsletters that will be useful or interesting to them.

> **Keep looking for ways** to improve your service, and keep up-to-date with whatever is happening in your business sector.

> **Regularly try your competitors' services** to see what they do, and how you can surpass their offerings.

> **Deal with problems** immediately and try to put things right for clients.

> **Maintain your passion** for what you do to generate enthusiasm and to make your clients feel excited about experiencing your service.

> **Remain alert for related services** you could offer; for example, if you are a personal fitness instructor, you could also offer a sports massage service or nutrition advice.

Generating trust

Your clients will trust you if you are honest about what you can and cannot do. If you are unable to offer a particular service, suggest another business that can. Both the potential client and the business will remember you.

Exceeding expectations

Personalize your service by getting to know your clients and showing you care. Own up to mistakes and apologize, and offer no-quibble refunds. Surprise your clients – perhaps by sending birthday wishes, even a small gift.

Learning from experience

Creating loyalty among clients

The key factor in winning loyalty will be the quality of the service you provide. Back that up with excellent customer service, as well as incentives such as discounted rates, special offers, easier payment terms, or other "rewards" for longer-term clients.

Understanding clients' needs

Do not assume you know what your clients want. Ask people for feedback and discuss ideas for improving services with them. Do this regularly, so that the services you provide can evolve to meet their changing needs.

Being easy to work with

Be welcoming and friendly, and put people at ease. Always reply promptly to messages from clients. Make sure it is easy to book, pay for, and even cancel your services. People will be more willing to sign up if they feel in control.

Taking payments

For your business to succeed, you will need to be able to accept payments electronically. Give customers several payment options, so it is easier for them to make purchases and for fewer sales to fall through.

Paying electronically

To enable a customer to pay electronically (using a debit or credit card either in person or online), you need to open an account with a merchant service provider, who will give you access to their e-payment system in return for a fee. Merchant services provide payment gateways (for online transactions) and payment processors (for use in person), and act as intermediaries to communicate between your customer's source of funds, typically a bank, and your own bank or other type of financial account. Some merchant providers can offer combined gateway and processor technology. If you make sales with the customer in person, you need a payment processor combined with a terminal – a device that reads the customer's debit or credit card, or the mobile wallet on their phone. Merchant services are widely available, and the convenience to both your business and your customers will easily outweigh the costs involved.

You may be able to manage without using a merchant account – for example by asking customers to pay via online transfers directly into your business bank account. However, merchant services not only offer the widest range of payment options, but they also help to streamline your payment system, helping you to provide refunds easily, as well as shouldering some of the risk of customers attempting to reverse transactions.

How e-payment systems work

With cash use on the decline, e-payment – making paperless transactions via an electronic medium – is fast becoming the main way of making purchases. In the seconds it takes for an e-payment, the customer's bank and your bank "talk" to one another through a payment gateway or processor. If the customer has enough funds, the transaction is approved, and payment usually follows later. You might also wish to accept cryptocurrency, such as Bitcoin by choosing a bitcoin payment processing provider (PSP) and opening a bitcoin account. Customers pay you from their bitcoin wallets, and bitcoins can be converted to your local currency after the sale.

1 **Customer provides account information**

Using a terminal, the customer inserts, swipes, or taps their card, or taps their phone. When shopping online, the customer inputs their card or digital wallet details.

2 **Authorization request sent**

The merchant service provider gathers the transaction data and sends a secure request via a payment gateway/processor for approval to pay the seller.

3 **Request approved or declined**

The customer's bank approves the purchase if there is sufficient money in their account; otherwise it declines.

OFFLINE PAYMENT METHODS

Not everyone is happy making online purchases via websites, so if you can offer a range of payment methods there is less chance of you losing sales.

> **Bank deposit** The customer pays into your business account before the order is dispatched.

> **Cash on delivery** A courier collects cash for you from the customer at the point of delivery.

> **Cheque or money order** The customer posts you a cheque or money order, which you deposit and then wait for the funds to clear.

> **Pay to an agent** A partner shop collects payment from the customer on your behalf and takes a percentage of the money as a fee for providing the service.

> **Cross-border payment platform** This is a computer program shared with a partner organization that enables direct payments to be made between countries.

✓ NEED TO KNOW

> **Acquiring bank** is the seller's own bank, which receives funds from the customer's bank.

> **Digital wallet** is any type of software that enables people to store their bank details in the cloud for making payments online. PayPal and GooglePay are examples.

> **Issuing bank** denotes the customer's bank, which has issued the debit or credit card in the customer's name.

> **POS (point-of-sale) system** is software that enables retailers to take customers' payments, send invoices, and manage data and stock inventory.

> **PSP (payment services provider)** is a payment gateway and a merchant service provider combined into one.

> **White-label platform** refers to a ready-to-use computer program that automates the sales and payment system.

69% of customers abandon a purchase due to a lack of payment options

Baymard Institute consumer survey, 2019

④ Authorization or decline sent

Approval or refusal is sent back through the card network via the payment gateway/processor. The seller sees the message and the order is fulfilled or declined.

⑤ Transaction sent for settlement

The merchant service provider may wait to gather transactions from several customers before sending them to the various banks to request the payments due.

⑥ Funds transferred to seller

For each transaction made, the customer's bank releases the correct amount of money owing and transfers it to the seller.

Fulfilling orders

If your business sells and delivers products, it is vital to develop an efficient system for fulfilling customer orders. Customers will value your reliability and your brand will inspire trust.

Meeting expectations

Over the past decade, advances in managing orders from sale to delivery have raised customer expectations of quick, convenient receipt of goods and their easy return. A positive experience at each stage strongly influences customers' purchasing behaviour, so a new retail venture needs to ensure each part of the process, from taking orders and packing goods to sending them out, is as fast and efficient as possible.

To facilitate this, make certain you have sufficient stock, stored as close to your premises as possible, so that products can be easily accessed, packed, and despatched. Keep careful records throughout.

Initially, you might use multiple spreadsheets to track incoming orders and costs, to review and update inventory, and to set delivery dates so customers know when to expect their goods.

As your online orders grow, however, you are likely to need order fulfilment software to help you to organize your systems – or

Managing the process

A basic fulfilment system should enable you to handle orders promptly, acknowledge receipt of them, keep a record of them manually or otherwise, and communicate with all parties involved – from the manufacturer to the customer. Keeping track of all your inventory (products and materials) is also crucial, so that you have what is needed to meet demand. Coordinate each stage with the next one to ensure a smooth process.

Take orders

When a customer places an order, check if the goods are in stock or when they will be available. When this is confirmed, send an email to the customer, supplying them with an order number and indicating an estimated delivery date.

Manufacture or retrieve the product

Create the product or retrieve it from existing stock, simultaneously updating the inventory and creating or ordering more items to meet future demand. Then carefully package, label, and prepare the parcel for despatch.

you may find it more efficient to outsource all, or part of, the process (see pp.50–51) to maintain a high standard of customer service.

E-fulfillment companies help with online sales, handling everything from storage to despatch. They can also tailor their services to your needs as a small business.

If this seems an attractive option, choose carefully, ensuring that the costs are manageable and that the company's values, services, and operation are a good fit with your brand.

✓ NEED TO KNOW

> **Fulfilment management** is the overseeing of the ordering process, from the initial sales inquiry to the delivery of the product to the customer.

> **E-fulfilment** refers to the processes used by businesses to sell products or services online.

> **Warehouse inventory** refers to all the goods and materials that will be for sale by the company.

60%
of people buy from the online retailer with the best delivery options

State of eCommerce Delivery Consumer Research Report, MetaPack, 2017

Distribute or deliver the package

Choose an appropriate delivery method. If the customer is local, you can hand-deliver the item; if not, send it by post or courier. Valuable items require an insured shipping method, or can be covered by a goods-in-transit insurance policy.

Notify customer

Notify the customer when the package ships and, if required, contact them on the day of delivery to confirm location, time frame, and any special instructions. The package should include instructions on how to return the item, if necessary.

Identifying initial costs

You will need to spend money on items to get your business up and running. Give some thought to what you need now and what can wait, and balance the cost of the essential items against your available funds.

Assessing your needs

Each business has different set-up needs so will require a shopping list depending on the industry, location, and business model. Identify the initial costs required for the basic set-up of your business. These start-up purchases could be for assets, such as stock and equipment, or one-off expenses, such as acquiring a licence and creating a website. Remember that once your business is up and running, you will also have ongoing expenses (see pp.78–79).

It is not always necessary to buy everything; items can be leased (see box, below), rented, or shared with other businesses. Think, too, about buying reconditioned items, which can be cheaper and are less wasteful for the environment (see pp.100–101).

INSURANCE, PERMITS, AND LICENCES

Depending on your business, you may be legally required to hold insurance, permits, and licences in order to operate. Seek advice to ensure your business is compliant.

STOCK

Raw materials and stock need to be bought and stored before you can sell. Buy the minimum amount of materials to meet sales forecasts in the business plan. This avoids spending too much on storage.

BUYING OR LEASING ASSETS

Some assets essential to starting your business might be very expensive, such as premises, or be continually updated, such as equipment or software. When deciding what initial purchases you need to make, consider whether it would make sense to buy or lease. If you decide to buy an asset, you own and control it, but will have larger upfront costs and have to pay for ongoing maintenance. If you lease an asset, however, you rent it for a fixed time, spreading payments over regular intervals. You avoid a large initial outlay, and payments may be tax deductible. Leasing is also appealing if there is a high risk of the asset becoming obsolete. However, if you intend to use an asset in the long term, it is generally more cost-effective to buy it than lease it.

PREPARING PREMISES

Whether it is an office or a shop, if your business requires premises you will need to make upfront payments. Some costs to expect include deposits and rent, health and safety checks, construction, and decorating.

UTILITIES

Getting your premises connected to telecoms, electricity, and water is vital. Many utility providers offer discounted deals for rates and installations to business users, so shop around before committing.

EQUIPMENT

All businesses need equipment , whether it is machines to make coffee or scissors to cut hair. Make a list of your minimum requirements to see what your budget allows before spending on non-essentials.

TECHNOLOGY AND IT

In addition to computers and software, you may also need technology and IT support specific to your type of business. This can involve a significant investment, so consider buying refurbished kit or leasing.

MARKETING AND BRANDING

You will need to design a brand and a marketing strategy. Anticipate the costs of hiring a graphic designer to create a logo and any promotion for the launch of your business.

WEBSITE

You will need to lease your website's domain name and its web-hosting service. You may also want to commision a web designer. Secure your website and the privacy of its vistors by including online cybersecurity.

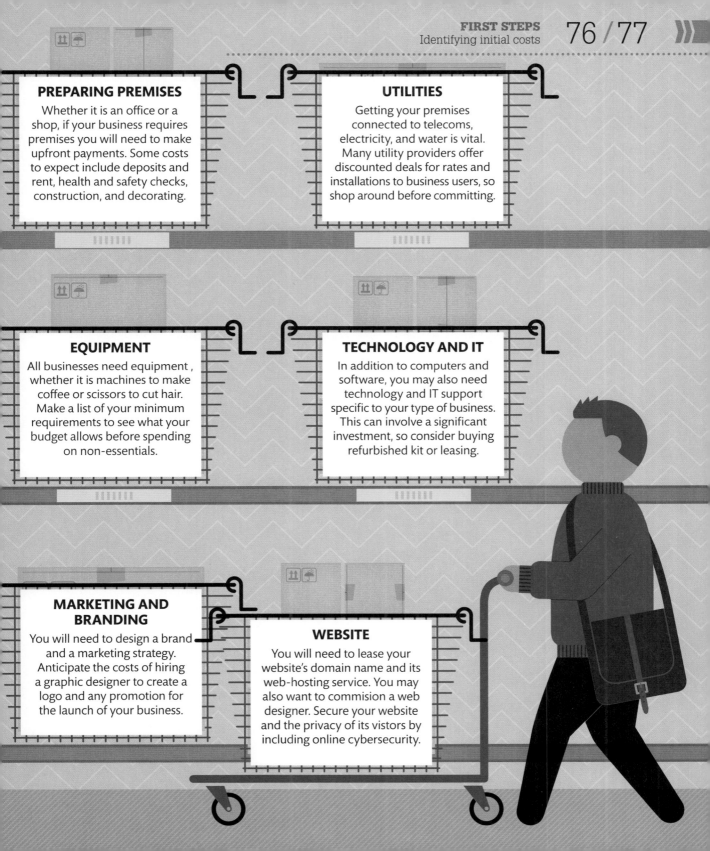

How much do you need to spend?

Working out your start-up costs can be overwhelming. Take a systematic approach and divide your expenditure by category, to calculate what you do – and do not – need to spend on.

Identifying potential costs

Accurately calculating exactly how much money you need to spend in order to get your business up and running is a critical step. It will help you assess whether you will be able to survive the first few months of operation, and will give you a clearer idea of whether you might need to raise additional funds. It is useful to think about your start-up costs as falling into three separate categories: assets, initial costs, and regular ongoing costs. You will then need to compare these three categories with your estimated monthly revenue for the first year. The comparison will give you a realistic idea of your business's financial health, alerting you to potential peaks and troughs throughout the year, and showing when you are likely to break even, and then start making a profit.

Estimating start-up costs

Create a spreadsheet so you can see at a glance the three main types of spending you will incur when you start trading. In the first column, note down business assets, such as those shown here, and their cost, plus the cash in the bank you need to get started. In the second, itemize initial expenses, such as branding or legal work. Add all these costs together to give you the amount you need to spend to get your business to the point of launch. In the third column, list regular ongoing expenses.

STARTING ON A SHOESTRING

If your finances are limited, be realistic, and prune your start-up costs to the bare minimum. For example:

❯ **Upgrade your computer**, rather than replace it, and borrow other items from friends and family.

❯ **Buy office furniture** and equipment from auction sites, secondhand shops, specialist resellers, and bankruptcy sales, or lease specialist equipment initially.

❯ **Create your own website** using a low-cost website building service, and publicize your business yourself on social media platforms using smartphone images.

❯ **Use a fixed-cost contractor** for tasks that require expertise, instead of taking on employees.

BUSINESS ASSETS

Equipment and items of value that your business owns. These can be tangible, such as a computer, or intangible, such as a patent.

Stock/inventory
Items required for retail, hospitality, wholesale, or manufacturing ventures

IT equipment
Technology such as desktop computers, laptops, and mobile phones

Office furniture
Ergonomic desks and office chairs to support staff wellbeing

Vehicles
Any mode of transport required for delivery or business travel

Prioritizing your needs

When assessing how much you need to spend, consider your assets first – the essential items and equipment you need to run your business. There will also be other one-off costs (see examples below). In addition, you will have ongoing expenses payable every month, quarterly, or annually. For each itemized cost, ask yourself if you really must incur it, and focus your spending on what is vital to run the business right now. Research the cheapest ways to get what you need, such as buying assets secondhand or hiring, rather than purchasing equipment (see box opposite).

INITIAL ONE-OFF COSTS

One-off costs that will be required to prepare your business to start operating. Unlike assets, they will be tax-deductible against income.

Premises (preparation)
Installing networks, health and safety adaptations, painting and decorating

Website (design and set up)
Creating and setting up your website, including security

Branding
Graphic design to create your logo and brand appearance

Legal work
Applying for permits and licences; giving advice on contracts

Advertising/marketing
Getting the message out about your business launch and product

REGULAR ONGOING EXPENSES

Regularly recurring costs that your business will face once it starts operating. Also tax-deductible against income.

Utilities
Payable for usage of electricity, water, internet, and phone

IT maintenance
Specialist help for managing and updating software, your website, and network security

Raw materials
Creating a product will require raw materials to be replaced

Consumables
Items that get used up such as stationery, refreshments, and toilet paper

Repayment of loans
Any amounts of capital and/or interest paid to lenders for debt

Wages
Usually paid monthly for any staff on the payroll

Contractor payments
For others who provide services on a temporary basis

Advertising/marketing
For regular paid promotions such as pay-per-click

How much do you need to earn?

Every enterprise needs to be financially viable, as most owners will expect to earn a living from it. When starting out, you will need to calculate your business costs as well as your living costs to work out your expected earnings.

Estimating your income

As a business owner you can draw a salary like an employee, but you may also take regular sums known as dividends. The business must first generate enough money to pay for all day-to-day running costs, such as rent or stock replacement. You will also need to put aside extra money for unexpected (contingency) costs and for financing growth. It is therefore vital to calculate how much money, after costs, your business is realistically capable of producing. In other words, when will it start to make enough money to give you an income that you can live on?

Income versus investment

There is a balance between taking money out of your business and retaining it to invest in future growth. In the early stages, your business is unlikely to make money as you may only have a few customers or clients. It is not unusual for owners to take only a small income or none at all. This may have to continue for some time to ensure your company has sufficient funds to remain stable, and to invest for the long term.

Working it out

To calculate the viability of a business idea, you need to compare how much money it will generate against how much you need to earn. From this you will get an estimate to use as a guide, because the company is not yet trading. You should be prepared to earn less at first in order for the business to survive.

However, it is important that your business can deliver a realistic income within a reasonable length of time. Work out these calculations so that you can add them to your business plan (see pp.104–105).

POTENTIAL MONEY IN THE BUSINESS

First make a realistic estimate of how much the business may earn over a period of 6–12 months. Then deduct all outgoings, including investment and contingency costs.

START-UP COSTS (which will eventually be repaid)	RUNNING COSTS	INVESTMENT AND CONTINGENCY COSTS
Premises	Staff costs	New or replacement equipment
Stock	Rent/mortgage	Product or service development
Machinery	Consumables and stock replenishment	Market research
Website	Utilities (broadband, gas, electricity)	Unforeseen emergencies

Calculate the amount of money that you will have to pay in taxes (see pp.90–91) and add this figure to your costs. The amount of money left after all deductions have been made is available for you as a salary or dividend.

> "Never spend
> your money
> before you have
> earned it."

Thomas Jefferson, 3rd US president

✓ NEED TO KNOW

❯ **Turnover** is the total amount of money taken by a business over a specified period of time.

❯ **Profit** is the amount of money remaining after costs/outgoings have been paid.

❯ **Retained earnings** is money kept in the business to support growth.

❯ **Dividends** are earnings from the company that are paid to owners or shareholders (typically annually) in the form of cash or shares.

YOUR REQUIRED INCOME

Working out what you need to earn is similar to working out what the business requires in terms of costs. Personal spending usually falls into the following categories:

DAILY LIVING COSTS	Groceries	Transport	Clothing
HOUSING	Mortgage/rent	Insurance	Maintenance
UTILITIES	Electricity	Water	Telephone
EXISTING DEBT	Personal loan	Credit card	
ENTERTAINMENT	Holidays	Eating out	Subscriptions
SAVINGS	Pension	Emergency fund	

Estimate how much you typically spend, and consider where savings can be made. Be realistic about how much you have to spend, rather than how much you currently do. Many banks have online forms that can help you itemize your expenses.

Funding your business

The biggest challenge facing you as an entrepreneur might be sourcing enough money to start your business. Be aware of the different types of funding that are potentially available to you.

Understanding funding

The simplest way to fund your new business is through your personal income or savings. You can then rely on cash from your first sales to develop the business further. This approach is called "bootstrapping", and it typically suits businesses with low start-up costs.

If you lack savings, or if your early sales are unlikely to be sufficient to support the business, then you will need external funding. Taking on debt is one option. Debt takes many forms, such as bank loans, business credit cards (see box, right), and asset financing (borrowing on the basis of your company assets), but

Types of funding

Choosing a funding route will depend on your personal circumstances, as well as the wider economic situation. For example, bootstrapping may work if your business is ideas-based with few overheads. You may feel taking on debt is a viable option if interest rates on borrowing are particularly low, whereas if you are skilled in social media, crowdfunding may suit. Equity funding avoids debt, but the expectations of investors will bring a different pressure.

82%
of UK start-ups use self-funding to start their business
Institute of Directors, 2016

Bootstrapping

This means funding the business from your own savings or income with little or no outside help.

PROS
- ❯ **No debt** means no repayments and thus no liability if income falters.
- ❯ **Good for business-to-business (B2B) enterprises**, for example, if you offer services or technology.
- ❯ **Suits web-based businesses** and those where staff work remotely.

CONS
- ❯ **Requires creativity and tenacity** to build a business with low funds.
- ❯ **You need skills** to negotiate long payment terms with suppliers.
- ❯ **Not a practical option** if you need large sums, such as to fund premises or to pay staff to work on site.

Debt

This involves borrowing money — bank loans or finance secured against your personal or business assets.

PROS
- ❯ **No need to sell equity** to outside investors, meaning you keep control.
- ❯ **Short-term borrowing helps** with cash flow issues in times of growth.
- ❯ **All profits are yours**, with no need to share with investors.

CONS
- ❯ **Loans mean detailed paperwork** in the form of a business plan and cash flow projection.
- ❯ **You may need security** for a loan.
- ❯ **Interest rates can be much higher** if your lender sees you as high risk.

in each case the money you owe must be paid back regularly over an agreed period of time. You might be eligible for a grant (see p.85), or you might consider equity financing, whereby investors put money into your venture in return for a share of your business.

Meeting obligations

Before getting into any financing agreement, read all the terms carefully. They will set out strict conditions on payment times and amounts, and specify whether the interest rate is fixed or fluctuates. There may be penalties for missed payments, perhaps also for early repayment of the full sum. Discuss how you will meet your financial obligations with an accountant. Remember, if you provide security, such as your house, to the lender, you risk losing this if you default on the debt. An equity agreement avoids debt, but comes with the "cost" of giving up some control over your business to investors.

BUSINESS CREDIT CARDS

A business credit card is a form of debt, but it can help you manage your cash flow. Before settling on a credit-card provider, make sure you compare a range of different cards aimed specifically at new businesses. Look for cards that offer management tools, such as the separation of business and personal expenses, and the option of obtaining extra cards on the account for your employees to use. A low-rate card is the best choice for paying back large expenses over time. However, you often need a good credit rating to be accepted for low-rate cards, and the lender may not offer cashback or other rewards that may appeal.

Crowdfunding

Individual investors put in cash in return for rewards, repayments, or a share in the business (see p.84).

PROS

> **Social-media platforms** offer many funding opportunities for start-ups.

> **You can reach people** worldwide.

> **Investors may opt for rewards**, so you do not have to repay in cash or give away shares.

CONS

> **Social-media platforms** need constant, expert management to ensure success.

> **Set your target amount too high** and you may fail to reach it.

> **Set your target too low** and you may not maximize your potential.

Equity

This depends upon investors providing funds in return for a share in the profits or control of your business.

PROS

> **Removes the burden** of debt and easies financial worries.

> **You benefit** from the expertise of experienced business developers.

> **Investors can help** build your business through their networks.

CONS

> **Likely to be time consuming** to find the right investors.

> **Investors share profits** and may want a return in less than five years.

> **You may lose** some control over the running of your business.

! BE AWARE

> **Be as accurate as possible** with your cash flow projections when applying for funding, so that you can be sure you will be able to meet your obligations.

> **Make sure there is enough cash** in your current account to meet monthly repayments if you are borrowing.

> **Agree on a strategic date** with your lender(s) when money will leave your account.

> **Schedule repayment dates** so that cash flows into your business account before money is due to be repaid.

Who might invest?

There are many types of investors who can help to finance your venture. You need to understand the implications of accepting each kind of investment, from making repayments to giving up a share of your profits.

How funding works

Any person, group, or organization willing to invest in your start-up can do so in one of two ways: by lending money to your business at a particular rate of interest, or by giving you a lump sum in return for shares in your new enterprise.

Many people, when considering loan investments, wrongly think that banks are the only potential lenders. In fact, anyone is legally allowed to lend you money so long as the loan is covered by a formal contractual agreement that sets out the amount being borrowed, the duration of the loan, the interest rate charged, and how much will be repaid each month.

The other funding option for a small business is called an equity investment – putting money into your venture in exchange for a say in the running of the business and a portion of its future profits. Once

again, it will not only be financial institutions that are attracted (or allowed) to put money into your business. Friends, family members, and business contacts are just

some of the potential investors who may want to help you get up and running, and at the same time be rewarded by a share of profits in the form of annual dividends.

Types of investor

Traditionally, small businesses were funded primarily by banks or perhaps wealthy relatives, but today the ranks of investors run from individuals with spare cash to groups of professional investors who specialize in funding start-ups with good growth prospects. Many countries have government agencies that assist new ventures via direct funding, providing grants, or linking them with potential investors.

Family and friends
People close to you may be willing to assist, but funding by family and friends requires careful management.

PROS
- ❯ **May offer useful advice** and expertise as well as funding
- ❯ **More likely** to offer preferential interest rates on loans
- ❯ **May be flexible** on repayment plans and dates

CONS
- ❯ **Risk of damaging relationships** if things go wrong
- ❯ **Discussing money** arrangements may be awkward
- ❯ **Additional pressure** for the business to succeed

Peer-to-peer
Potential investors range from business colleagues and staff members to individuals on peer-to-peer (P2P) lending sites.

PROS
- ❯ **Peers have a personal interest** in helping you to succeed
- ❯ **Peers will understand** the business environment of your start-up
- ❯ **Interest rates** offered by peers are usually better than bank rates

CONS
- ❯ **Risk of losing your reputation** should your business fail
- ❯ **Disagreements with peers** over how to run the business
- ❯ **Your credit rating may suffer** if you apply via a P2P site

Crowdfunding
Through crowdfunding you can reach a global audience for either a loan or a stake in the business.

PROS
- ❯ **Wide pool of potential investors** can be targeted online
- ❯ **Can raise money quickly**, and you control the terms of the funding
- ❯ **Funding appeal might go viral** and raise more cash than expected

CONS
- ❯ **May be more demanding**, since funders do not know you personally
- ❯ **You must reimburse investors** if you fail to reach your funding target
- ❯ **Fierce online competition** for investors' funding

Banks

While not usually equity investors, banks will still assess the stability and growth potential of your business before lending.

PROS	CONS
❯ **Simple debt agreement** with no say in business operations	❯ **May require a guarantor** or security against the loan
❯ **You maintain independence** in running your business	❯ **You need an excellent credit rating** for the best interest rates
❯ **Banks adhere** to government-imposed financial regulations	❯ **You need to provide evidence** of your ability to repay from revenue

Business angels

A wealthy private investor who puts money into a start-up in return for a stake in the business.

PROS	CONS
❯ **Can provide mentoring** and bring valuable experience	❯ **May wield more control** than you feel comfortable with
❯ **Will make quick decisions** and have cash available	❯ **You are giving away** a percentage of your future earnings
❯ **May enhance growth potential** with their vision and contacts	❯ **High expectations** about your performance and the rate of return

Venture capitalists

Professionals who manage pooled funds for investors seeking a return from funding new business growth.

PROS	CONS
❯ **You do not have to repay the money** (as with business angels)	❯ **When you sell** the business, your share will be less
❯ **Can give leadership** and also advise on day-to-day management	❯ **Board of directors required**, as well as frequent financial reporting
❯ **Provides opportunities** for collaborating with experts	❯ **Risk of losing your business** if it fails to perform well enough

Government, local authorities, and charities

National and local government bodies, as well as some charities, may award grants to new ventures (see pp.212–215).

PROS	CONS
❯ **Grants are essentially free** and do not need to be repaid	❯ **Often time-consuming** to go through the application process
❯ **Generally easy to access**, with plenty of information online	❯ **Plenty of competition** from other businesses for funding
❯ **Helps to build credibility** and promote your business	❯ **Restrictions and conditions** on how you spend the money

ACCELERATORS AND INCUBATORS

In most countries, two types of programme – accelerators and incubators – exist to support businesses at the start-up stage. Joining either type can encourage lenders to invest in your business.

❯ **Accelerators** are like intensive study courses, and they are either privately run or publicly funded. Start-up owners apply to join and, if selected, enter for a fixed term, usually 3 to 6 months. During this period, the owner receives a concentrated, rapid education on how to grow their business under the guidance of mentors. Private accelerator programmes may also offer to invest in your business.

❯ **Incubators** are less intensive but still provide education and tactical mentorship. These programmes are usually funded by a university or an economic development organization. With a focus on innovation, incubators typically run for a year or more and aim to provide an environment in which an entrepreneur can hone their business model.

"**Investors** are employees **you can never hire.** We made sure to **pick investors** that **thought like us.**"

Biz Stone, co-founder, Twitter

Pitching for investment

If you need to borrow to finance your start-up, you will have to persuade funders that your business is a good investment. Thorough preparation is key; be enthusiastic but also honest and realistic.

Preparing to pitch

Once you have identified potential investors, you will need to create a presentation – or pitch – to persuade them to back your business.

Research your potential investors' interests and current investments, and see if they match your plans. Make sure you can describe every aspect of your business, including your customers and competitors. You will also need to show a detailed grasp of finances, so have financial projections to hand, including expected turnover and profits in the short to long term.

Start your pitch with a short, engaging summary of what makes you and your business stand out from the crowd. This is known as an "elevator pitch" – deliverable in the time it takes to ride in a lift. Then describe what the business provides, highlighting the problem it aims to solve or customer wish it can fulfil, before moving on to your service or product solution.

The detail should follow. Outline the marketplace, competition, customers, operations, others involved in the business, and finances, using high-quality visuals, such as product examples, artwork, or digital presentations. Finally, set out what funds are needed and their exact purpose. Be sure to practise your pitch beforehand to get constructive feedback.

Online presentations

Pitching over a video-conferencing platform, such as Zoom or Google Hangouts, poses particular challenges. Practice your pitch using the platform's various functions and prepare for technical issues, such as losing connection while presenting – perhaps by having a colleague ready to take over. You are not in control of your audience's environment, which may be filled with distractions, so get to the point quickly. Since it is harder to read the room, make your presentation more discussion-based, asking questions and engaging with the audience, but allow for time delays and the possibility of talking over each other.

Presenting the pitch

Investors are likely to judge a business at least partly by the person making the presentation. Aim to appear confident but not arrogant, and professional without being inflexible and unwilling to listen. Build a rapport by introducing yourself clearly, making eye contact (or looking into the camera if online), and delivering a strong statement of why your business exists and why customers will buy its products or use its services. Watch the audience to ensure they are still engaged, and note points that raise particular interest as these may appear in later questions. Keep in mind the three key questions below, which may decide future investment. End with a statement of what you are looking for and establish what the next steps will be. It is usual to send a follow-up email a few days after a pitch.

What does the business offer?
Your business needs to offer a viable product or service in order to repay any potential investment.

"**When we are selling** our ideas, the audience must first **buy** *us*."

Peter Coughter, *The Art of the Pitch*, 2012

DO...

- **Keep it short** and to the point, and make your first sentence count.
- **Invite the audience** to ask questions, and listen to them carefully.
- **Make sure you** have evidence for claims (such as market research).
- **Show enthusiasm** for, and belief in, your ideas, demonstrate motivation.
- **Stay relaxed** – head up, with good posture.
- **Speak at a steady** pace, especially at the start of your pitch.
- **Use powerful images** to back up the messages in the presentation.

DON'T...

- **Be unrealistic** about financial projections.
- **Focus too much** on technical detail or jargon.
- **Assume your** audience will share your enthusiasm (you must persuade them).
- **Talk too much** about yourself – focus on the business.
- **Read directly** from a screen, or turn your back on the audience if presenting in person.
- **Fidget** – this can be distracting.
- **Overload visuals** with words, bullet points, and complicated graphics.

Who will buy?
You must show there is sufficient demand and the business can actually meet that demand. Otherwise, investment could be too risky.

What about the competitors?
Your business needs to either create a new market or beat its rivals to provide a realistic return on investment.

Balancing the books

To keep track of your business finances, you need a proper system in place. Balancing the books – or balancing the figures – is a method of ensuring that all monies entering and leaving the business are accounted for.

Keeping a record

Balancing the books – bringing the totals of debits and credits into agreement – is the basis of business accounting. Businesses typically balance their figures at month-end using double-entry bookkeeping (see below). This records every transaction as both a debit *and* a credit, making it easier to spot errors and helping to protect your business against fraud, whether from customers or clients, suppliers, or employees.

Managing your business accounts is vital, but if you are not confident, you could hire an accountant to do the work for you. Or, learn how to do it yourself.

The traditional way to record business transactions is to write them down in a ledger book and calculate the figures manually (see below). Alternatively, you can also use spreadsheets and simple accounting software, which is widely available. This allows you to easily record, store, sort, and retrieve information about your transactions, and to generate essential documents, such as sales invoices and financial reports. It can also highlight unbalanced transactions in your records, as well as calculate totals. However, ensure the software you use is up-to-date, so that it is in line with current tax rules and requirements.

How double-entry bookkeeping works

As the name implies, double-entry involves recording every transaction twice. A double-entry spreadsheet or ledger will have a debit column and credit column for each transaction, showing how one form of asset – cash – has been exchanged for another form of asset, such as stock for resale, a piece of equipment, or raw materials. Thus, all the cash you spend as part of the business over a set period is replaced by an asset or service you have bought. For example, if you buy $200 worth of stock on credit, add this amount to the debit column as inventory, and in the credit column as accounts payable. Repeat this for every purchase made, daily or weekly, throughout the accounting period.

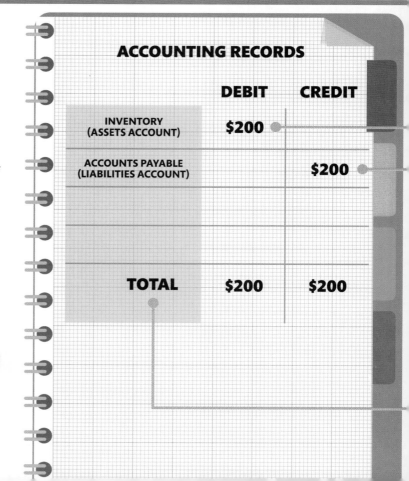

ACCOUNTING RECORDS

	DEBIT	CREDIT
INVENTORY (ASSETS ACCOUNT)	$200	
ACCOUNTS PAYABLE (LIABILITIES ACCOUNT)		$200
TOTAL	**$200**	**$200**

Producing financial reports

Creating an effective bookkeeping system allows you to produce financial reports to help monitor the financial health of your business, such as a balance sheet, (see box, below right). Prepare a profit and loss statement, also known as an income statement, to assess how profitable your business has been over a specific period – comparing revenues with expenses. Create a statement of cash flow (see pp.160–161) to show how money is moving through the business, and your ability to pay its bills. Use these reports to help you to make informed business decisions, such as setting budgets, assessing costs, and measuring business performance. Study them closely, looking for potential irregularities and problems as soon as they occur, in order to prevent them developing further.

Debits

Debits record all monies flowing into your business. Although the stock has yet to be sold, the debit entered represents the value of the extra stock that you have purchased.

Credits

Credits record all monies flowing out of your business. Although you have not yet paid for the stock, they will have to be paid for in the future, so they are entered as a credit.

Balanced total

Totals record the sum amounts of both the credit and debit columns, which should match or "balance". If the totals do not match, check the entries in both columns for errors.

✓ NEED TO KNOW

> **Assets** are the cash and resources owned by the business, including equipment and stock. It also includes accounts receivable, which are sales that have been made for which money is outstanding.

> **Liabilities** are the business debts, such as bank loans and accounts payable – money owed by the business.

> **Equity** is what is left after the total value of business liabilities is deducted from the total value of your assets.

> **Income** is your revenue – the money you receive from sales of goods or services, or from investments and dividends.

> **Expenditure** is the money you pay out for goods, materials, services, salaries, rent, utilities, etc.

THE BALANCE-SHEET EQUATION

Provided that your bookkeeping is correct, the assets on your balance sheet should equal the sum of your liabilities and equity. A balance sheet is like a health check for your business. If liabilities are proportionately low and equity high, you will be in a better position to expand – or weather downturns in the economy.

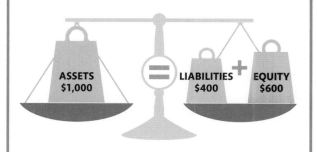

ASSETS $1,000 = LIABILITIES $400 + EQUITY $600

"Accounting is the language of business... a little study, early on... pays off big later on."

Warren Buffet, CEO of Berkshire Hathaway, 2014

Understanding business tax

All businesses are required to pay tax. Understanding business taxes will ensure you pay the right amount at the right time. It will also help you to set aside enough money to meet your tax obligations.

Paying your taxes

As a business owner, you will be responsible for paying tax on profits. How much your business pays depends on how much profit you make, and the percentage of tax you pay on that profit depends on how you choose to structure your business – as a sole entity (or sole trader), a partnership, or a company (see pp.26–27). Each of these legal structures has tax advantages and disadvantages, so thoroughly research which one gives you the most favourable rate of tax for your expected earnings.

In your first year, as you set up your business, you will usually have high expenses. However, these expenses can be deducted from your income, leaving you with a lower tax bill at the end of the year. This is difficult to predict, so it is important to monitor monthly profitability consistently (see pp.88–89) and set aside enough cash each month to pay your annual tax bill. You can complete your own tax return, but many business owners choose to appoint an accountant, who will advise on how to maximize any deductions you can claim.

"No government can exist without taxation."

Frederick the Great

Calculating tax

Regardless of whether you have a company or operate as a sole trader or partnership, you will need to register to pay tax and complete a tax return each year. On the return, you or your accountant have to show your income, and then subtract expenses to find gross profit on which tax will be calculated.

Revenue

Also called "turnover", this is the total amount of money your business receives from its customers in payment for its products and services.

Expenses

These are the costs incurred by running your business – such as rent, wages, raw materials, and stationery. Investing in your business also counts as an expense.

COMMON TYPES OF TAX

Business owners may have to pay many different types of tax, depending on the nature of their business, and the country in which it is registered (see pp.212–15). The most common types of tax include the following:

Sales taxes

In many countries, a sales tax, or value-added tax (VAT), is added to the price of most goods and services. Your business may be required to register for sales tax if turnover exceeds a certain threshold. The amount of sales tax you receive can be offset against sales tax paid out, and the balance is paid to the government.

Company taxes

If you set up your business as a company, you will need to register it in order to pay tax, file an annual tax return, and pay tax on profits. The tax rate will vary depending on national tax law, but is often a flat rate. Late tax payments usually incur a penalty, which is added to the total tax amount owing.

Income taxes

Sole traders or individuals in a partnership will pay tax on profits made through their business activities as though they were employees. If you are a director or employee of your company, and are paid dividends or wages from the company, you will pay tax on these personal earnings, which are treated separately from company tax.

Other taxes

It is common for taxes to be levied by local authorities and jurisdictions, even at city level. For example, in the UK, businesses with commercial or industrial premises pay business rates to their local authority, in addition to tax paid to the government. Small businesses can often claim a discount or relief on business rates, especially if profits are below a certain threshold.

Gross profit

This is the amount of money that remains after expenses and taxes have been deducted. Investing in the business increases expenses and therefore reduces gross profit.

Tax

This must be paid according to the tax system of the country in which the business is registered. Paying tax remains a legal requirement in most countries.

Net profit

This is the amount of profit left after tax has been paid. This amount is available for the business, or for the owner in the form of a dividend.

Setting up a business account

Setting up a dedicated bank account for your business is not always essential. However, it can be a sensible step, granting you access to useful banking services only available to business owners.

Understanding the benefits

Depending on your business type (see pp.26–27), you may be required to set up a business bank account that separates business finances from your own. A business account can offer advantages. Importantly, it allows you to clearly see how much money the business has available at any time, and when payments have been made or received. Plus it makes it easier to manage regular business expenses, such as stationery, utilities, or travel costs. A dedicated account means that your business can collect payments made by credit or debit cards, as well as online, which customers may expect. You can also exchange foreign currencies more easily. An account allows your business to build up a credit history, which may help you raise finance in the future.

Considering options

As well as traditional banks, there are also "fintech" organizations (see below, left), which provide a range of automated financial services. However, your choice will depend on many factors, such as whether your business makes mainly online consumer transactions, transactions with other businesses, or transactions in different currencies.

FINTECH

› **Fintech (financial technology)** developed as banking became increasingly digitalized. It provides services such as mobile payments.

› **Utilizing the technology** available on your smartphone, fintech has fewer overheads and offers cheaper options.

› **In regions such as Africa,** Asia, and India, where traditional banks can leave many smaller businesses at a disadvantage, fintech offers access to affordable payment services.

› **Start-up businesses** can use fintech to access finance from crowdfunding platforms rather than from traditional banks.

$4,754bn

is an estimate of the value of the worldwide mobile payment market

Mobile payment outlook 2023, Alliedmarketresearch.com, 2020

Choosing and opening an account

When you set up a business account, you will need to provide documentation to prove who you are, as well as details of the business. You need to be sure that the account meets your needs now, and will continue to do so in the future. You need to consider the different services, products, and resources each account provider offers. Before committing yourself, ask these questions (see right):

QUESTIONS TO ASK BEFORE YOU OPEN AN ACCOUNT

How easy is it to open an account?

It can take four weeks to open a business current account. Consider a savings account, if appropriate for your business.

Is there a relationship manager?

This person works with you on your accounts. Ensure you can contact them easily (face-to-face, phone, email).

Is there an introductory offer?

If there is an offer such as a free banking period, balance this against future monthly charges.

Does the bank provide advice?

Find out whether the bank offers advice and market expertise, for example, network events or investment advice.

What are the standing charges?

Typically these are payable monthly. Check also whether a minimum balance is required.

Is it easy to get an overdraft?

Ask about overdrafts and the terms or charges involved. See if there are any short-term or quick lending options.

What are the transaction charges?

Find out the bank charges for paying money in and out, as well as for mobile and online transactions.

How soon are deposits processed?

Find out how long it takes to process deposits, both large and small. This is important for business cash flow.

PROVIDING DOCUMENTATION

To comply with banking regulations, including those to protect against money laundering, you will need to provide the following documents to open an account in most countries:

Proof of identity such as a passport or identity card.

Proof of address such as a utility bill.

Business details such as the company registration documents from the relevant national institution, or legal documents, such as Articles of Incorporation.

Protecting your business

All business ventures involve an element of risk. Identifying key risks in advance and working out how to guard against them will increase your start-up's chances of success.

Assessing risks

To effectively plan for risks, you must first identify them. One way to do this is to carry out a simple risk assessment. This involves noting potential risks, from threats to your intellectual property (see pp.96–97) to employee accidents and fire damage, then evaluating how severely these risks would impact on your business and how likely they are to occur. You might find it helpful to create a chart (see top right).

Your assessment of a risk's likelihood should take into account past performance and also encompass possible future events. Make a plan of action for each weighted risk, and decide whether you intend to avoid, minimize, or accept it.

You might seek to avoid a risk by changing a supplier, or minimize a threat by altering a process. Where the risk seems small, you might choose to accept it, but monitor it. Another option is to guard against risks by transferring them to a third party, such as an insurance company (see below).

Types of business insurance

A start-up's insurance requirements will depend on the type of work you undertake, where the business is based, and what risks are involved. Identify your immediate insurance needs initially, then regularly review the situation as the business develops, adding extra cover as necessary. There are several key insurance products that you might consider for your new business; depending on the country you are operating from, and the nature of your business, some may be mandatory (see pp.212–215).

Product liability
Product liability insurance covers you in case a faulty product you designed, sold, or repaired causes injury or damage.

Business interruption
A policy for business interruption compensates you for financial loss suffered when activity is halted by an event such as fire or flooding.

Legal protection
The expenses and costs arising from a commercial legal action brought against your business are paid by legal protection insurance.

Employers' liability
Claims made by employees who are injured or become ill while working for you are covered by employers' liability insurance.

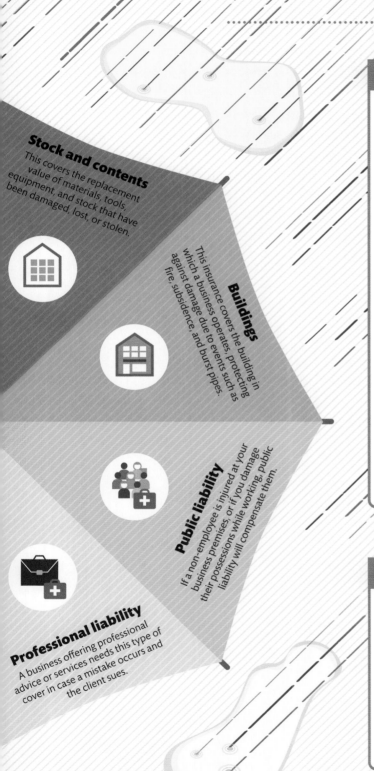

Stock and contents
This covers the replacement value of materials, tools, equipment, and stock that have been damaged, lost, or stolen.

Buildings
This insurance covers the building in which a business operates, protecting against damage due to events such as fire, subsidence, and burst pipes.

Public liability
If a non-employee is injured at your business premises, or if you damage their possessions while working, public liability will compensate them.

Professional liability
A business offering professional advice or services needs this type of cover in case a mistake occurs and the client sues.

VISUALIZING RISK ASSESSMENT

Once you have conducted a risk assessment, a good way to visually display your results is to create a risk impact/probability chart. The chart has two axes: one to show the likelihood (probability) that risks will become a reality, and one to show the severity of their impact if they do. Assign each of your risks a score for both probability and severity, then plot them between the axes. Prioritize risks that fall in the top-right (red) corner; those in the bottom left (green) corner will require less immediate attention.

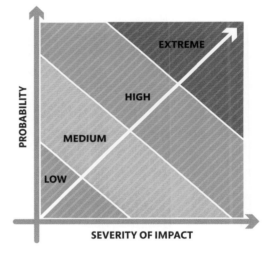

LICENCES AND PERMITS

You should also safeguard your business by ensuring that it is fully compliant with all local and national legislation, and that you have all relevant legal documentation. For example, certain activities, such as importing and exporting goods, and preparing and selling food may require a licence or permit, (see pp.212–215). Failure to comply can result in fines or even prosecution. Seek professional advice and regularly check to ensure your documentation remains current.

Protecting your intellectual property

Intellectual property (IP) consists of ideas and inventions that you have created, such as photographs, designs, and software. It is an asset that others may try to exploit, so take steps to protect it.

Keeping ideas safe

Exactly what counts as intellectual property varies from country to country (see pp.212–215), although it typically includes inventions, artistic works, works of fiction, commercial images (such as photographs or illustrations), and brand names.

The type of protection available depends on the nature of the work you have created. Some are automatically granted protection – for example, copyright for literary works and sound recordings. Some protections, such as trademarks and patents (see below), you will need to apply for. The relevant body in your country will handle these applications. Take care that your idea does not infringe on another's IP, particularly where other people's ideas have inspired you.

Consider the type of protection best suited to your needs. Single patents only protect rights in individual countries, so you may need to take out more than one.

Types of IP

An invention or idea is the basis of your success, and protecting this intellectual property could determine your long-term profitability. Businesses of any size, and individuals, can use IP protection. There are five main types of intellectual property: patents, trademarks, copyright, registered designs, and trade secrets. Depending on the specific IP, more than one type of protection might be necessary.

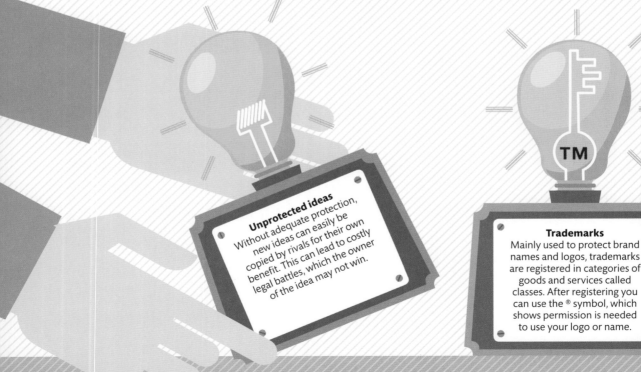

Unprotected ideas
Without adequate protection, new ideas can easily be copied by rivals for their own benefit. This can lead to costly legal battles, which the owner of the idea may not win.

Trademarks
Mainly used to protect brand names and logos, trademarks are registered in categories of goods and services called classes. After registering you can use the ® symbol, which shows permission is needed to use your logo or name.

Copyright
An automatic protection, this does not need to be registered. It protects original work involving skill, labour, or judgement, including books, visual arts, music, dramatic works, and software.

Trade secrets
Set up procedures to protect confidential information and trade secrets that give you a competitive edge. Protection against unauthorised use or disclosure is given under common law and by statute.

Patents
These apply to inventions that are new, involve a unique step, and can be used or made. They give the right to take legal action against those making, using, or selling without permission.

Registered designs
These cover a product's external design or shape; they are useful for immediate protection. For extra security, you might use both a registered design and a patent.

Staying safe in the workplace

As the owner of a business, you have a legal responsibility to protect staff, customers, and clients from harm. Proper safety procedures will help your operations to run smoothly, avoiding accidents and injuries.

Creating a safe work space

It is vital to protect your staff and visitors while they are in the workplace. Check with government and local authorities for the legal safety requirements applicable to your workplace (see pp.212–215). A hairdressers, for example, will present different hazards from those in a garage, or tech start-up. Almost all types of business premises – from a home office or studio, where clients or contractors may visit, to a retail premises or a manufacturing facility – need to meet basic obligations in order to keep workers and visitors safe. Carry out risk assessments and act on any issues that arise, instruct staff on safety procedures, and ensure that all equipment is installed correctly and regularly maintained. Safety precautions also help protect your premises and assets from damage due to accidents.

Protecting yourself and others

When planning or setting up a workplace, pay attention to these key areas to protect yourself and those working for you or visiting your premises. You could be prosecuted if your working conditions are found to be dangerous.

Hygiene

Provide regularly cleaned toilets with soap and hand-washing and drying facilities, as well as bins for secure waste disposal. If you offer hospitality services, you may need extra hygiene measures.

Food handling

Ensure staff involved in the preparation of food are trained to meet the legal requirements for food hygiene and storage, the proper cleaning of utensils and equipment, and pest control measures.

Fire

Follow government and local directives on the fire safety responsibilities of landlords and commercial tenants. Appoint key employees as fire marshals; hold regular emergency drills for all staff.

Toxicity

Avoid harm to people and animals by preventing their exposure to chemical or gas toxins, such as asbestos, cleaning agents, and machine fumes. Follow local regulations for the disposal of toxic waste.

Gas & electricity

If you are renting premises, be aware of the landlord's responsibilities to provide electrical and gas safety checks. Inspect for defective plugs, broken switches, and damaged cables; make repairs a priority.

Machinery & equipment

Fit guards around dangerous machine parts, display warning notices, and ensure operatives are fully trained. Protect equipment users against excessive noise, heat or cold, vibration, and radiation.

Trips and falls

Make sure that lighting is adequate and that floors are non-slip and kept free of obstructions. Clearly mark any sudden changes in floor height. Supply stable ladders for staff working at heights.

Personal protection

Issue staff with the appropriate clothing and equipment to give them adequate protection in their work, such as face masks, ear defenders, safety boots, gloves, and helmets.

Lifting and moving objects

Teach staff how to lift objects safely, and discourage moving items that could cause injury. Store heavy objects on low shelves. Supply trolleys or other equipment for moving large stock items and materials.

Vulnerable people

Some individuals – whether employees, clients, customers, or visitors – will need special consideration when on your premises; for example, pregnant women and people with disabilities.

Safety notices

Clearly display signs that follow local regulations and reinforce workplace safety procedures such as hygiene and waste disposal routines, hazard warnings, and what to do in the event of fire.

First aid

Give first-aid training to employees. Ensure that first-aid supplies are readily accessible and that injured persons get immediate attention. Appoint a safety officer to report and record all incidents.

Thinking green

Creating a business that focuses on sustainability or other green issues will not only help the fight against climate change, but can also boost your company's image and reputation.

Taking action

To become sustainable, a business must try to limit its carbon footprint as far as possible. It should take action to reduce any adverse effects while increasing any positive ones.

From a business point of view, a green image can be beneficial. More and more customers like to buy from companies that can show they care about the environment. When such customers buy a product or service, they want to know it was created sustainably. An environmentally responsible business also tends to attract employees who prefer to work for a company that takes an ethical approach.

Additionally, reducing waste – whether by using less electricity and fewer raw materials, or by reducing printing – helps to reduce costs. Sustainability pays other financial dividends, too, as more governments around the world impose taxes and restrictions on companies that pollute and damage the environment.

Achieving sustainability

One good way to think about the sustainability of a business is to divide it into three stages: The first is the inputs (source materials) it requires. If producing clothes, for example, that could be the fabric used, or if running a café, it will be the food ingredients. Consider where these materials come from. Are they produced sustainably? If not, are there other options, such as natural or recycled fabrics, or food products that carry the Fairtrade logo, showing they are produced ethically? With careful sourcing, greener options are affordable, especially if the business ensures there is minimal waste. However, running a green business might require more initial investment

Thinking local

Using local suppliers creates goodwill, benefits the community, and helps a business reduce its carbon footprint.

LOCAL RESOURCES

By sourcing raw materials and supplies locally, and hiring local staff, a new business can keep its fuel costs low and build good local relationships. Waste or unwanted goods can prove an invaluable resource for local innovative recycling ventures.

ENVIRONMENTAL STANDARDS

Your business willl need to follow the environmental standards imposed by the government (see pp.212–215). These cover activities such as waste disposal, and air and water pollution. You might also follow voluntary standards, such as choosing to produce only organic food. Compliance with mandatory standards is crucial to avoid penalties, whereas adopting voluntary standards can make a product more attractive to customers, and add value.

to get these things right from the start. The next step is to think about the energy it takes to make your product or deliver your service. Most businesses use fuel and water. Is there a way to reduce consumption, for instance, by using electric vehicles or working from well-insulated premises? The third is to think about the further effects of the product after purchase. What type of packaging was used? Is the item made from recycled materials and can it be recycled? Perhaps the packaging can be returned by the customer for a refill, which is also a good way of ensuring that the customer comes back.

Finally, a word of caution. Sustainability credentials can help promote a business and build a reputation, but it is important to keep checking that the venture stays environmentally friendly. A good name can be lost if people discover that claims are not genuine.

HELP TO SOLVE THE PLASTIC PROBLEM

While ecologists warn that our oceans are polluted with plastic waste, entrepreneurs are finding new ways to recycle plastic into desirable products. Some create fabrics from plastic waste, while others transform it into furniture, bricks, clocks, and fuels, or add it to asphalt to strengthen road surfaces. If you are going to use plastics in your product, make sure they are widely recyclable (see pp.212–215).

MUTUAL BENEFITS

When a new business draws on local resources everyone benefits from its success.

> **The new restaurant** with a menu using local produce served by local staff creates its own community identity.

> **The furniture restorer** who transforms old furniture into fashionable new pieces helps to reduce waste.

> **The company** that turns scrap cars and vans into fully electric vehicles benefits the local community and supports the global move to cleaner fuels.

"**Sustainable development is the pathway to the future we want for all.**"

Ban Ki-moon, Secretary-general of the UN (2007–16)

Operating ethically

If you take an ethical approach to business by acting honestly and openly with your customers and suppliers, you will gain a reputation as a fair operator.

Taking responsibility

Running your business in an ethical way is important and pays dividends. Customers prefer to buy from ethical traders, staff prefer to work for those who treat them fairly, and gaining a good reputation will help you to build a loyal following.

Think about how you would like your business to operate by setting out your values. For example, you may decide that your company will be dedicated to supporting the local community or committed to protecting the environment. Or you may focus on employee health and

Workplace
Identify how you can make your business a good place to work and ensure that you treat all of your employees fairly and equally.

Creating a code of conduct

Think about your business from different viewpoints to help you decide what to include in your code of conduct. The following headings are useful for most businesses, but you may want to add others, depending on the nature of your work.

Community
Think about how your business can contribute to the local community. You could sponsor a sports team or donate to a charity. Try to avoid causing any negative impacts on your neighbours with noise or pollution.

Environment
Think about the effects your business has on the environment (see pp.100–101). Identify ways you can minimize damage. For example, use recyclable packaging or adopt a cycle-to-work scheme to help your employees buy a new bike.

wellbeing. Once you have identified your core values, draw up a code of conduct: a rulebook for how you and your employees will act. This acts as a guide for how you and your employees will act. Everyone must understand how you expect them to operate. You can share your code of conduct with suppliers and customers. Whatever you decide to focus of conduct must be genuine. If you tell people you are an employer who values their staff but then you force people to work long hours, potential employees will hear about it and go elsewhere. Ensure you can do what you promise because it takes a long time to build a reputation and a short time to lose it.

Making the right choices

Your ethical stance may sometimes lead to difficult choices. If your code of conduct only allows you to buy from other businesses that trade ethically, then you may have to pay more for your goods. If you run a clothes shop, for example, you will not want to buy cheaper garments from factories with poor ethical standards. However, customers are usually prepared to pay a little more when they buy from companies they trust to take this ethical approach, so you may not lose out financially.

Suppliers and customers
Always choose to buy from suppliers who have an ethical programme in place. Buy locally to support the business community. Strive to be open, honest, and transparent with your customers.and build personal relationships with them.

Operations
Ensure that all operations in your business are ethical and transparent. Check that every employee and supplier involved in your business understands and is working to maintain your ethical standards.

CASE STUDY

Solarkiosk AG

Start-ups like Solarkiosk place ethics at the heart of their business. Founded in 2011, the German solar technology firm is "driven by the mission of universal access to energy". About 20 per cent of the world's poorest people live off-grid. Solarkiosk's flagship product is the E-HUBB, a solar-powered mobile kiosk that generates electricity. Kiosks are used to charge phones or cool medicines, but they also act as small businesses.

"**Real integrity is doing the right thing,** knowing that nobody's going to know whether you did it or not."

Oprah Winfrey, media mogul

Writing your business plan

Creating a business plan will help to guide you at each stage of your business and convince others of its viability. The plan acts as a road map to get you from where you are now to where you want to be.

Why do you need a plan?

When you start a business, it may seem clear where you want to end up, but not how you get there. Writing a concise business plan can give you focus and direction, explaining the objectives of the business, what it will sell, how you intend to win a market share, and how it will operate and promote products or services. You can use your business plan to secure funding or investment, set goals, monitor the business's performance, or reinforce your own belief in the venture. Take time to research and write a plan – the more thorough you are, the more likely the business is to succeed.

How to write a business plan

Write your business plan clearly and explain any technical terms. Back up your business proposition with key market statistics and accurate projections of sales and profits.

1. EXECUTIVE SUMMARY

> **A snapshot of your business** This may be the only part of your business plan that a busy investor looks at, so ensure it provides sufficiently compelling information. Although your business plan leads with the executive summary, it may be easier to write it last.

> **The name and structure** Clarify the basics of your business, summarizing quickly what it will sell and to whom. Consider starting with an "elevator pitch", a short pitch (see pp.86–87), which sells the business idea in brief, crystallizing its purpose and objectives.

2. THE BUSINESS

> **Ownership** Provide details about the founders and managers, and their roles. Include information on any relevant work experience, qualifications, and training – both received and planned.

> **Trading** State briefly where the business will trade from, and where it will buy the goods and materials it needs in order to operate.

> **Products and services** Describe – in fuller detail than in the summary – what the business will sell. Include images of products or of the proposed service in action. Touch on what makes your products or services different.

> **SWOT analysis** Review your business's strengths, weaknesses, opportunities, and threats (see p.155), and say how you propose to respond to them.

3. MARKET AND COMPETITION

› Customers Say who you expect your customers to be – the market segment. Identify any niche segments, based on market segmentation research (see pp. 40–41). Describe the customer profile and identify why they are likely to buy your product or use your service.

› Competition Compare your business to what is already out there. List competitors, their products, services, prices, and gaps in their offerings. State your USP – unique selling point (see p.23).

› Trends Include research to show whether the market is static or growing, and highlight any trends you have spotted.

4. MARKETING AND SALES STRATEGY

› Promotion Define the methods you intend to use to promote your product or service, such as press and publicity, advertising, or direct and online marketing.

› Social media Describe the social media channels you will use to build your profile, and what kind of posts you will share to attract customers.

› Pricing strategy Indicate how much each unit costs to make and deliver. Or, for a service, establish what customers might be willing to pay. Discuss the price point, showing how it compares to competitors', and state your anticipated profit margin.

› Sales methods Outline how you intend to find, reach, and retain customers. Describe the customer experience and how you will encourage repeat purchases.

5. BUSINESS OPERATIONS

› Premises and structure Describe the base from which your business will operate and any equipment you will use. Explain why this location is well positioned to serve your market.

› Day-to-day running Outline how your business will operate, including how customers will pay for goods or services, and how you will pay staff and comply with legal requirements, such as health and safety, and contingency planning. Include supply and distribution details about how products will get from A to B.

6. FINANCIAL FORECASTS

› Sales/costs Project your sales and costs (see pp.78–81), month-by-month, over at least one year, preferably three. Allow for seasonal fluctuations.

› Profit forecast Provide a gross profit figure (the predicted turnover of the business – all sales – minus the cost of sales) and a net profit figure (what remains after all expenses are deducted from total sales).

› Cashflow forecast Define the payment terms for your customers and suppliers, and forecast the cash flow over a 12-month period.

Writing an action plan

To turn your business strategy into reality, you will need to create an action plan. This sets out the specific steps that have to be taken to ensure that your business thrives.

Understanding the basics

Your action plan should be designed to follow through on your business strategy (see pp.36–37). Your strategy outlines the overall direction of your business and the major decisions you need to take – such as identifying who your customers will be, and what your business will look like in five years' time. However, your action plan should provide precise details about your goals and the actions needed to achieve them in the day-to-day running of your business.

When writing your action plan, involve your colleagues, so you can create and share new ideas. Inviting others to contribute also means that you are more likely to earn their commitment to making your venture a success.

Getting started

Start by thinking about the different aspects of your company – such as marketing, production, and finance. Depending on how complex your business is, you may want to write a plan for

each sphere. Make sure that there are no conflicting deadlines in your plan, and that the various aspects of your business will not have to compete for the same resources. If your business is small, you may be able to cover all of your activities in a single plan.

To measure the success of your action plan, specify deadlines by which key tasks have to be completed, and meet regularly with your staff to discuss any changes that need to be made. Be prepared to update your plan as necessary.

Making a plan

In this example, a mountain tour guide company wants to tell potential customers about their new winter routes, so they develop an action plan based on marketing. More complex steps in the plan, such as the social media campaign, will benefit from having their own, more detailed, action plans.

THE GOAL

To increase awareness and sales of the tour guide company's new winter mountain routes

KEY STEPS TO TAKE

Email existing customers about the new winter routes, offering discounts

Arrange advertising on hiking and mountaineering websites

Run a social media campaign that publicizes exciting features of the new routes

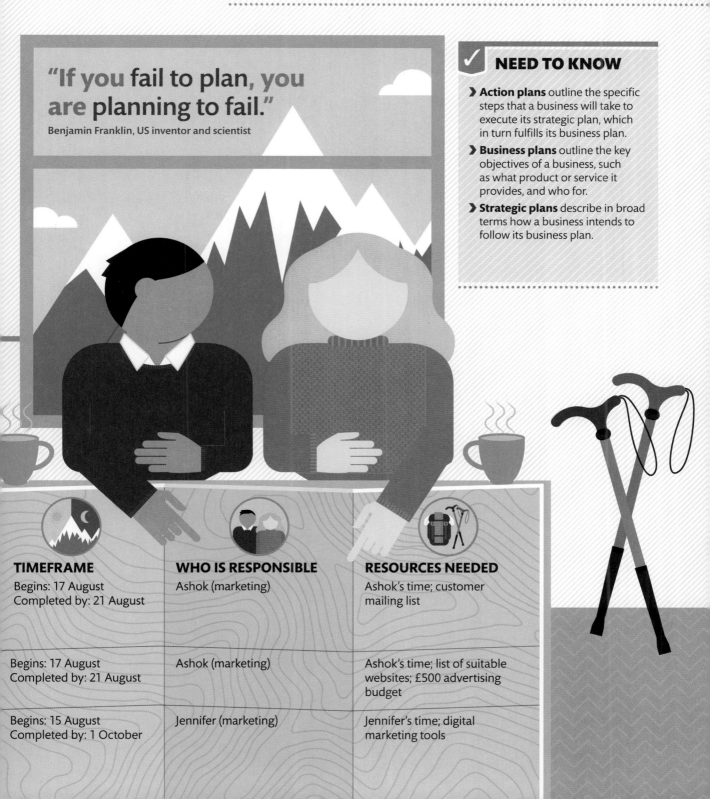

"If you fail to plan, you are planning to fail."

Benjamin Franklin, US inventor and scientist

✓ NEED TO KNOW

❯ **Action plans** outline the specific steps that a business will take to execute its strategic plan, which in turn fulfills its business plan.

❯ **Business plans** outline the key objectives of a business, such as what product or service it provides, and who for.

❯ **Strategic plans** describe in broad terms how a business intends to follow its business plan.

TIMEFRAME	WHO IS RESPONSIBLE	RESOURCES NEEDED
Begins: 17 August Completed by: 21 August	Ashok (marketing)	Ashok's time; customer mailing list
Begins: 17 August Completed by: 21 August	Ashok (marketing)	Ashok's time; list of suitable websites; £500 advertising budget
Begins: 15 August Completed by: 1 October	Jennifer (marketing)	Jennifer's time; digital marketing tools

Understanding consumer rights

When starting a business you need to recognize your legal duties towards customers. From the outset, make sure you are aware of consumer legislation, which affects both goods and services.

Selling products

Consumer laws protect consumers against unfair selling practices and unscrupulous vendors. Wherever your business operates, you need to understand the rights your customers enjoy under national and local law. These rulings are encompassed not just in consumer legislation but also, for example, in food safety, electronics, and labelling laws.

In some countries, such as the United States and Australia, individual states apply their own rules in addition to national law. Legislation can even be shared between nations, as it is for member countries of the European Union. There are also increasing efforts to internationalize consumer law, particularly because of global trade via the internet. The International Consumer

A customer's basic consumer rights

Government bodies and consumer watchdog groups firmly defend consumer rights and will investigate unresolved complaints against businesses. Before you start trading, check local and national government websites (see pp.212–215), and those of consumer-championing organizations, for guidance and information relevant to your type of business. Rights will vary from country to country, and even region to region, but are likely to cover the same fundamentals of buying goods or services – quality, being fit for purpose, delivery, returns, and repairs. If you sell handbags, for example, you would have to meet consumer rights in all these areas.

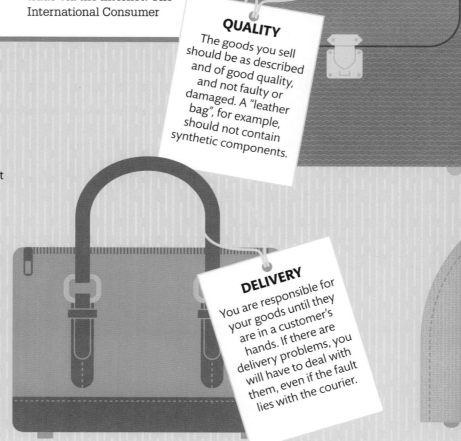

QUALITY
The goods you sell should be as described and of good quality, and not faulty or damaged. A "leather bag", for example, should not contain synthetic components.

DELIVERY
You are responsible for your goods until they are in a customer's hands. If there are delivery problems, you will have to deal with them, even if the fault lies with the courier.

Protection and Enforcement Network (ICPEN), for example, works to ensure minimum standards of consumer protection for cross-border purchases.

Providing services

Consumer rights apply just as much to services, such as plumbing, hairdressing, and building, as they do to products. If you provide a service, you need to be aware of laws that demand certain basic standards, including reasonable care and skill, binding contracts, specified price, and delivery within an agreed timeframe. If you fail to deliver your service to the agreed standards, you may have to repeat the service or provide compensation.

A knowledge of consumer rights will highlight what protection you might need against any legal action, such as product liability insurance (see pp.94–95). It will also help you to meet your customers' expectations. An issue that is fairly resolved may renew a customer's faith in your business.

> "Customer service should not just be a department, it should be the entire company."
>
> Tony Hsieh, internet entrepreneur

FIT FOR PURPOSE
Your goods must be fit for purpose and meet reasonable customer expectations. For example, a laptop bag should be able to hold a laptop.

RETURNS
If an item is not fit for purpose, a customer can demand a refund or replacement within a certain number of days.

REPAIRS
If an item develops a fault, you should honour the customer's right to a repair or replacement. A bag with loose stitching will need to be repaired free of charge.

GETTING
GOING

Setting up your workspace

No matter where you base your business, planning and organizing your workspace will improve efficiency, productivity, and wellbeing, as well as mimimizing risks to health and safety.

Assessing your needs

A successful workspace is one that allows your business to operate effectively, while also ensuring that your needs and those of your staff, clients, and customers are met. These needs will depend on the nature of the business: the ideal workspace for a car mechanic is very different to that of an accountant working at home. In each case, however, a well-designed workspace that functions efficiently can help to reduce accidents and illness, or stress-related problems, while increasing productivity and wellbeing (see pp.172–173).

When planning your workspace, consider who will be using it and the tasks they will be performing, ensuring that furnishings are appropriate, and that devices and facilities are easy to use and fit for purpose. Importantly, check that your workspace is in line with any relevant health and safety regulations (see pp.212–215).

The basics

A business that takes care of employee needs by providing comfortable and safe working conditions – from reliable equipment to a comfortable temperature – will enjoy higher productivity and fewer days lost to absenteeism. Although employees' specific needs will vary according to the type of work they perform, there are some basic requirements that are common to most workplaces.

55%
of typical employees spend the majority of their time away from their desks

iofficecorp.com, 2020

CALCULATING SPACE REQUIREMENTS

Buying or renting workspace is a major cost, so you will want to use your space optimally. The typical allowance per desk worker can vary from 4.5m–9 sq m (50-100 sq ft), and will include height as well as floor area, but check local regulations (see pp.212–215). There are many free online tools to help you calculate your requirements. When calculating your needs, take into account space for people to circulate and any unusable areas. Open-plan designs in which people share facilities can save on space, but won't suit all types of businesses. Also allow space for additional staff down the line.

IT EQUIPMENT

Virtually every business requires a computer, if not several, together with a Wi-Fi or wired connection. You may also need printers, which in turn require space to store paper and ink. Check that your workspace has enough electrical sockets for equipment, and that they are located near to workstations.

SUITABLE FURNITURE

You will need to provide furniture that supports good posture and that employees can adjust to suit their various needs – particularly if they will be sitting for long periods or may incur strains over time. Many businesses lease their office furniture from specialist suppliers.

LIGHT AND SOUND

Employees will need good lighting to work effectively. Aim for as much natural light as possible – fluorescent lighting should be avoided as it can cause eye strain. Protect staff from high levels of noise or vibration, whether through office design, limiting the use of noisy equipment, or using protective gear.

VENTILATION AND TEMPERATURE

Ensure your setting has good ventilation and clean air. A comfortable temperature may depend on the kind of work being done (sedentary work versus physical labour), but temperatures should be adjustable and take into account heat generated by equipment.

HYGIENE AND SAFETY

You must provide access to toilets and drinking water, and will also need to regularly clean your premises. Designate a suitable area for staff to prepare food and drinks. First-aid facilities, smoke detectors, and fire extinguishers are also mandatory (see pp.98–99).

WORKING SPACE

Certain tasks require more space or equipment than others, or can be hazardous or noisy, so plan for this. Other work may involve a need for confidentiality or quiet concentration, and require the use of a private area. If possible, also allow a communal space for informal staff gatherings.

ACCESS

The space must be suitable for all staff, including anyone with a disability. When setting up workstations and facilities, allow enough room to move around freely and safely. Allow sufficient storage for both work-related and personal items to keep floors clear of obstructions and maintain a clear path to fire exits.

Planning a website

To succeed in today's marketplace, an online presence is essential. A professional-looking website will help you to grab and retain people's attention. Careful planning will save you time, effort, and money – and deliver a better result.

Thinking about content

A website's look and feel are important, but engaging content is what really attracts visitors to your site. Before writing any text, taking photos, or drafting designs, outline what the content of your website will be when it launches, how it will be structured (see below), and how you will amend and add to the content as your business develops.

Consider your site's purpose: a site that provides content (information), for example, has very different requirements to one through which people wil be making purchases (see panel, right). Think about your target audience and investigate what kind of content is working well on similar sites, from instructional videos to picture stories.

Choosing a domain name

Deciding on the right domain name – your website's address on the internet – is as important as selecting the right business name (see pp.58–59). The domain name and business's name don't need to be the same, although this can be helpful. Your domain name should describe the business, and contain key words for search engines. For example, a bike repair shop might

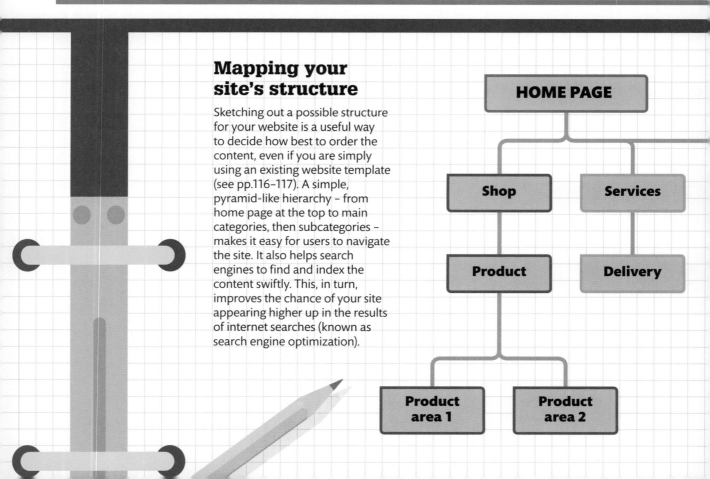

Mapping your site's structure

Sketching out a possible structure for your website is a useful way to decide how best to order the content, even if you are simply using an existing website template (see pp.116–117). A simple, pyramid-like hierarchy – from home page at the top to main categories, then subcategories – makes it easy for users to navigate the site. It also helps search engines to find and index the content swiftly. This, in turn, improves the chance of your site appearing higher up in the results of internet searches (known as search engine optimization).

HOME PAGE

Shop

Services

Product

Delivery

Product area 1

Product area 2

choose a domain name that includes the words "mend" and "bike". A short name that is simple, easy to type and memorable is best. You should also avoid numbers and hyphens, as they can be confusing.

Select the appropriate domain extension for the business. Commercial businesses tend to use ".com", while ".net" is more appropriate for internet, email, and networking services. If you want to appeal to a more local audience, there are also country- and even region-specific extensions, such as ".au" for a business in Australia, or ".uk" for one in the UK.

To obtain your domain name, visit a domain name registrar, check if your preferred domain name is available, and pay a fee to lease the name. You will also need to use a web-hosting service, which allows your website to be accessed on the web. Some companies provide both hosting and domain names.

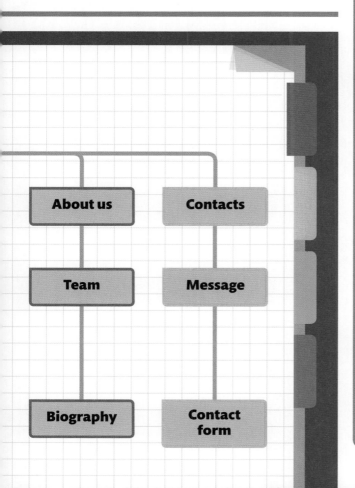

WHICH TYPE OF WEBSITE?

Your website's purpose will influence the design and whether the site is static (always shows the same content) or dynamic (shows different content according to the user). Many sites that aim to provide information, called content websites, are static, while e-commerce sites – online shops – tend to be dynamic, with pages tailored to the needs of individual customers who visit the site.

Content websites

A content site might give a general overview of a topic, such as caring for cats; focus on a specific aspect, such as breeds; or narrow to key terms, such as a particular breed. You can secure funding for content sites in various ways: a cat site, for example, might be funded by a pet food company or have links to an e-commerce site. Other ways to generate income include advertising and affiliate marketing (see p.35). If your site is instructional, you might offer products, such as ebooks, or services, such as courses, seminars, or consultancy. Social media offers another way to be visible (see pp.140–141).

e-Commerce websites

An e-commerce site showcases goods, such as pet foods, and allows customers to make online purchases. Like real shopfronts, such sites need to be eye-catching and regularly updated. The ordering and payment process should be straightforward and hassle-free (via a trusted system, such as PayPal) with a clear return/refund policy.

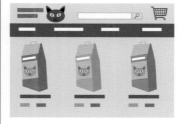

Designing and building a website

An attractive, user-friendly website gives your business the edge on its competitors. Take time to examine all your possible options, and choose carefully to ensure the site will meet your present and future needs.

Build for usability

Whether its purpose is to provide information about your company or to sell goods or services, your website must be accessible and easy to use. To get started, you will need a web-hosting service (see pp.114–115). Some website builders offer combined web hosting and templates, which is an attractive option, but may not meet all your needs. Shared web hosting, for instance, means sharing hardware with multiple other users, which can slow down your website's operating time, and some website builders are not "search engine optimization" (SEO) friendly (see pp.118–119), making it harder for users to access your content. A content management system

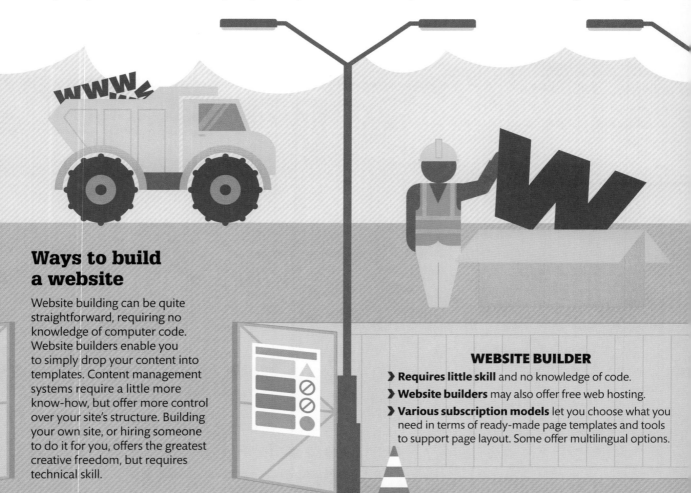

Ways to build a website

Website building can be quite straightforward, requiring no knowledge of computer code. Website builders enable you to simply drop your content into templates. Content management systems require a little more know-how, but offer more control over your site's structure. Building your own site, or hiring someone to do it for you, offers the greatest creative freedom, but requires technical skill.

WEBSITE BUILDER

> **Requires little skill** and no knowledge of code.
> **Website builders** may also offer free web hosting.
> **Various subscription models** let you choose what you need in terms of ready-made page templates and tools to support page layout. Some offer multilingual options.

(CMS) offers more design options and your own choice of web host, whereas creating your own site from scratch requires web-design expertise.

However you build your website, your homepage should set the scene with a clear statement that summarizes the business. Use minimal text, bold images, and a consistent design throughout to help users identify key information and navigate easily.

Make it mobile-friendly

By 2022, monthly global data traffic will be 77 exabytes. To meet this challenge, it is worth ensuring that your website is also "responsive", meaning it is optimized to fit a screen of any size (even a watch) and still be clearly read.

"Users often leave web pages within 10–20 seconds, but stay much longer if they perceive value."

Jakob Nielsen, "How long do users stay on web pages", nngroup.com, 2011

CONTENT MANAGEMENT SYSTEM (CMS)

> **Requires some skill** but offers more control over design and features. WordPress is the most popular CMS.
> **Software enables** users to create, store, search, and manage content that is typically stored on a database.
> **Useful for sites** with changing content, such as blogs.

BUILD FROM SCRATCH

> **Involves programming** a website line-by-line with code.
> **Time-consuming**, but ensures design freedom rather than relying on templates, resulting in a unique website.
> **Requires knowledge** of coding and web development fundamentals, such as HTML and CSS.

Attracting website traffic

Increasing the "visibility" of your website will help potential customers or clients to find it. There are various things you can do to make your site more likely to get picked up by search engines trawling the web.

Making your site more visible

To view your website, potential customers or clients must first be able to find it. You can make this easier in several ways, such as by promoting your website online, through social media and advertising, and, most importantly, by making your website easy to find using search engine optimization (SEO).

Understanding SEO

Search engines, such as Google, collect data from every page on the web, then use algorithms (mathematical processes usually in a computer program) to turn the data into search results. The higher the algorithms rank your site, the higher it will appear in the list of search results, and the more likely it is to be seen (see p.215). There are things you must do to improve your search ranking, such as including keywords in your site's content. These are words or phrases that people might use as search terms when looking for your products or services, and which search engines will pick up. Your site's title page (as it appears in your website's code), links from other sites to yours (called backlinks), and the words that you use in your links (phrases with hyperlinked text), can all help to grab the attention of search engines. Sites that are regularly updated with good content will also rise in the ranks.

Driving traffic

Focusing on factors that improve search engine optimization (SEO) is an essential strategy. Having lots of backlinks to your site, for example, is something that search engines rate highly. Some strategies for driving traffic (increasing visitors to your site) are quick and cheap; others may require more investment or the hiring of expert help, depending on your skill set.

SEO
SEO is not a one-off task: you will need to keep up-to-date with what factors will help search engines to rank your website higher in search listings, such as keywords and backlinks, and update your website content accordingly.

KEYWORDS
Research keywords using a keyword tool, such as Keyword Planner or Keyword Explorer. Insert those words and phrases relevant to your business within the first 160 words of your web page, using each keyword only once.

BACKLINKS
The higher the quality of your content, the more other websites will want to link to yours. Provide HTML links in your messages to copy and paste. An easy way to get backlinks is to sign up to online business directories, then link from the directories to your website.

The first page of Google search results captures

71%

of traffic clicks

Philip Petrescu, Moz.com, 2014

NEED TO KNOW

> **Broad targeting** means aiming at a mass audience.

> **Narrow targeting**, also called interest group targeting, is seeking a specific group of consumers.

> **Cookies** are files placed on a website user's computor, used to track returning visitors

> **Data management platforms** are software tools that track website visitors with cookies, and pull together a profile of customer demographics and habits.

> **Keyword targeting** is using keywords relating to your product to improve your ranking in search engine results.

CONTENT

Generate interesting content and keep it fresh, updating it as often as possible. It will not only be useful to your customers but will also boost your search ranking. Also post content on other sites, such as YouTube, that will link to yours.

SOCIAL MEDIA

Create a profile of your business on the main social-media platforms, and post when you know your audience is active or online. Offer further content that can be accessed via a link to your website (see pp.140–141).

MARKETING

Build a customer database and ask permission from your customers to send them marketing information. Then run an email marketing campaign with an offer, including a link to your website.

ADVERTISING

Try pay-per-click social-media advertising in different channels, targeting customers by age, location, or other criteria (see pp.139). Monitor and then adjust keywords and targeting. Display your web address offline, on business cards, shopfronts, or vehicles.

Data protection

It is crucial to protect all of the financial data and any other sensitive information stored on your business computers from cyber attack. Taking a few basic measures can make the difference between safety and disaster.

Staying secure

Small businesses are more likely to suffer a cyber attack than large ones, as they have less to spend on security and rarely have in-house IT teams. However, effective precautions can be cheap, or even free.

Many cyber attacks target technical weaknesses in computer systems. Make sure your computer hardware includes antivirus software and firewalls (programs that block unauthorized access), and keep them turned on. This will place barriers between your computer

Information security

Protecting your business from online criminals is essential, as successful attacks can be financially damaging and undermine customer and investor confidence. You also have a legal obligation to protect customer data (see pp.212–215). You must take protective measures before any computer systems go live.

Budget for your cybersecurity needs
To safeguard your data, purchase appropriate equipment and software, and seek specialist advice.

> **Back up** all business-related data daily and store it securely – and separately from any computer
> **Store data** on a hard drive and a cloud storage service. A cloud software subscription buys cybersecurity software for all your computers
> **Pay for risk analysis** and have the software installed by a certified technician

Introduce essential cybersecurity
Around 80 per cent of security breaches can be prevented by installing software to protect systems and control device usage.

> **Install and switch on** firewall programs
> **Install and activate** antivirus software
> **Update software and firmware** (software fixed into hardware)

> **Control the use** of USB drives and memory cards
> **Protect passwords** and make sure they are as strong as possible

network and potential attackers. Criminals may also try to gain access to data through human vulnerability. To avoid this, train staff to recognize potential attacks, such as phishing, where emails are used to trick the receiver into giving away passwords and user names, or malware programs, which install on a computer when you click on a link or email.

Seek free data protection advice from business organizations and government agencies. Also be sure that you meet any cyber security regulations.

63%
of data breaches involve stolen, default, or weak passwords

Verizon, Data Breach Investigations Report, enterprise.verizon.com, 2016

✓ NEED TO KNOW

> **Malware** is short for malicious software – any program that damages a computer's operating system and the data it contains.

> **Ransomware** is malware that infects a computer and demands a ransom to be paid electronically in return for restoring the computer to normal.

> **Denial of service** is a cyber attack that floods computer or web systems with bogus requests that stop users from connecting, allowing criminals to gain access.

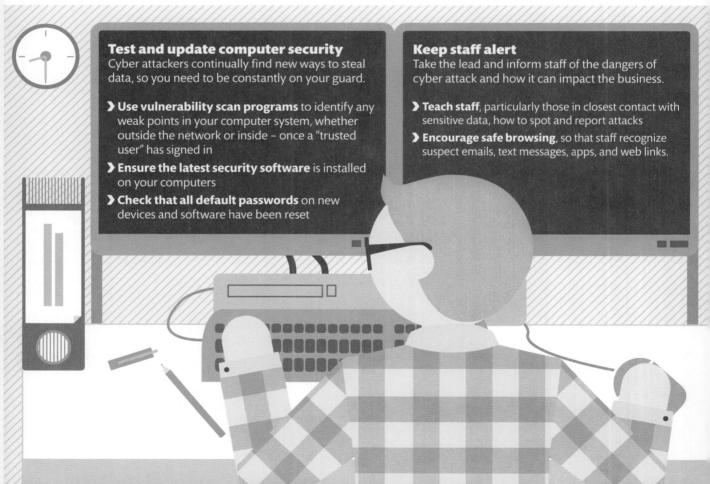

Test and update computer security
Cyber attackers continually find new ways to steal data, so you need to be constantly on your guard.

> **Use vulnerability scan programs** to identify any weak points in your computer system, whether outside the network or inside – once a "trusted user" has signed in

> **Ensure the latest security software** is installed on your computers

> **Check that all default passwords** on new devices and software have been reset

Keep staff alert
Take the lead and inform staff of the dangers of cyber attack and how it can impact the business.

> **Teach staff**, particularly those in closest contact with sensitive data, how to spot and report attacks

> **Encourage safe browsing**, so that staff recognize suspect emails, text messages, apps, and web links.

Finding the right talent

Attracting the right people to work for you will give your business a competitive edge. Although you may not be able to afford permanent staff, there are other ways of bringing talented people on board.

Identifying your needs

Before looking for potential employees, think carefully about the work that needs to be done. Taking on staff is a big commitment, since recruitment (see pp.124–125), induction, and training all take time and money. Consider whether you could outsource the work to another organization instead (see pp.50–51). For example, many small businesses now outsource their accounting and payroll activities. This avoids the need to employ dedicated staff, allowing you to focus on running the business. Decide if the work is short-term or requires specialist skills, such as web design or marketing, and whether it could be

undertaken on a freelance basis. A specialist freelancer can provide the expertise you need, for the duration of a specific task or project.

Alternatively, if the work is seasonal, or for a limited time period, and requires specific skills or experience, you may wish to employ someone on a fixed-term contract. This approach can provide the help you need without a long-term commitment and its associated costs.

(see pp.124–125)
(see pp.50–51)

DO'S AND DON'TS

When looking for the right people to fill roles in your business, here are some factors to keep in mind.

Do

> **Try several sources** to find suitable talent

> **Identify several candidates** in case one turns the role down

> **Keep in touch** with skilled people you may need in the future

> **Consider referrals** from trusted contacts but interview them carefully along with everyone else

Don't

> **Promise** anything that you are unable to deliver

> **Rush into** making a decision; consider all candidates carefully

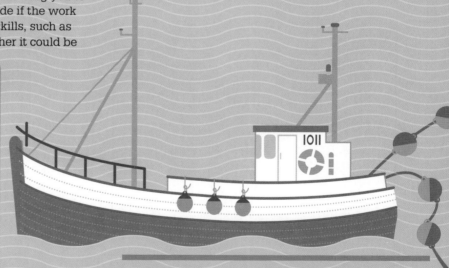

Catching the talent

Once you have decided upon the type of candidate you need and how you want to employ them (on a freelance, contract, full- or part-time basis) you can select the best way of finding them. Commonly used sources are:

Attracting candidates

If your company has a good reputation, it will attract the best candidates. To find out what makes an employer appealing, ask your own employees, find out how other managers run their businesses, and study advertisements to see how other companies entice their talent. Having a good reputation is vital, but whatever you tell candidates about your business must be genuine. If you promise training, for example, and do not provide it, they may leave, and your time and effort will have been wasted.

84%
of job seekers say a company's reputation matters

www.glassdoor.co.uk, 2020

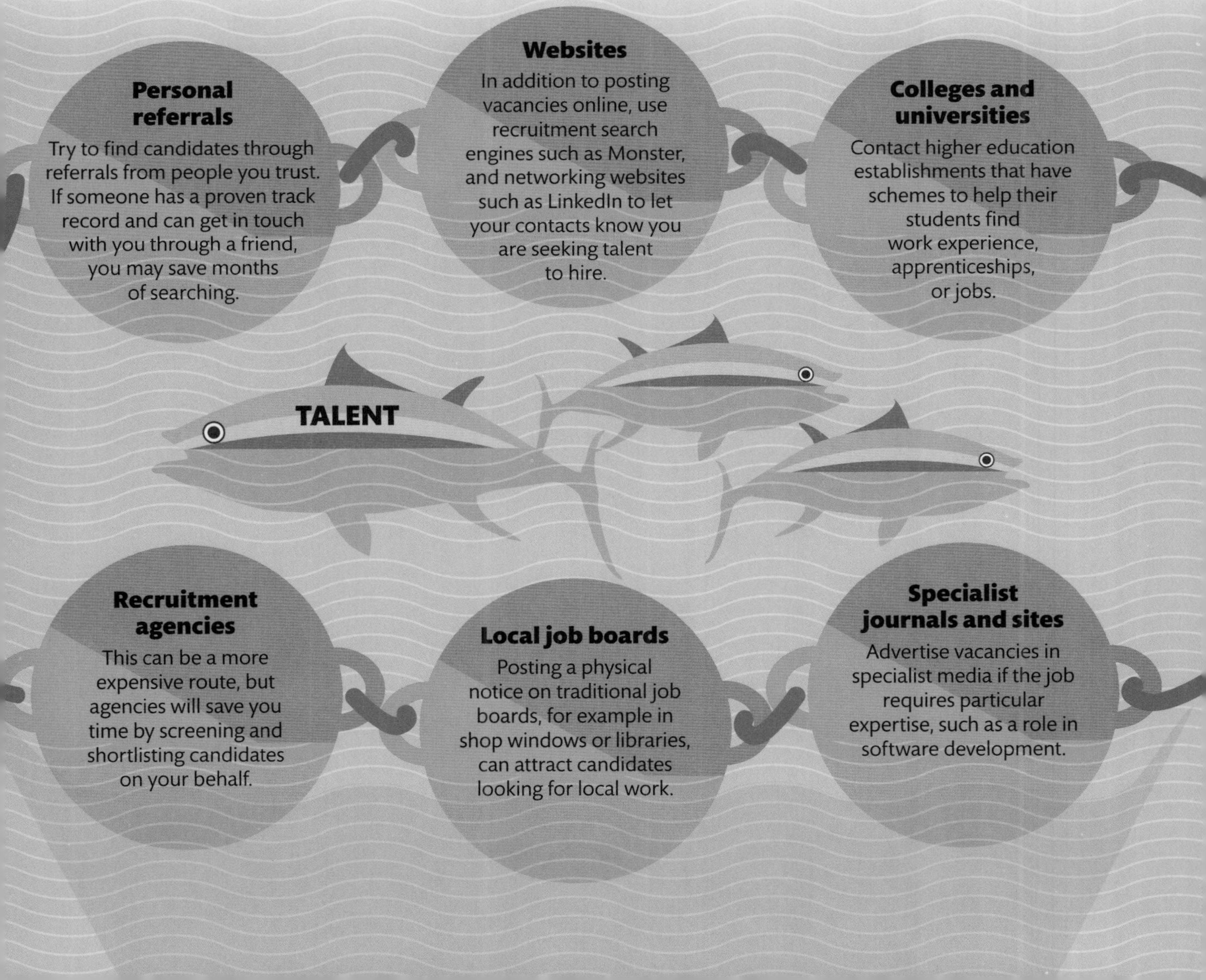

Personal referrals

Try to find candidates through referrals from people you trust. If someone has a proven track record and can get in touch with you through a friend, you may save months of searching.

Websites

In addition to posting vacancies online, use recruitment search engines such as Monster, and networking websites such as LinkedIn to let your contacts know you are seeking talent to hire.

Colleges and universities

Contact higher education establishments that have schemes to help their students find work experience, apprenticeships, or jobs.

TALENT

Recruitment agencies

This can be a more expensive route, but agencies will save you time by screening and shortlisting candidates on your behalf.

Local job boards

Posting a physical notice on traditional job boards, for example in shop windows or libraries, can attract candidates looking for local work.

Specialist journals and sites

Advertise vacancies in specialist media if the job requires particular expertise, such as a role in software development.

Recruiting staff

To find employees with the right skills, knowledge, and attitude for your business, you need to plan the recruitment process in detail – from advertising the role and creating a job description, to interviewing and making a decision.

Hiring effectively

Taking on the right person is a time-consuming process, so it is essential to plan ahead. Think about the role and the qualities of the person who is most likely to succeed at it. Having the right skills is key, but characteristics, such as the ability to work in a team or use one's own initiative, may be equally important. If someone has to work alone in an office, for example, they will need to be confident enough to handle queries without deferring to someone else. Experience of a similar business is also invaluable, affording insights into different ways of doing things. Looking at advertisements for similar jobs will give you an idea of the typical salary and the key skills for the role.

Finding the right person

A job description will help you attract and assess candidates, and decide who to interview. Planning the interview in detail will guide you towards choosing the right person.

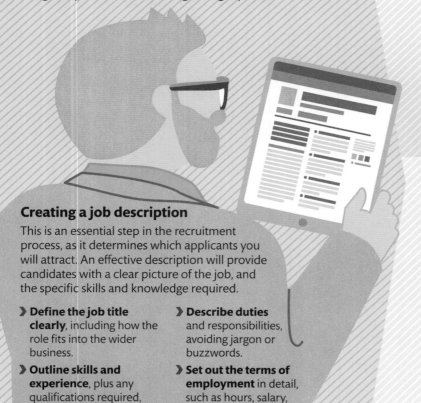

Creating a job description

This is an essential step in the recruitment process, as it determines which applicants you will attract. An effective description will provide candidates with a clear picture of the job, and the specific skills and knowledge required.

> **Define the job title clearly**, including how the role fits into the wider business.

> **Outline skills and experience**, plus any qualifications required, being reasonable in your expectations.

> **Describe duties** and responsibilities, avoiding jargon or buzzwords.

> **Set out the terms of employment** in detail, such as hours, salary, location, sick pay, and holiday allowance.

Reviewing applications

The job description provides a guide for assessing candidates. Use the skills and qualities you have listed as a checklist to decide if candidates will meet your needs.

> **Divide applications** into three groups: likely, not sure, and unlikely.

> **Focus on skills** and experience rather than personal details such as someone's name, which may bring an unconscious bias.

> **Look out** for someone who has experience in the area you need but will still have things to learn in the role.

> **Make notes** as these will help form questions at the interview stage.

> **Keep on file** candidates who are not right for this job but might suit a future role.

There are many channels for recruitment (see pp.122–123), including online job sites and talking to friends. Think about the the best place to find the person appropriate for your post and begin the recruitment process. Decide who will be involved, and what your timescale and budget will be.

Next, create an induction plan to introduce the new recruit to their colleagues and the business.

! BE AWARE

❱ **Make sure** that all interview questions are non-discriminatory and relevant to the role.

❱ **Avoid** personal questions about marital status or religion, which could lead to legal action.

❱ **Be mindful** that health and disability are also sensitive areas.

30%
of the global workforce is **seeking a job** at any one time
Business.linkedIn.com

Shortlisting and interviewing

A shortlist identifies the most suitable applicants for interviewing. You may wish to conduct short telephone interviews first to screen out unsuitable candidates. Plan the timing and order of the interview, and make a list of questions to ensure consistency.

❱ **Let the candidate know** in advance what form the interview will take and roughly how long it will be.

❱ **Put the interviewee** at ease and encourage them to talk.

❱ **Ask open questions** that cannot simply be answered with a "yes" or "no".

❱ **Watch how** they react to your questions and listen carefully to their responses. Make notes.

❱ **Find out** what motivates the interviewee. Ask what they like doing most or least.

❱ **Ask the candidate** to describe specific work situations that illustrate their experience.

❱ **Devise a test** to check the skills of the candidate.

❱ **Introduce the interviewee** to staff afterwards — less formal situations often reveal how likely an individual is to fit in.

Choosing the right person

The interview should reveal which candidate has the best skills and experience. Make sure you feel that the candidate has the right attitude for the job; this can be hard to change later.

❱ **Make sure** that you can justify the reasons for your choice.

❱ **Call** the successful applicant to offer them the job. Ensure you know their salary requirements before doing this.

❱ **Draw up** a contract setting out the conditions of employment to send to the new recruit.

❱ **Notify** and thank the unsuccessful candidates. You may want to give them constructive feedback.

Do you need a manager?

As your business grows, you may have to think about hiring a manager. Understanding the responsibilities and skills of a manager will help you weigh the advantages against the cost of their salary.

Sharing the load

Even if you have the time and skills needed to oversee every part of your venture at the start, that may change as your business develops. You could find yourself pulled away from your priorities, or without the skills to take the business further.

Recruiting a manager could reduce your workload and bring in much-needed expertise – but it is a big decision. A managerial salary will add a significant extra cost to the business, and you may be apprehensive about handing over authority to an outsider.

Remember, you could bring a manager onto your team as a temporary measure to begin with, to see if this is right for your business.

Looking ahead

While you are still able to run the business yourself, consider how it might

Coordinating your business

A skilled manager will pull together all the different areas of a business to produce a successful outcome. They will have an overview of what everyone is doing, observe what is going well and where the problems are, and take action as necessary. A good manager will be adept at the following skills:

Directing project

Agrees and sticks to timescales and budgets, and makes sure targets are met and goals achieved

Managing staff

Provides support, motivation, and essential training to help staff perform their roles effectively.

Organizing resources

Makes sure people have what they need to get their work done effectively.

develop – you may need to take on staff, introduce new products, or carry out more ambitious marketing. Think about how much of this you could manage on your own, and identify areas where you would benefit from experienced help. Also consider your existing workload, and how it will increase as the business grows. Planning ahead will highlight the skills and experience you may need in a future manager, as well as which parts of the business will most benefit from your own skills. This will also give you a timeframe within which to find, and budget for, the ideal candidate.

Do not rush the recruitment process (see pp.124–125). A highly capable manager may need some persuasion to join a new business, especially if it means resigning from an existing position.

IDENTIFYING A GOOD MANAGER

When choosing a manager, look for someone who is:

> **Full of ideas** that are relevant and fresh.

> **Confident** enough to challenge and improve existing methods.

> **Versatile** and capable of thriving with minimal supervision.

> **Trustworthy and personable**, inspiring loyalty in employees.

> **Passionate** about coaching and developing a team.

Maintaining order
Puts efficient processes in place so staff understand what to do, and ensures consistency in what is being done.

Communicating
Establishes good channels of communication so all employees understand their role and what is happening elsewhere in the business.

Getting things done
Observes activity across the whole business to assess the effectiveness of work processes and the wellbeing of staff, ensuring tasks are completed, and roles are fulfilled.

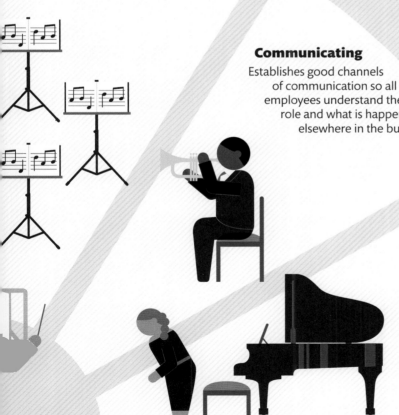

"**Managers** are the most creative people **in the world.**"

Maharishi Mahesh Yogi, Indian guru and businessman

Diversity and inclusion

A diverse and inclusive workplace makes for a more successful business. Recruit from a wider pool of talented people and create an environment where all are welcome and appreciated, and feel able to contribute.

What is diversity?

Diversity extends beyond considerations of race, gender, and disability. More broadly, it encompasses all the characteristics or qualities that make a person different from yourself. When recruiting, there is a subconscious tendency to look for people who are like you, so pay attention to diversity to help you to move away from that bias and think more openly.

This is not just to ensure legal compliance: firms that embrace diversity are likely to be more profitable, so it is good business sense to have a welcoming outlook and reflect the globally connected marketplace.

Research carried out by US management consultants McKinsey & Co., showed that diverse businesses are more successful at winning top talent, score higher on employee satisfaction, have a deeper understanding of their customers, and are better at decision-making.

Diversity is about recruiting and doing business with a broader range of people, while inclusion involves sustaining an open and welcoming work atmosphere. A new business needs to strive to promote an inclusive culture, where people feel safe to make suggestions, without worrying how their views will be received.

Why diversity matters

Encouraging diversity brings many benefits to a business. Not only will your firm be able to draw on a wider pool of talent with fresh ideas, but it will also be in a better position to connect with a range of customers. A diverse company will also have a better understanding of the wants and needs of that wider audience.

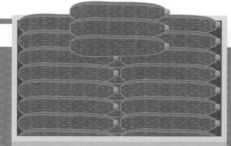

STRATEGIES

Set in place a plan to encourage diversity from recruitment and induction, through to marketing. Everyone involved must understand the benefits, and not see a focus on diversity as merely compliance with the law. Social media used to promote the business should both depict and engage with a wide range of individuals and groups.

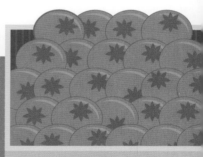

BENEFITS

People who think in the same way are likely to come up with a similar, limited range of ideas. Involve a diverse group of people, however, and creativity will soar. Diversity improves innovation as people bring their different perspectives, and feel freer to propose original, even unconventional, ideas.

Understanding unconscious bias

Studies have shown that people can have preferences they are not aware of that may guide their choices – a state known as unconscious bias. These preferences are often based on stereotypes and beliefs that are ingrained and unconscious. Many organizations offer "unconscious bias training" that aims to bring these hidden prejudices, held by everyone to a greater or lesser extent, to light. Further research indicates that these biases can affect who is recruited even when candidates have identical CVs, so identifying and addressing these preferences is key to becoming a more open and diverse workplace.

ANTI-DISCRIMINATION LAWS

Many countries across the world now have anti-discrimination laws of some kind (see pp.212–215), in order to stop businesses from discriminating against individuals based on protected characteristics. These characteristics can include age, disability, race, religion, gender, or sexual orientation. Every individual must be dealt with fairly, equally, and in accordance with national law, all the way through the employment lifecycle – from placing an advertisement for an employee to equal treatment in the workplace. Business practices are falling under greater scrutiny. It is not only a matter of criminal law; in some countries, civil law may also apply, meaning that an employee could claim for personal compensation if an employer is proven to have discriminated against them.

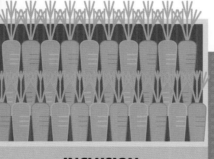

INCLUSION

It is also important to follow through on a pledge to encourage diversity by making sure all members of staff are made to feel welcome. This may mean being flexible to accommodate different ways of doing things. Keeping an open and honest dialogue with all your employees will help everyone feel heard and valued.

"Diversity is being invited to the party; inclusion is being asked to dance."

Vernã Myers, US activist

Using a customer data system

The better you understand your customers or clients, the better you can meet their needs and encourage them to keep coming back. Customer relationship management (CRM) software can help you with this.

Understanding CRM systems

Your customers and clients will expect to be able to access your business online, whether to order goods, find special offers, book appointments, or just ask questions. These interactions (known as "touchpoints") can tell you a great deal about your customers – what they are interested in, what they buy and when, how often they shop, and how much they spend. CRM software is widely available online to help you capture and analyse this data. You can use it to ensure your business offers your customers what they want, when

Using a CRM system

A CRM system works by collecting and analysing data about customers' or clients' purchasing and communication history with your business. You can then use this data to better understand and target your customers and clients. Even a simple CRM system will help you in building customer relationships, improving customer service, and increasing the productivity and profitability of your business.

Gathering data from customers and clients

Existing and potential customers can interact with your CRM system in many different ways. Encourage this at every opportunity, so you understand their needs and expectations before they do business with you, and at every step along the journey. The more data the system collects, the more you can learn. Here are some ways to achieve this:

Create a website
Create an eye-catching website that draws users in and promotes your business. Use it to sell the brand and get people talking about you.

Use social media
Create a business profile and post relevant content. Aim to engage customers and clients in a conversation.

Send regular e-communications
Email newsletters tailored to the interests of clients and customers. Write a blog and post videos online about your business.

Reward customers
Offer incentives to customers for recommending your business. Reward repeat customers.

Promote products or services
Give regular discounts and special offers to attract attention to your business.

Meeting customers
Plan events, where you can engage with customers and clients. Invite people to sign up to your mailing list.

Improve customer experience
Impress customers and clients by exceeding expectations. Offer a personalized service, quality goods, unique packaging, and prompt delivery.

Follow-up complaints
Handle and resolve complaints properly. Where purchases require installation/service, follow up with customers and clients promptly, and provide detailed FAQs on your website.

they want it, and at a price they are willing to pay. You can also use CRM software to manage how you communicate with your customers and clients, by automatically emailing personalized invoices, receipts, reminders, and marketing material or promotional offers.

Investing in CRM

You may feel that you want to delay installing a CRM system until your business is established. However, the better you understand your customers or clients, the more competitive your business will be. There are many systems available, including bespoke ones, so look online to find independent advice from a CRM consultant.

✓ NEED TO KNOW

> **Contacts** are existing clients or customers who have already purchased a product or service from a business.
> **CRM technology** captures and analyses customer data automatically through their transactions.
> **Data analysis** examines the information gathered to help the business operate more efficiently.
> **Leads** are potential future customers or clients.
> **Net promoter score** measures customer or client satisfaction by their willingness to recommend products or services to others.

"The sole purpose of business is to create and keep customers; profits are the reward."

Francis Buttle, professor in customer relationship management

Using customer data

Capturing as much data as possible will give you a broad insight into your customers and clients. You can then organize and analyse this data into useful information to guide future business decisions.

> **Identify customers' characteristics** including their buying habits, seasons, and times of purchase, as well as special interests – this can help you target these specific groups.
> **Highlight patterns and trends**, such as fashions and growing interests, which reveals areas you can tap into and exploit. You can also spot new and growing markets, and those in decline.
> **Analyse marketing responses** to monitor the effectiveness of your campaigns. If customers do not respond, you know you need to try a different approach.
> **Target customers or clients** who are high spenders with customized marketing.

Using customer insight

A CRM system will reveal how the behaviour of customers and clients changes over time. This information can strengthen your business, enabling you to:

> **Understand your customers'** preferences and expectations, allowing you to meet them now and in the future.
> **Ensure your marketing** campaigns are targeted and effective.
> **Compete more successfully** against your rivals, especially those without a CRM system.

Preparing for launch

Before taking your business live, build in a pre-launch stage when you can test each component – from branding to product – and tweak as necessary to ensure you achieve the best possible launch.

Preparing to launch

Careful pre-launch planning will ensure that your business is fully prepared for lift-off. This is the time for crucial small-scale testing of your product or service, branding, website, marketing approach, and any other key component of the business. Getting feedback from a sample of your target audience a few months in advance of your launch will give you time to adjust your approach, if necessary, to address criticisms, and to incorporate helpful new ideas.

To keep costs low, discuss your ideas with as many friends, peers, and family members as possible – especially those who match the characteristics of your target customer (see pp.40–41). Show them what you plan to launch, and get their honest opinions.

Ask those who match your target customer profile which social media or internet forums they use; their preferences will help you to decide which external

groups to survey to gain more objective judgements. If you are building a new website to support your business, consider creating a landing page with a countdown timer to your launch date. To gather names, add an offer to attract potential customers to sign up and stay informed.

Globally, only

55%

of all product launches take place on schedule

www.gartner.com, 2019

Test strategy

Having created a product to appeal to a certain audience, you now need to find out where those people gather (virtually or physically), and seek their opinions. Approach them via a website that sells your type of product, host a brief online survey, conduct shopping-centre or store interviews, or use a focus group, if affordable.

Testing and trialling

Methods for refining your product include click-testing on a website frequented by your target customers; running a trial in a store; and holding a pop-up event.

Feedback mechanisms

Talk to family, friends, and colleagues. Online, budget for a brief survey; question customer groups; set up a web page to solicit reactions and advice.

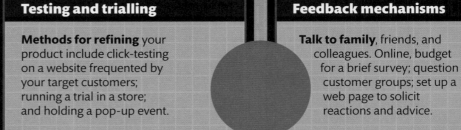

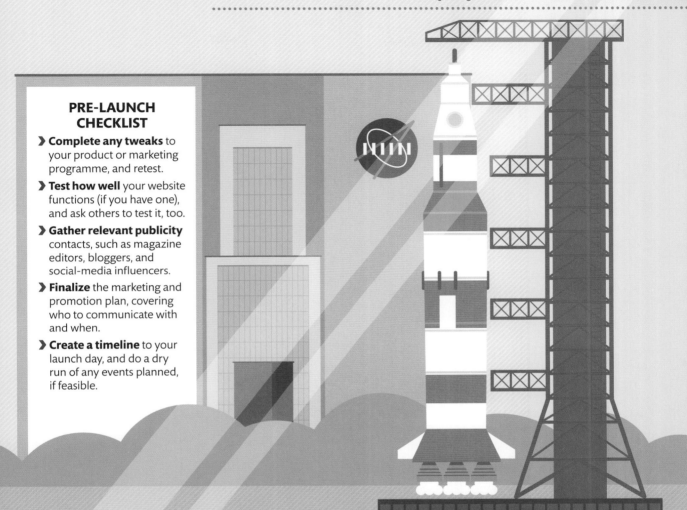

PRE-LAUNCH CHECKLIST

> **Complete any tweaks** to your product or marketing programme, and retest.

> **Test how well** your website functions (if you have one), and ask others to test it, too.

> **Gather relevant publicity** contacts, such as magazine editors, bloggers, and social-media influencers.

> **Finalize** the marketing and promotion plan, covering who to communicate with and when.

> **Create a timeline** to your launch day, and do a dry run of any events planned, if feasible.

Use focus groups

Setting up a focus group is not cheap but can be highly effective. You need a venue, 5 to 10 participants who match your customer profile, and a mediator to moderate and ask them well-designed questions about your product offering.

Spreading the word

Before spending money on costly marketing campaigns, consider using low-cost methods of promoting your products or services yourself to generate sales.

Telling the world

Marketing your products and services is essential in order to attract sales. While your budget may not allow for professional campaigns at first, there are steps you can take to spread the word at minimal cost. Known as "organic marketing", this approach simply requires your time, energy, and creativity.

Organic marketing involves any means of getting your message out to potential customers and clients. This can include writing a blog, attending local fairs, handing out samples of your product, or posting your business details on free online directories.

This approach is less direct than conventional advertising, so the benefits may be slow to materialize. However, research shows that more than 70 per cent of consumers ignore paid-for advertising and have greater trust in "word-of-mouth" messages, triggered by customer experience, as they appear to be more authentic. As such, even when you can afford to undertake more traditional marketing techniques, organic methods are well worth continuing.

Creative approaches

The primary aim of marketing is to promote sales, and should work in conjunction with your public relations activities, (see pp.136–137). When using organic marketing, be creative, and use as many methods and channels as possible, to target potential customers and clients. However, always ensure your approaches are consistent with your brand and company values.

USE YOUR CONTACTS

> **Ask friends and family** to talk about your products and services to everyone they know, both on- and offline.

> **Approach business** contacts and former colleagues to help promote your venture.

REPRESENT THE BUSINESS

> **Attend industry events**, where you can talk about and show your products or services. Share your details and build contacts.

> **Participate in community events**, such as fairs and shows, to meet potential customers and clients. Demonstrate what you offer.

MAKE MORE ONLINE CONTENT

> **Demonstrate and promote** your products and services on online video sharing sites and forums.

> **Write blogs and articles** that feature your products and services.

> **Publish positive testimonials** from satisfied customers. Encourage customers to post feedback.

TARGET SOCIAL MEDIA

> **Join all relevant** social media groups and highlight your business.

> **Develop social media** relationships with complimentary businesses. 'Like' and share their posts.

> **Befriend popular influencers** to attract their followers to your profile and website, if you have one.

TRY OTHER TACTICS

> **Come up with quirky** or controversial products and campaigns to attract attention.

> **Offer free samples** and "mini" versions of your products or services to encourage trial purchases.

USE ALL CHANNELS

> **Build a website**, even just a basic one, to promote your products and services.

> **Post your business details** on all relevant local and online business directories with links to your website.

> **Use online auction sites** to sell and promote your offering.

OFFER PROMOTIONS

> **Offer friends-and-family** benefits to existing customers.

> **Reward customers** for referring your products and services to their friends and contacts.

> **Use giveaways** and competitions as an opportunity to get people to try your products and services.

84%
of millenials do not trust traditional adverts

McCarthy Group, 2014

Creating a buzz

While marketing encourages the sale of your products and services, public relations (PR) aims to promote your business and brand. It is a valuable tool to help gain interest, customer loyalty, and sales.

Understanding publicity

As a new business owner, it is important to learn how to use PR to generate and maintain a positive image of your company and brand. It is key to establishing your brand's personality (see pp.60–61), and can strongly influence how willing people are to deal with you, including customers, suppliers, and even investors.

PR is an ongoing process that starts by creating a public image of your brand, what it is, and what it stands for. It then uses publicity to carefully manage how the business or brand is perceived externally.

Generating media coverage is a vital PR tool in order to reach your audience. For example, a journalist or online influencer writing about your business will give you valuable, free publicity. When launching your business, publicize the story behind your brand, and why you launched it, (see pp.62–63). Plan events, such as open days, enter for relevant trade or community awards, and share interesting news stories about your business. Take advantage of free internet monitoring services, such as Google Alerts, to keep track of any media mentions, as well as to follow competitors.

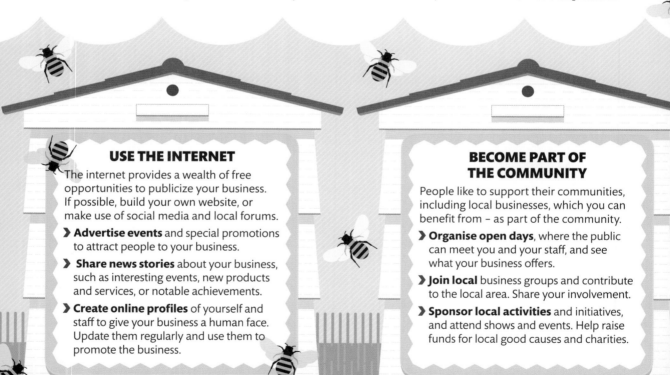

USE THE INTERNET

The internet provides a wealth of free opportunities to publicize your business. If possible, build your own website, or make use of social media and local forums.

> **Advertise events** and special promotions to attract people to your business.

> **Share news stories** about your business, such as interesting events, new products and services, or notable achievements.

> **Create online profiles** of yourself and staff to give your business a human face. Update them regularly and use them to promote the business.

BECOME PART OF THE COMMUNITY

People like to support their communities, including local businesses, which you can benefit from – as part of the community.

> **Organise open days**, where the public can meet you and your staff, and see what your business offers.

> **Join local** business groups and contribute to the local area. Share your involvement.

> **Sponsor local activities** and initiatives, and attend shows and events. Help raise funds for local good causes and charities.

"A good PR story is more effective than a front page ad."

Sir Richard Branson, entrepreneur

Spreading the word

Generating publicity need not be expensive, especially if your customer base is local. Identify your target customers (see pp.40–41) and develop publicity and PR activities with them in mind. Most people like promotions, with special deals and free giveaways, but some may respond better to information via direct mail, whereas others are likely to prefer social-media posts. Here are some ways to generate publicity and get people talking about your new business.

BE CREATIVE

The point of PR is to get people interested in, and talking about, your business. Think of quirky ways to promote your brand that will capture the attention of others.

> **Create posters and flyers** that will amuse or inspire those who see them. Make them available online for people to share and repost.

> **Occasionally offer novelty** products or services, unique to your business.

> **Launch innovative competitions**, such as local treasure hunts or online puzzles.

BE THE FACE OF YOUR BUSINESS

As business owner, you are central to your brand. Use your knowledge and enthusiasm to generate positive PR.

> **Engage with local media** and develop a good relationship. Invite them to events, share stories, and send press releases.

> **Become the expert** in your field to raise your personal profile and give greater credibility to your business.

> **Speak publicly** at local and industry events. Join and start campaigns.

Advertising

As well as promoting your business with marketing and PR activities, you can further increase your visibility by paying for advertising, using the medium best suited to your target audience.

Choosing your channel

Once you have launched your business with a promotion, paying for advertising can broaden your reach. In a competitive market, it is important to use the right means of communication for your target audience. For instance, if your message is for an older demographic, traditional advertising in printed publications or on the radio can be more effective,

TRADITIONAL ADVERTISING		
	PROS	**CONS**
DIRECT MAIL	❯ Reaches local/specific target market, such as restaurant diners ❯ Delivered directly to people's homes/offices ❯ Low cost	❯ May be regarded as junk mail and discarded ❯ Typically low response rate
NEWSPAPERS	❯ Fast publication process ❯ Themed specialist sections may allow for targeted advertising ❯ Can include coupons	❯ Offers no control over advert placement ❯ Competition for attention with other material on page (including competitors) ❯ Short shelf life and lower-quality printing
MAGAZINES	❯ Is often in circulation for months ❯ Specialist titles and themed sections allow focused adverts ❯ Quality printing adds cachet to the brand	❯ Accurate circulation figures are hard to source ❯ Advance planning is necessary to secure slots ❯ Is more costly than newspapers as it reaches a more targeted demographic
RADIO	❯ Inexpensive and easy production process ❯ Useful for reaching a target audience ❯ Good for creating immediate sales	❯ Listeners tend to "switch off" during adverts ❯ Frequent adverts are required for an impact ❯ Increased competition and higher cost for "rush hour" slots
BILLBOARDS	❯ Highly visible, clear message, seen repeatedly at all times ❯ Reaches people faster and more cheaply than other media	❯ Format limits message length ❯ Competition for prime sites ❯ Digital billboards are more effective, but much more expensive than static billboards
CINEMA	❯ Potential to impress with creative, professional production ❯ Captive audience ❯ High impact	❯ Limited audience numbers ❯ Audience may enter cinema only after adverts are shown
TELEVISION	❯ Offers local, national, and global reach ❯ High impact with vision/sound ❯ Adds cachet to brand	❯ Generally more expensive than other channels ❯ Repetition may cause viewer fatigue ❯ Viewers may ignore or skip adverts on catch-up television/internet streaming

although more expensive than online options, via the internet or mobile technology. Online advertising is more flexible, as it is not limited to a scheduled publication or broadcast. Response rates, which you need in order to work out the return on your investment (ROI) (see p.152), are also easier to accurately track with online advertising. Look at the pros and cons of each option to decide on the most effective and affordable way to reach your customers.

"**In 2017, internet advertising overtook all other forms of advertising spend in the UK.**"

Department for Digital, Culture, Media & Sport, 2019

ONLINE ADVERTISING		
	PROS	**CONS**
ADVERTS EMAILED IN NEWSLETTERS	❯ Relatively affordable. Requires good software and a list of email addresses ❯ Offers ability to send out bulk emails ❯ Easy to track the response rate	❯ Building a mailing list takes time; buying one in can be expensive ❯ Adverts may not reach the right audience ❯ Emails can be deleted or marked as spam
PAY-PER-CLICK DISPLAY ADVERTISING	❯ Affordable, as you only pay when someone clicks on the advert ❯ Can be visually eye-catching and build brand awareness ❯ Makes it easy to target special interests/topics	❯ No guarantee that website users will click ❯ Advert-blocking tools can stop users seeing adverts ❯ Lower click-through rate than pay-per-click adverts on search engines (paid search adverts)
PAID SEARCH ADVERTISING	❯ Similarly affordable, as search engine only charges when visitors click on the advert ❯ Success is the number of clicks, so easy to track ❯ Higher click-through rate than for other pay-per-click banner and display adverts	❯ Requires lots of testing to establish most effective keywords ❯ No guarantee that those who click will buy ❯ No direct correlation between budget and results
MOBILE ADVERTISING	❯ Generally cheap to develop ❯ Quick and easy to track advert effectiveness ❯ Can target specific demographic groups, thanks to geo-location technologies ❯ Can engage individually with users	❯ Creating a consistent advertising campaign for different screen sizes and systems is tricky and can be costly ❯ Users may be annoyed by the intrusion ❯ Negative experiences are quickly shared
SOCIAL MEDIA SPONSORSHIP	❯ Sponsoring a social media influencer who connects with your target audience raises awareness of your brand ❯ A positive mention of your product or service encourages brand loyalty	❯ Large followings do not necessarily guarantee high engagement ❯ The appeal of influencers, especially celebrities, can fluctuate
SOCIAL MEDIA ADVERTS	❯ Easy to target a specific audience ❯ Increased brand visibility and recognition ❯ Cheaper than conventional advertising	❯ Continual posts and updates can distract user attention away from placed adverts ❯ Requires constant monitoring to maintain users' interest and find new users

Making the most of social media

Thanks to social media, your business can engage with existing and potential customers anytime, anywhere. To make the most of it, you need to target the right platforms and use the most effective strategies.

Picking the right sites

Start by deciding what you want to achieve on social media, this could be to build your brand, reach new customers, or engage better with existing ones. Review the platforms your competitors use; this will help you decide which are most relevant for you, and may inspire new ideas. To further guide your choices, ask your customers which platforms they use, and compare any profiles you have built up of them – and of customers you aim to attract – to the user demographic information found in the business tools on most popular platforms.

Once you have decided on your plan, you need to bring it to life. Start by creating compelling content, including posts, images, or videos, and post it on the most appropriate platforms (see right).

Creating a strong profile

Begin by choosing a username, which starts with the @ symbol, called a "social media handle", for example, @mycompanyname. Aim for a strong, consistent username across all platforms, and ideally one that matches your website domain name (see p.114). Use the same logo or personal photograph across all platforms, too, so that your business is easily recognized. Then, add an attention-grabbing summary of the business and keep it updated.

SHARE CONTENT ACROSS DIFFERENT PLATFORMS

> **Repeat consistent messages** but reshape content to suit different platform styles.
> **Tweak messages** to suit the vocabulary and the tone of each platform.
> **Boost impact** by using the full character limit for each platform.
> **Check images** and resize them as necessary for each platform.

EXTEND BUSINESS REACH

> **Target the maximum** number of users who see your content.
> **Use hashtags** – "#" followed by words with no spaces, such as #hotdog – to create phrases that are easy to search for, including your business name.
> **Encourage engagement**, using likes, comments, and shares.

Choose the right social media

Six key sites; look out for new ones, too.

> **Facebook** – use to showcase your products and services.
> **Instagram** – share videos and photos, and engage with customers.
> **Snapchat** – post to 12–34 age group, and offer discounts and promo codes
> **Twitter** – post breaking news, announcements, and promotions.
> **LinkedIn** – post professional content, as well as jobs, to build credibility.
> **YouTube** – post educational and instructional videos.

EXISTING CUSTOMERS
Engaging with existing customers can result in repeat sales and greater loyalty.

CREATE CONTENT

> **Post compelling** content.
> **Plan consistent**, regular, scheduled content updates.
> **Personalize** content to suit your target audience.
> **Use strong images** or lively infographics to draw attention.
> **Tailor** content to the platform but keep a clear brand focus.

MAKING IT WORK

> **Use free online tools** and analytics (see pp.212–215) initially to track and measure performance of social media interactions.
> **Respond to any negative comments** on sites in a positive way, and avoid defensive or inflammatory replies.
> **Add your social networking profile** links to your website, email signature, promotional materials, stationery, and business cards.

Follow the trends

> **Identify "influencers"** – people with a large social media following – in areas relevant to your business and that best match your brand.
> **Subscribe to social media blogs** (online articles and commentaries) to learn about the latest trends.
> **Look online at Google Trends** for a broad view of the topics that are the most searched for online.
> **Join relevant online forums** to see what members are talking about and interested in. Start and lead threads on subjects involving your business.

Invest in advertising

> **Choose the most relevant platform** to your business and customers, and try to steer users, or "traffic", to your own website.
> **Use online adverts** that target buyers by geography, shopping patterns, personal interests, and other demographic pointers.
> **Create compelling** offers to attract attention and customer interaction.
> **Make sure adverts** have a clear, simple graphic design, punchy memorable headlines, or both.

If you have a website

> **Link to your website shop**, which is where customer sales are actually made.
> **Keep website content** up to date, with news, blogs, new products, and trends.
> **Promote website content,** such as blog posts and images, on your social media platforms to generate website traffic.
> **Encourage the sharing** of website content on social media by adding "sharing" tools to web pages that link to Facebook, Instagram, and other sites.

POTENTIAL CUSTOMERS
Raising your profile will attract new customers, who may spread the word about you.

Networking to build your business

As the owner of a start-up, you need to make connections so that your business becomes better known and gains some support. As your business grows, these connections may become mutually beneficial relationships.

Meeting in person

Online technology provides plenty of good ways to connect, and video-conferencing platforms have come into their own since the global pandemic. Apps such as Zoom, Microsoft Teams, Google Hangouts, and Skype offer facilities for people around the world to see each other in real-time, host meetings, share visuals, and vote on decisions.

However, where possible, face-to-face contact, especially when meeting someone for the first time, is an easier way to establish a rapport. A significant part of communication is body language; being able to see and interpret a person's reactions helps both understanding and the flow of conversation. It is also a better way to build credibility and establish trust.

Face-to-face networking need not be daunting. Think about it as a way to gain personal exposure, which will create opportunities and grow the business. Set a goal to meet more people, have meaningful interactions, and build personal and professional relationships. Look for professional networking events as well as special interest groups and associations linked to your area of business where you can go along and make connections.

Maintaining relationships

Networking is not just about seeking out new contacts. Imagine two lists. The first is your target list, containing people to get to know, or types of people to connect with, for example, influencers in your sector. The second list contains all your current contacts. Choose the relationships to maintain and strengthen, and plan to have a weekly coffee or phone call with at least one of these people. Do not assume anything; asking open questions may reveal connections. Always aim to help contacts as far as possible, even if it is just emailing a link to an article.

HOW TO NETWORK EFFECTIVELY

There are some important ways in which you can make your face-to-face networking more successful.

> **Dress professionally**.

> **Listen carefully** to the people you meet to find shared interests. Then, politely move on to meet others.

> **Aim to develop relationships** rather than sell something.

> **Exchange a well-designed business card** with people you want to connect with.

> **Follow up** with an email or connection via social media.

Veejay Nahar-Watson
Managing Director
Any Business
vnaharwatson@
anybusiness.com
www.anybusiness.com
+12 3456 789012

MAKING IT WORK

> **Nurture and maintain** your current contacts by staying in touch, but do not add people to your emailing list without their permission.

> **Trust remains** the basis of any relationship, so be sure to follow through on any offers to share information that you make when you meet someone.

> **Inform your contacts** when you are launching a new product or service and seek input from those with relevant experience.

How to network in person

Consider people, from peers in the same sector to industry experts, who would make good connections. Face-to-face opportunities include breakfast meetings, conferences, and business clubs; joining a regular group is more likely to result in enduring relationships.

Make friends early

Most people want to give someone starting out a helping hand, so begin networking as soon as you can, and quickly build relationships with your peers.

Be interested

Curiosity and a genuine interest in the other person is the start of any worthwhile relationship. Converse equally, share information, and be authentic in all interactions.

Build your list

Gradually compile a list of contacts, and identify those that could be helpful to you. These are not necessarily the most senior; consider those likely to be mutually supportive, also.

Be helpful

Think of networking as trading. Have some ways in which to help others, such as offering recommendations, useful information, or professional contacts.

RUNNING YOUR BUSINESS

Encouraging customer loyalty

Building a base of loyal customers or clients will help you to generate a steady, sustainable income stream, and bolster trade in times of uncertainty. Faithful customers who refer others to you also help to boost your business.

Understanding loyalty

Some customers and clients will come back regularly to you because you are familiar and they are short of time. It takes more effort and they could feel like they are taking more of a risk to find a new place.

Other customers might buy from you because you have the cheapest prices, but they may easily be lured away by a discounting competitor. These customers are hard to keep loyal, but if you back up sales with great customer service, you will at least receive some positive reviews.

The most loyal customers will be those who value the quality of your product, service, or brand, and who enjoy the experience of purchasing through your business. Gathering and acting on feedback from your customers (see box, right) will improve your interaction with them; that, in turn, will help boost loyalty.

Promoting referrals

A loyal customer base can, in effect, become an extra promotional arm for your business. Market research shows that up to 85 per cent of consumers trust online reviews as much as they do word-of-mouth referrals. The challenge is to persuade loyal customers to take the step of either telling other people about your business or brand, or leaving an online review.

77% of consumers say they stayed loyal to specific brands for 10 years or more

www.inmoment.com, 2018

Creating a bond

It is easy for most customers and clients to research products, brands, and service providers online, so they will have high expectations. Attentive, personalized customer service is a vital tool in holding on to customers and developing an emotional connection with them.

Key to this emotional bond is making memories for the customer as they interact with you. Remembering names, making transactions surprisingly straightforward, and offering customers something special can all be memorable. In short, ensure that every aspect of the customer experience is positive, eliminating any negatives.

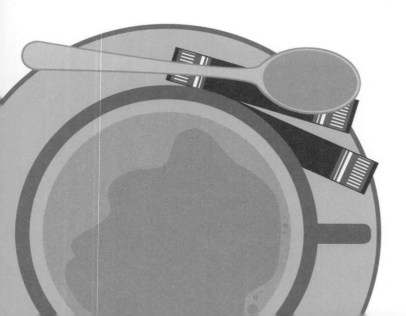

A referral scheme, such as offering a discount for the customer who refers a friend, as well as a discount for the friend, can be effective in promoting recommendations.

Ask customers and clients to leave an online review if they have had a positive experience. Invite them to do so when they are at their happiest – this is typically just after they have received the product or service you have sold them. Offering a prize or some sort of incentive may encourage customers or clients to respond.

COLLECTING CUSTOMER FEEDBACK

Gathering information about what customers need and want can enable a business to improve products and services, thereby building loyalty.

❱ **Simple surveys** can be sent by email, with statements evaluated on a scale of 1 to 10.

❱ **If your business has an app**, insert one or two pop-up questions relevant to the page the customer is currently on.

❱ **Live chat** on your website allows customers to ask questions and be asked for their opinions.

❱ **Post prompt replies** to negative reviews and offer to remedy complaints immediately.

❱ **When face-to-face** with customers, ask about their needs and note what they say.

❱ **Monitor website activity**: how long do visitors spend on your website, what do they click on, and how often do they return?

Enhancing the customer experience

To earn the loyalty of your customers and clients, try to ensure that every step in the consumer journey is as convenient and enjoyable as possible, from ease of finding products and hassle-free purchasing, to prompt, reliable delivery and excellent after-sales service.

Offering engaging content

Engage customers with your products and services by giving them useful information, or inspiring them. This will encourage them to keep coming back to you, giving you an edge over competitors.

Insider offers and social action

Rewarding loyal customers with gifts and discounts is one approach to earning loyalty. Alternatively, supporting a cause or community the customer cares about will also engage them.

Managing expectations

When it comes to the logistics of delivery in particular, customers appreciate being kept informed of when their product or service will be delivered, and what level of quality and service to expect.

Outstanding customer service

Consistent, thoughtful customer service is important in building loyalty. This might include speedy personalized replies to customer emails, or trying to exceed your clients' expectations.

Building customer relationships

All customers and clients are valuable to your business – especially those who return, support your brand, and advocate it to others, which you can encourage by building strong relationships.

Keeping customers satisfied

Anyone who buys products or services from your business is valuable, although some customers and clients are more valuable to you than others. While those who make single, one-off purchases have value, the best are those who not only return, but who also support and recommend your business to others.

While some people will only ever make a single purchase, you can encourage others to develop stronger bonds with your business. The first step is to understand who they are and what they need (see pp.40–41). Once you know this, you can create products and services that meet those needs, then promote them in the most appropriate way to reach your target audience.

To build relationships with your customers and clients, get to know them. Speak to them face-to-face, engage with them on social media (see pp.140–141), and use a customer data system (see pp.130–131). You can then use what you learn to ensure that your products and services not only meet their expectations, but exceed them. Prove to them that they can trust and rely on you through the quality of your offering, customer service, and aftercare.

Marketing
Identify potential customers and clients and develop marketing material designed to attract their interest towards your business.

Communication and campaigns
Use marketing campaigns specifically aimed at your target customers (see pp.140-141) to build interest in the products or services you offer.

Quality and reliability
Provide good-quality products and services that exceed your customers' and clients' needs and expectations.

How to build relationships

Building relationships with your customers and clients is a gradual process that starts with your business appearing relevant to them. Once you have caught their attention, you need to inspire sufficient interest for them to make a purchase. From this point, use your understanding of your customers or clients to develop and sustain good relationships.

Prospective customer
A potential customer becomes aware of your business and may be persuaded to buy from you.

Single purchase
The customer knows more about you and what you offer, which appeals to them enough to make a purchase.

CUSTOMER SERVICE

Customer service and experience are key areas where your business can compete. While some customers and clients will be impressed by a flashy website or stylish premises, all appreciate feeling valued and cared for, which requires time and thought – not money.

Regularly review how you interact with your customers and clients, and how well. Think about every aspect of your business, and the products or services you offer, from your customers' perspectives. What would they think? How would they rate you? Are you better than your rivals? Then think about your customers and what matters to them. Why do they buy from you? What do they come back? Pay attention to the smaller details, as it is often the little things that people notice and appreciate – and remember.

You can also target your marketing more effectively by offering tailored promotions, and communicate with your customers or clients as valued individuals.

NEED TO KNOW

❯ **Customer experience management** is the tools and processes a business uses to manage and improve interactions with its customers.

❯ **Customer journey** describes the entire purchasing lifecycle, from initial interest, through purchase, to aftercare.

❯ **Loyalty schemes** encourage return business, offering rewards to clients or customers based on the amount they spend.

❯ **"Sticky" customers** are loyal consumers who return to your business to make more purchases.

"Loyalty programmes made 46% of French customers feel more valued in 2019."

www.statista.com, 2020

Support and service

Engage with your customers as individuals and give excellent, personalized service. Offer guarantees and good aftercare service to inspire confidence.

Loyalty schemes

Offer customers emotional benefits, such as rewards for making purchases, and discounts for their friends and family. Add them to your mailing list and communicate regularly.

Regular customer

The customer knows they can rely on your products and services, and trusts you enough to make regular purchases.

Valued customer

The customer begins to feel valued and makes regular purchases in preference to other businesses.

Advocate

The customer makes regular purchases, feels loyal to your business, and actively recommends it to others.

Working with other businesses

As a new business owner, it can be well worth seeking mutually beneficial relationships – with your suppliers and also with companies whose goods or services complement what your business offers.

Collaborating with others

Although your business must compete against its rivals, it can benefit from good partnerships with other companies whose interests align with yours. As every business has its own strengths and weaknesses, a collaboration with another company may help fill a gap in your business model or provide a service that you need. For example, if you repair mobile phones but lack direct access to customers, it could be mutually beneficial to partner with a retailer who sells phone accessories and has space available. Alternatively, you may be a start-up whose innovative product or service.

Types of alliance

Working with other businesses can help support your start-up – by securing goods or services that you need or by providing something that complements or fills a gap in your business model. However, the partners and suppliers you choose must be right for your business, and you will need to work with them to sustain the relationships. Any agreement must benefit the business; if it does not, be prepared to walk away if necessary.

PARTNERSHIPS

To develop a successful partnership, you will need to work with a business whose products or services complement what your start-up is offering, helping to draw in new customers and provide extra value to existing customers. Whether you are looking at companies in the same industry or ones who provide a service, such as web design and maintenance, plan carefully before you enter a partnership, and consider the following tips on what to do and what to avoid doing.

DO...

> **Choose a partner** that meets your criteria, such as their financial status, willingness, goals, and personality.

> **Formalize the agreement**, recording what each party expects and offers.

> **Set realistic expectations** to ensure that they are met as agreed.

> **Maintain communication** and discuss any problems early, so you can take swift remedial action.

DON'T...

> **Limit partners by location**, as the best may be on the other side of the world.

> **Accept the first offer**; instead negotiate for the deal that suits all parties the most.

> **Be tempted by size**, as the biggest partner might offer more opportunities, but these may not be right for you.

> **Ignore issues**, as they are unlikely to disappear. Timely, shared resolutions can strengthen a relationship.

attracts the support of a larger company. Working with another business can give you fresh ideas and expand your experience. You should also build excellent relationships with suppliers to enable you to work together to support each other's business long term.

Forming alliances

The internet and social media have made it easier to find potential partners, but be sure to discuss your plans in detail before you commit to a collaboration. Explain to any prospective business partner what you want to gain from the relationship, and weigh up what is expected in return – it is vital to agree on shared outcomes. While you do not need to create

NEED TO KNOW

> **Horizontal alliances** occur between businesses that are in the same industry, and who may have been competitors, but have decided to work together.

> **Vertical alliances** are partnerships between businesses at different stages in the same supply chain; working with a supplier is a common example.

a legally binding contract, a clear, written agreement will help to avoid any misunderstandings and will underline the strategic objective you both aim to achieve too.

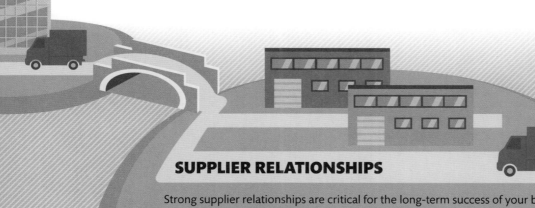

SUPPLIER RELATIONSHIPS

Strong supplier relationships are critical for the long-term success of your business, but it may be prudent to have more than one supplier if your company is dependent on a single item. Examples of ways in which suppliers can impact a small business include the quality of goods and services; the timeliness/reliability of deliveries; competitiveness and innovation; and financial implications/payment terms. Here are some simple ways to ensure mutually beneficial supplier relationships:

DO...

> **Develop personal relationships**, as suppliers value familiar customers, and are more likely to deal fairly with those that they know and trust.

> **Share information** with a supplier, particularly on critical lead times (and that way you will avoid surprises).

> **Agree and stick to all terms**, especially those that involve payments.

DON'T...

> **Cancel orders** without plenty of notice, and only do so when unavoidable.

> **Forget your supplier** is also in business, and therefore needs to fulfil their own objectives and make a profit.

> **Play one supplier off** against another to secure an advantage, as both may eventually cease to trade with you.

Is your marketing leading to sales?

Marketing is vital, but can be costly. Assess the effectiveness of your marketing activities, and monitor where most of your sales are being made to ensure that your campaigns count.

Investing in marketing

Marketing is a creative process and it is often viewed as being one of the most exciting parts of the business. However, since several factors can cause an increase in sales, the effectiveness of your marketing campaigns can seem hard to measure. For example, after delivering new flyers locally, you need to be sure that any subsequent increase in trade was not simply the result of more people moving to the area.

You need to view marketing as an investment, and understand which marketing approach will best engage with customers and drive sales, particularly as marketing is an ongoing and cumulative process.

Measuring success

Even for start-ups, digital marketing is an affordable and valuable option, and there are many free online analytical tools available (see pp.212–215) to measure its effectiveness, such as Google Analytics, which you can set up online without specialist knowledge. These record data such as the number of new visitors to a website, number of page views, clicks on paid adverts, and the rate at which sales have been made. Offline campaigns can also be measured by counting response rates to flyers and adverts featuring discount codes.

As well as measuring the response rate to marketing activities, you need to assess the financial return. To do this, look at a specific time period, and divide your total marketing spend by the number of new customers attracted. This gives a figure known as the customer acquisition cost (CAC). Next, estimate how much money an average customer will spend with you over their lifetime, the customer lifetime value, (CLV): to do this, multiply the product value by the number of times it is purchased, then multiply this by the average customer lifespan. If it costs $200 to acquire each customer, who will spend only $20 over their lifetime, you will need to review your campaign.

6. FINE-TUNE
Use customer feedback and your market research to fine-tune your product, promotional messages, sales, and service.

5. GIVE GREAT SERVICE
Build on the relationship, turning the sale into repeat purchases, word-of-mouth recommendations, and loyalty.

The marketing cycle

The marketing process should begin with a good understanding of your customers' needs. Using this information you can adjust your offering and craft a strong marketing message. Give great service to keep customers engaged, and use their feedback to hone your marketing campaigns.

1. RESEARCH
Get to know your customers, product, market area, and competitors.

2. CUSTOMIZE
Adapt your product, price, and distribution to suit your customers' needs and your market.

> "Email marketing has the highest return on investment for small businesses."
>
> Campaign Monitor, 2019

3. MARKET
Create and communicate your message to your intended customers to interest and attract them.

4. SELL
Close the sale with your customer, ensuring the process is hassle-free.

TRACKING SALES

Looking at overall sales may not provide all of the information necessary for you to make the best marketing decisions. Here are some ways to look at sales from different perspectives; they will help determine the best areas in which to invest marketing funds.

> **Keep records** for each day, week, month, quarter, and year, and compare with previous time periods.

> **Break figures down** to understand the best-selling products or services.

> **Identify which customers** make the most/largest purchases.

> **Record sales** made to new and existing customers – look out for repeat purchases.

> **Identify and compare** the best sales channels, such face-to-face retail or online transactions.

ANALYSING SALES DATA

As a business owner, you can collect sales data from many different sources (see pp.154–155). However, in order for it to provide meaningful information, it needs to be organized and analysed. For example, data such as a list of customers who bought a particular item does not reveal anything, but when organized by source, it could reveal that most sales were made to new customers. Use simple spreadsheets to analyse data.

Analysing business performance

You need to keep checks on which parts of your start-up are working as you had hoped they would, and which are not. Using key performance indicators (KPIs) gives you helpful snapshots of your business in action.

Understanding KPIs

Key performance indicators (or KPIs) are targets that you set for crucial business areas, such as marketing, sales, and finance, and against which you check progress regularly (weekly, monthly, or quarterly).

Set your KPIs carefully. Too many KPIs – or poorly chosen ones – will overwhelm you with unhelpful data. Ideally, start with a small number that relate directly to your business plan and the aspects most likely to bring success. Communicate your KPIs to your employees, perhaps displaying them as a "dashboard" (see below). Clearly defining KPIs and how they will be measured – whether as quantities or as ratios or percentages – will ensure that everyone understands them.

The KPI dashboard

When sharing the KPIs for your business, the best way is to display them graphically. You can either do this manually but drawing a simple chart or even just write them as percentages on a poster. Alternatively, make use of free online software to create digital "dashboard". However you present your KPIs, use them as a tool to motivate yourself and your staff by highlighting areas of success and where improvements are required.

Marketing
› **Company website** The level of traffic
› **Internet** Keywords in top 10 search results
› **Social medi**a Levels of sharing, liking, and retweeting of posts
› **Email campaign**s Percentage of customers responding and buying goods
› **Advertising** Units sold per $1,000 investment

Sales
› **Customer lifetime value** Total amount of money generated by the average customer
› **Upselling** Percentage of product buyers who also take a service package
› **Conversion time** How long it takes to close a sale
› **Regional sales** What is selling where and in what quantity

Customer satisfaction
› **Turnover** Proportion of customers making repeat sales, or continuing a service
› **Website** New visits to a site versus repeat visits
› **Feedbac**k Percentage of high-scoring customer reviews
› **Complaints** Ratio of complaints to number of customers

Make targets realistic, neither so high that they are unachievable, nor so low that they hold back growth. Updating your KPIs regularly will stop them from becoming obsolete (you may need to drop some and devise new ones as your business evolves). A good set of KPIs will act as a compass and show you if you are on course to meet your goals.

SWOT analysis (see box, right) is another useful tool. It identifies internal and external factors that could affect the performance of your business as a whole.

SWOT ANALYSIS

SWOT asks open-ended questions to address the Strengths, Weaknesses, Opportunities, and Threats influencing a business. Identifying these factors can help you understand their positive or negative impacts on performance.

> **Strengths** What is your business best at? Does it have any intellectual property (see pp.96–97), special skills, or financial resources?

> **Weaknesses** What is your business not good at? Why do people not like/buy its products? Does it rely on outdated technology? Is it missing strategic alliances (see pp.150–51)?

> **Opportunities** What external changes can your business exploit? Do competitors have weaknesses that could benefit your business?

> **Threats** What might competitors do that could impact your business? How might changing social or shopping trends undermine your business plan and affect profits?

Employees

> **Employee satisfaction** Proportion of satisfied staff as indicated by surveys

> **Staff turnover** Percentage leaving over time (high turnover rates are costly)

> **Absence and sickness** Average work days lost per staff member

> **Health and safety** Number of accidents at work

Operations

> **Products** Percentage of product defects

> **Output** How many units produced per operating hour/day

> **Efficiency** Percentage of tasks or deliveries completed in the allocated time

> **Overheads** Actual use of energy, water, and rent against budgeted use

Financial

> **Customer payments** Percentage of customers paying on time

> **Expenses payments** Proportion of invoices paid in 30 days, 90 days, etc.

> **Profit margins** Gross and net profit compared to desired levels

> **Inventory turnover** Time taken to offload stock

Maintaining momentum

Once you are up and running, it is vital to maintain momentum. Developing your business is an ongoing process – you will need to keep researching ideas, building products, seeking new markets, and growing your customer base.

Continual development

In order to achieve the objectives you set in your business plan (see pp.104–105), which can be months or even years ahead, take steps to maintain your business momentum. This means constantly trying to improve what you do and how you do it, and looking for ways to reduce costs and increase profits. It also involves searching for new products and services to offer, and improving those you already have. This is particularly important with your marketing activities, which play a significant role in attracting customers and sales.

There is no specific process to maintaining momentum. Instead, treat it as a fundamental objective, and share it with everyone involved in your business. To improve your chances of achieving it, set yourself goals and measure the results. For example, you might aim to reduce the cost of your materials by 10 per cent within the first year of trading, or to attract a new customer group within six months.

Making it happen

Maintaining momentum is important in all aspects of your business, but critical in your marketing activities. Customers can easily lose interest and be tempted away by competitive rivals, so continually developing and perfecting your marketing is essential. Here are some examples of different approaches you could take.

Develop contacts
Attend workshops and events, listen and ask questions, use networking resources such as LinkedIn.

Identify partners
Collaborate with businesses that enhance your brand; look for sales channel and supplier opportunities.

MAKING IT WORK

❯ **Borrow ideas from successful rivals** to improve how your business operates. Read trade articles in the media to discover the approaches they used.

❯ **Share the need to maintain momentum** with everyone involved within the business in a simple statement. Use it as a reminder for them and yourself.

❯ **Do not be blinded by short-term success**, which can easily vanish unless you continually improve and develop your business.

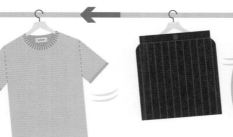

Create a marketing plan
Build a calendar of activities with deadlines for advertisements, events, trade shows, and online activity.

Schedule offers
Plan regular deals, often linked to promotions, such as free trials, discounts, two-for-ones, and coupons.

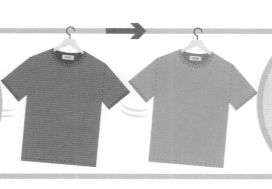

Apply for awards
Apply for relevant sector and local awards. This is useful for PR, building customer trust, and motivating staff.

Master sales
Know your target customer, design campaigns, capture customer information, and generate sales leads.

Develop loyalty/referrals programmes
Retain existing customers and acquire new ones by offering incentives.

Review, measure, and improve
Set goals, regularly review them, and build on whatever works best.

DEVELOPING NEW PRODUCTS AND SERVICES

Regularly reviewing your products and services and developing new ones is one of the most effective ways to improve what your business offers customers. It can be costly and risky, but also rewarding. Here are some points to consider:

> **Keep lists** of potential product ideas from customers, family, competitors, and articles in the media.

> **Test concepts**, offering samples to customers or testing new services on selected clients to see if an idea is worth pursuing.

> **Analyse the market**, looking at trends and your competition to assess any new opportunity and its potential sales.

> **Develop the product**, using customer or client feedback, as well as any relevant market analysis.

> **Test the market** by trying out the new offering on customers who fit your target audience profile.

> **Launch the product** using social media, email newsletters, and seasonal fairs to kickstart sales.

Managing your finances

Ongoing financial management is essential to ensure your business has the funds it needs, when it needs them. This means you must maintain accurate financial records from the beginning.

Keeping records

Effective financial management relies on accurate bookkeeping, (see pp.88–89). This allows you to see how much money the business has at any time. It is all-important when calculating your profit and loss statement (also see pp.88–89). Before you begin trading, you will need a system to record all sources of income and expense. You can either do this manually, or by using online software. You should also record the type of income or expense. For example, selling an asset creates a one-off lump sum, whereas regular transactions better indicate income. Similarly, buying an asset is a one-off cost, whereas regular expenses give a clearer picture of your outgoings.

Understanding business costs

There are two types of business cost: fixed costs (also called overheads) and variable costs. Fixed costs are the same no matter what business activities occur. This makes them easy to predict and account for. However, being fixed, they are difficult to reduce. In contrast, variable costs relate directly to business activities, so can go up and down. This makes them harder to predict at first, but you may be better able to do so over time. As variable costs relate to business activities, you can take steps to reduce them when necessary.

FIXED COSTS

This cost is a set expense for your business, but it can change over time. Examples include:

Rent or monthly mortgage costs, which have to be paid. When interest rates change, the amount you pay can either go up or down.

Insurance costs on your premises and machinery are fixed for the duration of the premium, usually a year. The cost can vary from year to year.

Licences to play music or sell alcohol are essential for hospitality businesses, such as restaurants, hotels, and bars.

Wages for permanent staff must be paid in line with employment contracts. As staff numbers alter, the amount you pay will change.

Making predictions

Keeping clear, ongoing records over time will help you to predict your expenditure and income. This is important to help you plan ahead for seasonal variations in trade, when sales may decline or costs rise. It can also help you forecast profit or loss projections – how much money your business may make or lose in the future – which is valuable for long-term planning. Accurate forecasts are essential if you are seeking external finance or presenting to potential investors.

Exactly how you keep records will depend on you and your business. However, there are many online tools available for little or no cost. The key thing is to choose a system that works, and to stick with it. You need to maintain thorough records, especially if you take cash or electronic payments.

Keep receipts for all business costs and expenses. It is harder to look for missing items at the end of the tax year than it is to file them on a regular basis.

82%
of businesses fail because of inconsistent or insufficient cash flow

www.smallbizgenius.net, 2020

VARIABLE COSTS

This cost fluctuates in line with business activities, although you can predict it. Examples include:

Material costs relate to how much of a product you make or sell, for example, the ingredients used in a food-related business.

Hourly wages for temporary staff may be at a set rate, but the number of hours will not. These will change according to your needs.

Utilities (gas, water, electricity) are partly fixed costs, as you have to use them. They are also variable, as cost varies according to how much you consume.

Commission to referral sites and third-party selling platforms can be a significant cost to online traders. Some may even see it as a fixed cost.

✔ NEED TO KNOW

› **Business costs** are those directly incurred in the running of a company, such as stationery, materials, and equipment.

› **Prospective costs** are those that may occur in the future. These cannot be accounted for until they arise, but they can be predicted.

› **Questionable costs** are those that can be fixed or variable. This includes utilities, as the business must have them, although the cost of using them varies.

› **Depreciation** is the gradual decrease in the value of an asset owned by the business. It is a fixed cost, as it counts as a loss on a profit and loss statement.

Managing budgets and cash flow

Your start-up may have healthy sales, but without a regular inflow of cash you will not have enough money to pay your bills. It is therefore vital to keep a keen eye on cash, and to budget wisely to ensure that you do not run out of funds.

Managing budgets

Cash is the lifeblood of your business. From the outset, make sure that you have a reliable system for tracking the money coming in and going out (see pp.88–89 and pp.158–59). These figures give you the basis for estimating how much cash you will need at any one time to meet your expenses. Regularly comparing the actual money flowing in and out to the figures you estimated in your business plan budget will highlight any discrepancies. You can then adjust your budget and, if necessary, your spending. Keeping your fixed costs (such as rent) as low as possible at the start enables you to allocate most of your money and any profits to steady cash flow, and grow your business.

Although some start-ups have access to cash reserves that enable them to run with a planned loss, most cannot. It is wise to keep a solid cash reserve aside to cover a potential unplanned loss that might otherwise be unsustainable. Running out of funds is one of the main reasons why new businesses fail.

How to improve cash flow

However good you are at generating new sales, maintaining cash flow should be your priority, since it enables you to pay your rent and wage bill at the end of each month. Ensuring that money flows into your business promptly and only goes out as necessary will determine the survival of your start-up. There are several ways of doing this, including invoicing immediately and chasing late payments. At times, it may help to sell goods at a discount, to run special offers, or to find ways to spread your business or supply costs. An accurate monthly cash flow statement, reporting the actual inflow and outflow of money, enables you to monitor the situation and decide which steps to take.

KEEP CASH FLOWING IN

Depending on the nature of your business, one or more of these steps may help maintain your cash flow.

❭ **Invoice immediately**, as soon as work is complete, to avoid unnecessary payment delays, or ask customers to pay a deposit or the full price up front.

❭ **Chase late payments**, setting up a process to ensure that no payments are missed. Consider offering future discounts for early payments.

❭ **Generate cash** by selling items of otherwise slow-selling stock at a large discount.

❭ **Increase sales** by lowering prices or running special offers to encourage purchasers.

RUNNING ON A LOSS

All start-ups need a healthy cash flow. However, some companies, such as Amazon and Tesla, turned traditional financial advice upside down by failing to make a profit in their early years. Many technology companies now build loss-making into their plans. From an early stage, they are helped by large investors who seek long-term rewards. By contrast, most new businesses hoping to raise capital have to get a bank loan or find investors who may demand a significant share of their assets.

✓ NEED TO KNOW

❯ **Burn rate** measures how fast a new business uses its capital before making a profit.
❯ **Financial deficit** is a loss. It occurs when costs exceed the money coming into a business.
❯ **Financial surplus** is the same as profit, which occurs when income exceeds business expenses.
❯ **Liquidity** is the ability to turn earnings into cash.
❯ **Net worth** can be calculated by deducting the total liabilities of a business from its total assets.

$38k
the average amount owed to small businesses in Australia

www.kochiesbusinessbuilders.com.au, 2020

YOUR BUSINESS

To fuel and grow your business, you need to have a continuous, positive cash flow. This is generated by sales and is supported by careful accounting and financial management. Also make sure that you have contingency funds in place for emergencies.

Contingency

Keeping some funds in an emergency savings account ensures that your business will survive a crisis.

MANAGE CASH FLOWING OUT

Spreading your business's costs (both fixed and variable) can help smooth your cash flow.

❯ **Use a company credit card** to defer business costs and possibly earn rewards on what you spend.
❯ **Pay suppliers on their terms**, such as within 30 days, to keep cash in your account for longer.
❯ **Review regular costs**, exploring other suppliers to find better terms, and seek one-off discounted offers.
❯ **Limit the stock you hold** by using accurate sales forecasts, and use suppliers who deliver quickly.

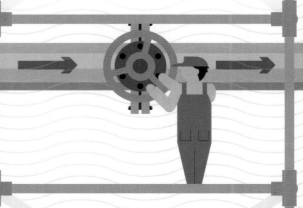

Establishing a culture

Bringing a positive attitude and approach to your business right from the start will help to motivate you and your staff. A shared culture will shape the personality of your business and how it operates.

Deciding your values

The term "business culture" describes the approach and style of your business – it is how you and your staff operate on a daily basis. Cultures develop and evolve over time, although you can establish a set of values that reflect what you want the business to achieve from the beginning. You cannot dictate a culture – it is the people working for the business who bring it to life. However, you may want to initiate a process that involves your staff and others connected to the business, including advisors or investors, to agree on a set of core values that are right for you.

Choose simple, meaningful values (see pp.24–25), such as honesty and accountability,

Creating the culture

Start to shape a successful culture by leading all staff and others involved in the business in a simple shared process to define meaningful values.

Get people talking

Find out what matters to individuals. Look at how other businesses have expressed their values and consider what works well and what does not.

Capture ideas and discuss

No idea is a bad one. Write down all the ideas about positive values. Explore the values and how they might relate to your business.

Organize and rationalize ideas

Group values together. Rank them according to how much difference they could make to the business. Combine similar values until you have around 10 in all.

rather than a list of buzz words that are hard to interpret or uphold. Once you have chosen your values, you must incorporate them into your business practices and processes. For example, if innovation is one of your values, allow people to take risks and make mistakes without being penalized.

You should also communicate your values to your customers, clients, and suppliers, so they understand your business better, which will help to foster more positive relationships.

LIVING YOUR VALUES

In order to instil your culture into the whole of your business, take a holistic approach.

❯ **Begin by incorporating** the values into all sections of the business.

❯ **Communicate the values** to all those you work with.

❯ **Actively demonstrate** what you mean by the values in your dealings with staff, customers, clients, and suppliers.

❯ **Adopt values** based on what is achievable now, not in the future.

❯ **Create a memorable** mnemonic (a memory-assisting word), such as ICE – Innovate, Create, Excite.

❯ **Avoid meaningless clichés**, such as "There is no 'I' in team".

❯ **Use active language**, such as "Do the right thing" (Alphabet, Google's parent company).

❯ **Use your values** to help guide recruitment and decision-making.

Ensure everyone understands

Discuss what each of your chosen values means in practice. How will they benefit customers or clients? How will they help the business succeed? How realistic are they to achieve?

Pick the winning ideas

Place the values in level of importance. Choose the top seven values that reflect the personality and aims of the business. Discuss how to put these values into action.

Incorporate the values

Integrate the values into every aspect of your business, changing practices where necessary. You could add them to your marketing materials, if appropriate.

Managing the business

Running your own business is rewarding, but as it grows, it can be hard for one person to deal with every aspect. You may need to bring in people to manage different areas of the operation.

Identifying skills

At the beginning, you are likely to take on most roles in your business to keep costs down. Even after you take on your first employee, you will probably still oversee all areas of management, such as production and finance. However, as your business expands, you will reach a point where holding all the management responsibility means that you are restricting opportunities to develop and grow.

To avoid this situation, plan ahead and identify where your skills are of best value to the business and also note where they are less effective. This exercise allows you to start to consider recruiting new managers (see pp.126–127), or developing your existing staff in order to share management responsibility. For example, if you excel at sales but find IT a challenge, recruiting an IT manager will allow you to concentrate on what you do best.

Sharing responsibilities

Your start-up probably cannot afford to employ a whole team of managers, but you maybe able to recruit one or two to oversee linked tasks, such as customer service and sales, or operations and production. As your business grows, so can your management team, allowing each member to specialize in a given area of responsibility.

Production/operations

Plans, coordinates, and controls the systems used to produce goods or services.

Human resources

Plans staffing; recruits and trains employees; develops the culture and values of the company.

MANAGEMENT STRUCTURES

When recruiting managers into your business, it is important to create a formal management structure, with clear lines of authority and responsibility. In doing so, the manager has a clear understanding of their role and place in the business. It also allows any staff they manage to understand the chain of command. In large, established businesses, the management structure typically includes multiple levels. However, in small ones, it is likely to have just two or three levels, with you at the top.

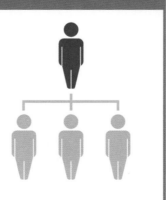

Dividing functions

While you may manage everything at first, developing an effective management team is always something you should plan for, in order for the business to succeed. Divide your business into functional areas, with a manager overseeing each area, or spanning related areas, and with you in overall control.

Sales/marketing

Promotes and sells existing products and services, and plans new ones.

Finance

Takes responsibility for money in and out of the business, produces financial reports; develops financial plans.

Customer services

Plans, provides, and promotes excellent customer service; sets service standards.

MAKING IT WORK

Over time, management structures can be changed to suit the needs of the business. A function-based structure (see left) is widely used, but there are others to consider:

❯ **Team structure** suits businesses that need rapid responses to problems, although it can be hard to maintain overall control.

❯ **Network structure** is "flat" (non-hierarchical), decentralized, and flexible. Its agility suits creative and technology companies; its low overheads are appealing to start-ups.

Information technology

Plans, implements, and maintains technology infrastructure; develops data management and communication strategies.

"Never doubt that a small group of committed people can change the world."

Margaret Mead, US cultural anthropologist

Managing a team

As your new business grows, your focus may change from working directly on tasks yourself, to team management. Setting clear, SMART goals and establishing shared core values will help your team to thrive.

Investing in your team

Employing staff can be a major expense for your new business, so it is vital that you make the most of your team. Employees are likely to be more motivated if they are well managed, have clear goals, and are rewarded for successes. Even a small business needs a sense of shared values and culture. When you and your colleagues establish a positive work culture and shared core values (see pp.162–163), it can make your business a satisfying place to work. Set a good example by arriving early and being positive and polite, even under pressure. Consistency is a quality that employees value.

People work best when they know what is going on, so set clear objectives for your team, and ensure information is shared freely around the business.

SMART management

The SMART approach enables you to set and achieve clear objectives for your team. Each objective is measured against five criteria, it must be: Specific, Measurable, Achievable, Realistic, and Time-based. This ensures that you and your colleagues approach tasks in a consistent way.

S – Specific
Set precise goals using specific figures or quantities. Make sure to establish an exact target – an increase of 50 per cent in productivity, for example – so your team knows precisely what they need to achieve.

M – Measurable
Ensure that you can quantify your objective. Establish a measurement system to record progress made towards your goal. This enables you to assess the success of the task once it is completed.

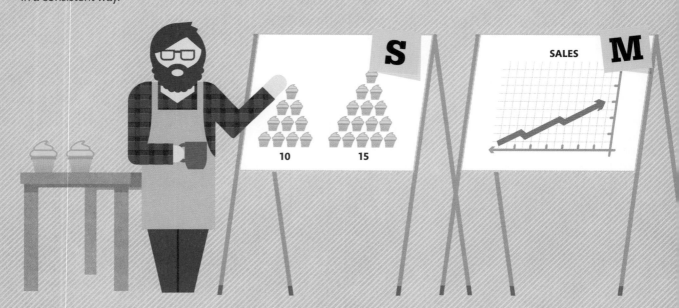

Make sure to share problems and possible solutions, and ensure that mistakes are treated as learning opportunities. Holding regular staff meetings and posting business updates on noticeboards are good ways to encourage open, honest communication.

> "Train people **well enough so they can leave,** treat them **well enough so they don't want to.**"

Sir Richard Branson, British business magnate

ENCOURAGING FLEXIBILITY

While the business is evolving, it is important to keep staff costs to a minimum. You need your team to be flexible, as well as productive. You may need your team to perform tasks outside their normal roles or work unsociable hours. Employees are often willing to adapt to new demands if they feel they are being treated fairly. Remember to:

> **Talk to staff** before changing their roles or hours.
> **Show flexibility** in return, such as accommodating employees' need to start early and finish early.
> **Listen to employees** who may know more detail about the tasks involved than you.

A – Achievable
Set goals that you can achieve. Assess whether you have enough staff and if they have sufficient capacity to meet your goal. If your current systems cannot accommodate this, you may need to hire additional staff.

R – Realistic
Determine realistic goals. Consider whether your objective is possible in practical terms. For example, do you have adequate equipment? If not, you will have to source more equipment before you assign the task.

T – Time-based
Establish a timeframe. In order to achieve your goal, your team may need training or you could need more storage space or better equipment. Take these factors into account and set realistic deadlines.

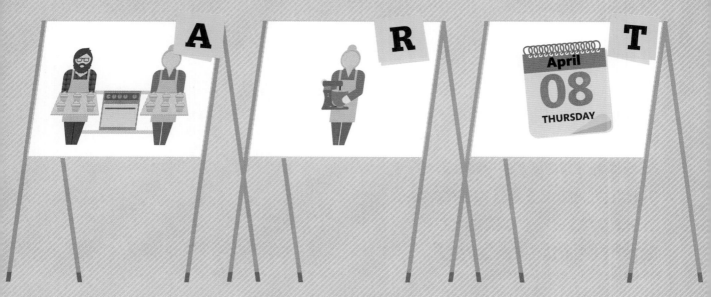

Retaining talent

You have to invest time and money to hold onto the best employees. Build good relationships with your staff and help them develop their skills, so that you do not lose them to competitors. Aim to create a workplace in which everyone can thrive.

Valuing your employees

New recruits bring fresh ideas and skills to a business, but over time good employees also develop a deeper knowledge of how things work. They get to know customers and suppliers. They understand the systems used by the business. They build relationships with other team members. Losing them can upset customers and colleagues. Even worse, if your competitors recruit them, it can give those businesses an advantage.

Get to know and value your employees as individuals. Understand what motivates them and how they like to work. This will help you pick up on any issues that are bothering them well before they consider moving on.

Persuading staff to stay

Hearing that a key employee wants to leave is never good news and it can even feel like a betrayal. The first step is to have an open and honest conversation to find

How to retain talent

There are three main strategies for retaining your best people. The first is to create an environment in which employees enjoy working and can thrive. They need to feel fulfilled and valued, and have enough autonomy to use their skills and experience. This is particularly important for small businesses where it is not always possible to pay high salaries. The second is to provide staff members with opportunities to develop through training, mentoring, and new challenges. The third is to understand what value each person is adding to the business and reward them fairly. Try to avoid only finding out what someone's contribution was after they have left.

1 A good place to work

❭ Treat your employees with respect and fairness
❭ Keep your employees informed
❭ Allow your employees to express their views
❭ Offer flexible working arrangements
❭ Give staff the resources they need to work well

"**Employees are a company's greatest asset – they're your competitive advantage. You want to attract and retain the best.**"

Anne M. Mulcahy, CEO of Xerox Corporation

out what led them to hand in their notice. Perhaps they feel undervalued because they are not getting the recognition or reward they deserve, or they are seeking promotion and new challenges. Ask if there is anything you can do to keep them. You may be able to make a counter-offer and persuade them to stay. However, think about the effect your offer may have on other people in the business. You will also need to recognize their contributions.

If your employee is determined to leave, accept their decision with good grace. Ensure there is enough time for a handover to a new person. If this is not possible, ask them to type up the important aspects of their job, including key contacts and advice for the newcomer.

CASE STUDY

Multi-Ply Components

Multi-Ply manufactures carbon fibre components for X-ray equipment around the world. To retain their best employees, they are flexible and come up with creative solutions to retain the people they want. When a valued employee was offered a higher paid job with a major employer locally, they discussed why he wanted to accept the offer. Although Multi-Ply could not match the higher pay, they could offer him a better work–life balance and a better job title.

2 Ways to develop

> Involve your employees in new projects
> Appoint internal mentors for more junior staff
> Encourage your employees to access training
> Make sure you undertake training yourself

3 Appropriate rewards

> Thank employees personally for good performance
> Allow time off at the end of a stressful project
> Celebrate successes with the whole team
> Pay a fair salary
> Offer a profit share

Running a sales team

Generating sales and dealing with customers are vital to most businesses, and require expertise. If you do not have the skills to do this yourself, recruiting and motivating dedicated sales staff is the best route to success.

Finding the right salespeople

Whether you plan to hire a dedicated sales executive or team, or to adopt selling responsibilities yourself, it is important to pinpoint the skills or qualities needed to best sell your product or service. For example, a salesperson adept at building trust and long-term relationships will help a business reliant on a small number of repeat customers. While someone persuasive who can identify large numbers of potential customers will suit sales of one-off products or occasional services. If competition is fierce, an experienced salesperson

Steering the team

Sales staff should be encouraged and motivated to work to the best of their abilities – and pull together as a team. Set high, but achievable, sales goals that provide staff with the incentive to push themselves, but in the knowledge that they have your full support. Be transparent about how the business is performing and all areas of its operation. Promote two-way feedback so that staff are clear on sales progress and you know their concerns, and you benefit from their new ideas. Invest in sales training, so staff develop new skills and feel valued.

Set expectations

> **Ensure** staff know what is expected in terms of sales targets and level of customer service.

> **Define** a clear team structure and ways of working together.

can provide compelling advice that steers a customer towards making a purchase. Make sure to incorporate the desired qualities into your job description (see pp.124–125) when recruiting for a sales role.

Representing the business

Salespeople may be the only contact customers have with your business. They represent the face of the organization, so you need sales staff you can trust to handle customers well, who believe in your business vision, and operate in a way that reflects its values. It takes time and hard work to build a positive brand reputation and customer loyalty, all of which can be lost easily through bad sales experiences.

! BE AWARE

❯ **When setting goals** for sales staff, do not lose sight of other business objectives, such as customer satisfaction and profit margins.

❯ **Ensure targets** are set against goals that will stretch staff. Easy targets can breed complacency.

❯ **Encourage drive** and determination in staff but watch out for rivalries that can unbalance a team. Use different approaches towards different personalities.

❯ **Leave selling** to sales staff. You should not be in competition with them but rather be their guide.

> "I have **never worked a day in my life** without selling. **If I believe in something, I sell it, and I sell it hard.**"
>
> Estée Lauder, US businesswoman, 1985

Empower staff

❯ **Allow** staff the freedom and authority to interact directly with customers.

❯ **Trust** them to manage customers and to learn from mistakes.

Push the positives

❯ **Create** a culture of achievement by sharing long-term strategies and good-news stories.

❯ **Reward** the team for their successes.

Establishing a healthy workplace

If you employ people, you will need to consider their wellbeing in the workplace. By supporting your employees' physical and emotional health, you can help them to reach their full potential.

Encouraging wellbeing

Wellbeing is a combination of feeling both physically and emotionally well. People with a sense of wellbeing tend to be more energized, motivated, and positive, as well as more resilient under pressure.

Employees with these qualities are likely to have a significant, beneficial impact on your business. Looking after your employees will enable them to perform at their highest level, and you can develop a reputation as a business that cares for its staff, so that prospective employees will be keen to join. Poor wellbeing, with staff who are unable to work effectively or who are absent altogether, has the opposite effect, and can prove costly. According to a 2019 paper from the World Health Organization (WHO), depression and anxiety in companies of all sizes costs the global economy $1 trillion per year in lost productivity.

Looking after employees' wellbeing

Studies into wellbeing at work show that employees need a sense of purpose. They want to feel they are contributing to the success of the business, that their efforts are valued, and that they have some control over what they are doing – guidelines and instructions are useful, but it is more important for staff to feel that they have the autonomy to decide exactly how to do their work.

Employees must also be able to cope with the demands of the job. Providing appropriate training will help, but watch for signs of anxiety, and make sure that people know that it is all right to say if they have a problem.

Fairness

People who feel they are being treated fairly at work are more likely to be well motivated and positive. When you make a decision that affects someone, be transparent and open, and make sure they understand why you made your decision. Ensure pay and conditions are fair for all employees.

Appreciation

Thank people for their efforts; even when something has not gone completely to plan, it will still help to raise morale. Appreciation can be a financial reward or bonus, but simply expressing your thanks in public for a job well done is effective, too. Most importantly, your thanks must be genuine.

Creating the right conditions

Strive to create a working environment in which your employees feel contented and fulfilled. You will need to make the workplace physically safe (see pp.98–99), and provide sufficient lighting and heating for the cooler months.

Develop a culture in which employees flourish, and look forward to coming to work (see pp.162–163). This does not mean there should be no rules or discipline; people understand these must exist, as long as they can see the purpose of them. Aim to create an environment where each person feels genuinely satisfied with their work, and the way in which they are managed.

LEGAL RESPONSIBILITIES

Although the specific details may differ around the world, employers in most countries have legal responsibilities for the health and wellbeing of their employees (see pp.212–215). These typically include:

> **Undertaking an assessment** of any potential risks to people working in the company.

> **Preparing a health and safety** policy stating what will be done to make the workplace safe.

> **Having a suitably equipped** first-aid kit and ensuring everyone knows where it is.

> **Assessing employees' risk** of workplace stress and taking action to prevent them becoming overly anxious.

Expectations

Most people find it stressful if things are unclear, or if they are unsure of what is expected of them. Set out clear aims and carefully selected goals to motivate people, and give them a sense of how they are contributing to the success of the business. Set up regular briefings to keep them informed of their progress.

Listen

Get to know your employees individually. Talk to them, and listen to what they say. In this way, you not only show that you value their unique contributions to your business, you will also be able to sense more quickly when something is wrong. Ensure that no one is afraid to talk to you.

IDENTIFYING STRESS AT WORK

Stress leading to anxiety is a major problem in the workplace, so be alert for these signs. Be prepared to talk to individuals if you think they may have a problem.

> **Increased absences** People have time off work for various reasons, but taking more time off than normal or arriving late may be a sign of anxiety.

> **Withdrawing** Those who are anxious may isolate themselves, avoid engaging with others, and prefer to be quiet and alone.

> **Becoming over-emotional** If an individual is moody, argumentative, or reacting in a way that is out of character, it is worth investigating.

> **Working long hours** A heavy workload might pressurize people to work longer hours than usual, or fail to take adequate breaks during the day.

Managing and resolving conflict

Conflict can happen in any business and at any level. While debate can lead to a positive outcome, constant arguing will undermine your business unless you learn how to manage and resolve it.

Understanding conflict

Most disputes that occur within your team will be short lived and minor, and it is impossible to prevent them all. Instead, aim to limit the damaging aspects of any friction between colleagues. Make sure to resolve any conflicts that occur between yourself and team members, tailoring your approach to the situation. Take advantage of new ideas or outcomes that result.

Resolving conflict between people can be time consuming. Learn when to intervene, and when to simply observe and monitor. Only take action when you have to, and encourage individuals to take responsibility for finding a solution. When serious conflicts arise, speak to those involved but look beyond what people tell you (see box, right) for the real reasons behind the issue. It is important to be calm, rational, and unbiased. Do not be drawn into the argument, but try to put people at ease. Listen carefully to what they are saying and look for evidence to back it up.

Preventing conflict

The best way to prevent unhealthy conflict is to create a working environment in which everyone feels able to say what they think and express their feelings. This will help stop problems from escalating. If, for example, someone is feeling under pressure to meet a deadline but they do not feel able to ask for support, they may become stressed. This can then result in a loss of confidence, leading perhaps to a period of absence from work, and feelings of tension

Handling conflict

In 1974, American professors of management Ken Thomas and Ralph Kilmann published a model for resolving conflict. Widely used today, it sets out five possible approaches. Most people have a natural preference for one of the approaches, but understanding and being able to utilize all five modes will help you to handle conflicts with or among your colleagues more effectively. With trivial issues, for example, avoiding can be the best approach. However, for issues that must be resolved decisively, competing may be the better option.

Avoiding
This approach involves withdrawing from a situation or postponing dealing with the conflict until a better time. It works for minor issues, such as trivial disagreements when you cannot invest time or effort.

Accommodating
This means accepting another person's position at the expense of your own. The opposite of competing, this approach is helpful when you know that your colleague is right or you want to protect a working relationship.

or conflict. It is also essential that your colleagues understand their goals and know how to achieve them, because a lack of clarity may lead to misunderstandings and disagreements in your workplace.

Create space for both formal and informal communication. Get to know and understand your team members. This makes it easier to pick up on any causes of tension.

CAUSES OF CONFLICT

To resolve conflict, you need to understand its root causes. Do not simply take things at face value — look for the underlying reasons. These causes commonly fall into the following groups:

> **Different personalities and working styles** can clash, when people prefer to behave and work in different ways.

> **Stress caused by pressure**, such as demanding deadlines or a lack of training, can cause tempers to fray.

> **Lack of clarity** can lead to misunderstandings between people with opposing views and opinions.

> **Sense of being undervalued** or "not heard" at work can make people become dissatisfied and argumentative.

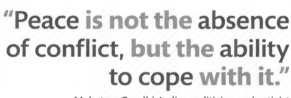

"**Peace is not the absence** of conflict, **but the ability** to cope **with it.**"

Mahatma Gandhi, Indian politician and activist

Compromising

This entails finding a mutually acceptable solution, giving both sides something, but not all of what they want. It suits many situations, whether you are handling conflict between yourself and a team member, or mediating a dispute among colleagues.

Collaborating

This approach means searching for a position that fully satisfies both sides. It involves digging deeper into the sources of conflict. Use it when an issue is important and merits the time and effort invested.

Competing

This involves pursuing your concerns at the other person's expense. Competing relies on using power and your ability to argue. It is useful when there is a time pressure and reaching a solution is vital.

Managing staff performance

Whether you have one part-time worker or a hundred full-timers, your staff will have a huge impact on your business. When employees perform well and realize their potential, it makes a big difference to the success of your business.

Setting expectations

As a business leader, one of your most essential tasks is to assemble and maintain a high-performing staff. The keys to this are three-fold: recruiting the right people, making sure that everyone knows what you expect of them, and regularly monitoring performance. If an employee is under-performing, you will need to act before the issue becomes more serious.

It is good practice to set out your expectations of performance levels on the first day that someone starts work. Take time to talk to the new recruit, get to know them, and let them know they can speak to you if they do not understand something or if they encounter a problem. It is better to know if something is awry early on than to discover it much later simply because someone has been too hesitant to approach you. Mistakes happen. It is important to learn from them and make sure they do not happen again.

CONDUCTING PERFORMANCE APPRAISALS

Hold a formal, structured discussion about personal performance with each member of staff at least once a year. Meet with them in private to talk about how their work is going. Use the meeting to agree goals, monitor progress, and discuss concerns.

> **Give the employee** plenty of advance warning of the meeting's time, location, and duration.
> **Make it a conversation** rather than an interrogation.
> **Use the time** to discuss the employee's ambitions and training needs, as well as their immediate work.
> **Allow time** for them to feed back to you about what is working for them and what is not.
> **Do not shy away** from discussing any performance problems you have picked up.
> **Make notes** to summarize the meeting – including any actions that have been agreed – and send them to the employee.

"Empowering employees is the key to keeping them."

Anita Roddick, founder of The Body Shop

Motivating staff

Defining achievable goals for each employee is the best way of getting across your expectations and motivating your staff. But take care to ensure that targets for individual staff members do not undermine collective working. Setting the wrong targets can result in employees competing with each other rather than cooperating and sharing information.

If you get to know your staff as individuals it will make it easier for you to spot if something is wrong. Adopt a "walk-and-talk" strategy, regularly mixing with employees to find out how they are and whether they are coping. Let them know what is happening in the business, and remind them of their value in the workplace. Remember that if staff feel appreciated, they are more likely to perform well.

! BE AWARE

There is considerable legislation around discipline and dismissal. Ensure that your business has a policy that reflects this, and that all staff are aware of it. If in doubt, engage the services of a legal professional. Be sure to:
> **Gather** relevant evidence.
> **Give** the employee an opportunity to improve.
> **Be fair** and impartial.

Failing to follow the law is likely to result in a claim for unfair dismissal (see pp.212–215).

DISCUSSING PERFORMANCE PROBLEMS

If a member of staff is not performing as well as they should, act quickly to prevent the problem escalating and affecting your business. Speak to the person informally to establish what can be done. If this does not work, then you will need a more formal meeting.

> **Gather evidence** of any poor performance in advance. Let the person know why you are meeting.
> **Be firm but fair**, making sure you focus on the problem and not on the personality of the individual.
> **Be calm** and supportive: it is likely to be a difficult and possibly stressful experience for the employee.
> **Explain the situation** as you see it, then invite the employee to respond.
> **Work together** to agree on a performance improvement plan; this is better than imposing one.
> **Put your agreement in writing** and fix a date for a follow-up meeting.

Streamlining business processes

A process is a series of activities that are linked together to deliver a particular product or service. Mapping your processes will enable you to visualize how efficiently your business is organized, and reveal any areas for improvement.

Creating a visual representation

Mapping out the key processes that your business uses will help ensure that your operations run as efficiently as possible – reducing costs and waste. It will also highlight which activities within your key processes that are worth investing in, or even eliminating.

The concept of process mapping originated in manufacturing, where raw materials are transformed from their natural state through a series of steps into the finished product. However, you can use process maps for any type of operation – from a restaurant business receiving a booking, greeting the diner, taking their order, and serving the food, to a gardening business, which involves buying in

seeds, growing plants, and then selling them to customers. In each case, the aim is to identify each step and its relationship with others. Creating a map is not complicated, and simply involves recognizing each step of the processes within your business, and sketching them out in sequence to create a visual representation of all the activities involved.

Understanding value

Once you have created a map, you can examine each step of your process, and find ways to streamline it. This will help to eliminate wasted time and effort, and reduce costs. However, you can also use the map to assess the value of each step.

Using a process map

A business-process map can provide revealing and valuable information. Consider each step or activity your business uses to complete each key process. For example, if your business delivers a service, map out every activity you undertake from start to finish. You can now assess each activity to decide whether it is essential or not. Similarly, you can also identify whether it adds value to your business or not. While essential tasks must be retained, nonessential ones that add value are also worth keeping. Review your processes regularly, as new technology may enable you to simplify them.

Nonessential/ value-adding

Activities like these benefit your business but could be eliminated if they cease to add significant value.

Activity 2

Starting point

Activity 1

Essential/value-adding

Activities like these are valuable to your business and customers. Consider investing in them.

Business processes are often described as "value-adding" or "non-value-adding". The former are part of the operation that adds value directly to customers or clients, such as physically making a product, or performing a service, such as delivering food to a customer. Non-value-adding processes are support services, such as IT or accounting, which are essential for the running of a company, but are invisible to customers, and do not add direct value to them.

As your business grows, try to ensure that your value-adding and non-value-adding processes are in balance. Since all processes incur some cost, such as material or staff costs, spending more on value-adding processes should result in a better return on investment. Beware of neglecting your non-value-adding processes, however, as failing to produce your accounts or monitor cash flow, for example, could cause a serious problem for your business. Both types of process can easily be mapped by thinking through each step that must be taken (or, if your business is already running, by observing), and putting it into your business-process map.

BENEFITS OF A BUSINESS MAP

A process map of your whole business will give you a full overview of the operation, and can also be used to inform others – both within, and outside, the business. By mapping out each step clearly, and how it relates to the others in the sequence, you can use it to ensure that everyone involved with the business knows exactly how it functions. This can be useful when talking to potential investors or when inducting new recruits, allowing them to see and understand how the business works.

"There is nothing so useless as doing efficiently that which should not be done at all."

Peter Drucker, US management consultant

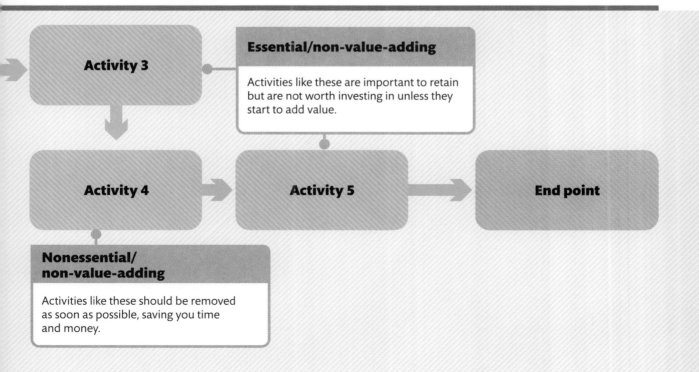

Activity 3

Essential/non-value-adding

Activities like these are important to retain but are not worth investing in unless they start to add value.

Activity 4

Activity 5

End point

Nonessential/ non-value-adding

Activities like these should be removed as soon as possible, saving you time and money.

Managing your supply chain

A supply chain is the network of people, processes, and activities required to deliver the products or services you sell. Creating an ethical and efficient supply chain will save you time and money, and increase profitability.

Understanding supply chains

A supply chain is like a series of steps that you have to take in order to deliver a product or service to your customer or client. Every business has a supply chain, although some are longer and more complex than others. For example, an ice-cream shop may only require ice-cream, spoons, and cartons to do business. In contrast, a baker will need to source ingredients and packaging from various suppliers, make the products, package them, then either sell them directly or deliver them to the customer. If any link in your supply chain fails, you will lose time, potentially incur extra costs, and disappoint your customer or client. Similarly, if your supply chain is poorly organized or includes unnecessary steps, you will waste time and money (see pp.178–179).

Managing a supply chain

The strength and efficiency of your supply chain plays a key role in how reliably your business can deliver its products and services. To save time and money, aim to create a chain that is robust and efficient.

It should also be flexible enough so that if a single link breaks it can be quickly repaired, and not disrupt the other links in the chain. Start by reviewing your chain and look for ways to strengthen each link.

Understand your supply chain
Know what each link in the chain is and how it connects to the next. Research all of your suppliers and ensure they meet your ethical standards, and can abide by your code of conduct (see pp.102–103).

Identify potential weaknesses
Examine each link and look for possible weaknesses. Consider what the impact of those weaknesses would be for your business.

Create contingency plans
Plan ways of avoiding problems should they occur. Create contingency plans and ensure you can put them in place quickly if the need arises.

Managing your supply chain

To ensure your supply chain is strong and effective, you need to understand how it works, and where potential weaknesses are before you can find ways to improve it. For example, if your business makes and sells necklaces, you may have a bead supplier in China, and a designer and jeweller in France who make the necklaces before sending them to you to sell in your shop. What would happen if your bead supplier failed to send the beads in time and your jeweller could not meet your agreed delivery date? Once you understand what could go wrong, you can put plans in place to mitigate any risks. You can also look for new ways of doing things; perhaps you could buy in ready-made necklaces as well as creating them from scratch, so that you would always have stock available.

79%
of companies with high-performing supply chains achieve above-average revenue growth

www2.deloitte.com, 2020

Streamline your supply chain
Look for ways to streamline your supply chain for maximum efficiency. Perhaps you can use technology to cut down on the time it takes to do things.

Seek professional advice and insight
Talk to your suppliers to gain insights into how you could do things better. Ask them about their experiences with other clients.

Review your supply chain regularly
Things change so keep reviewing your supply chain to check it still works in the same way, and that it still runs smoothly.

Improving the business

Even if your business is currently performing well, you can never assume that it will continue to do so. To remain competitive, it is important to regularly improve your processes to ensure you are offering what your customers expect.

Reviewing your business

Many small business owners spend much of their time dealing with unexpected problems, such as customer complaints, quality issues, and late deliveries. As a result, they have less time to spend on planning and growing their businesses. The best way to avoid this is by streamlining your processes (see pp.178–179), and improving performance (see below).

Improving business performance involves looking at your operations and processes, and identifying ways in which they could function better. You can do this slowly and incrementally over a period of time, by analysing each stage and activity in your business to determine how it could be done more effectively and efficiently.

Another way to make improvements is through "step change". This means rethinking your business, and making bold and rapid changes. For example, you may scrap entire products or services from your range, or decide to outsource activities currently performed inhouse. (see pp.50–51). However, the safest way is to improve and change your business slowly and methodically over time.

Improving your business should be continuous, not a one-off exercise. Invite your staff to be part of the process, so that they are prepared for change (see pp.204–205). You should create a culture in which everyone observes what is happening and feels able to make suggestions for how things could work better.

Improving performance

It is essential to review your business processes regularly, to ensure that everything is working well. One way of improving performance is by using the "Sand Cone" model. Although this approach was devised for manufacturing, it can be applied to services, too. The model divides the capabilities of a business into a hierarchy of priorities: quality, speed, flexibility, and cost. For optimal performance, the model suggests that you begin with quality; move on to speed; then improve flexibility; and finally look at cost. If you use this method, remember to be patient – you need to believe that your costs will decrease in time.

1. Quality

Quality comes first. Unless you deliver quality products and services first time, every time, you risk upsetting customers and clients, and wasting money. Getting it right first time means there is no rework and there is consistency in delivery time, so your processes are reliable.

2. Speed

Reliable processes are costly, so you need to look at how to run them faster. Doing things quickly reduces costs, but quality can suffer, so work on delivering quality quickly. Can you speed up delivery, for example, by using new technology?

Entrepreneurs typically spend 68% of their time firefighting and only 32% on long-term planning

The Alternative Board, 2016

Cost

Flexibility

Speed

Quality

OPERATIONS MANUAL

As your workforce grows, you might want to consider creating an operations manual, which is a document that explains exactly how your business functions. Although they vary from business to business, they typically detail the steps used to complete your business processes; staff roles and responsibilities; best practices; and emergency procedures. Having a record of every business function is more than just a tool to train new employees – it serves to record valuable knowledge in the event of staff leaving the business.

An operations manual also makes your business far more attractive to prospective buyers. If you plan to sell or franchise your business, it is evidence that the business can run without you being present.

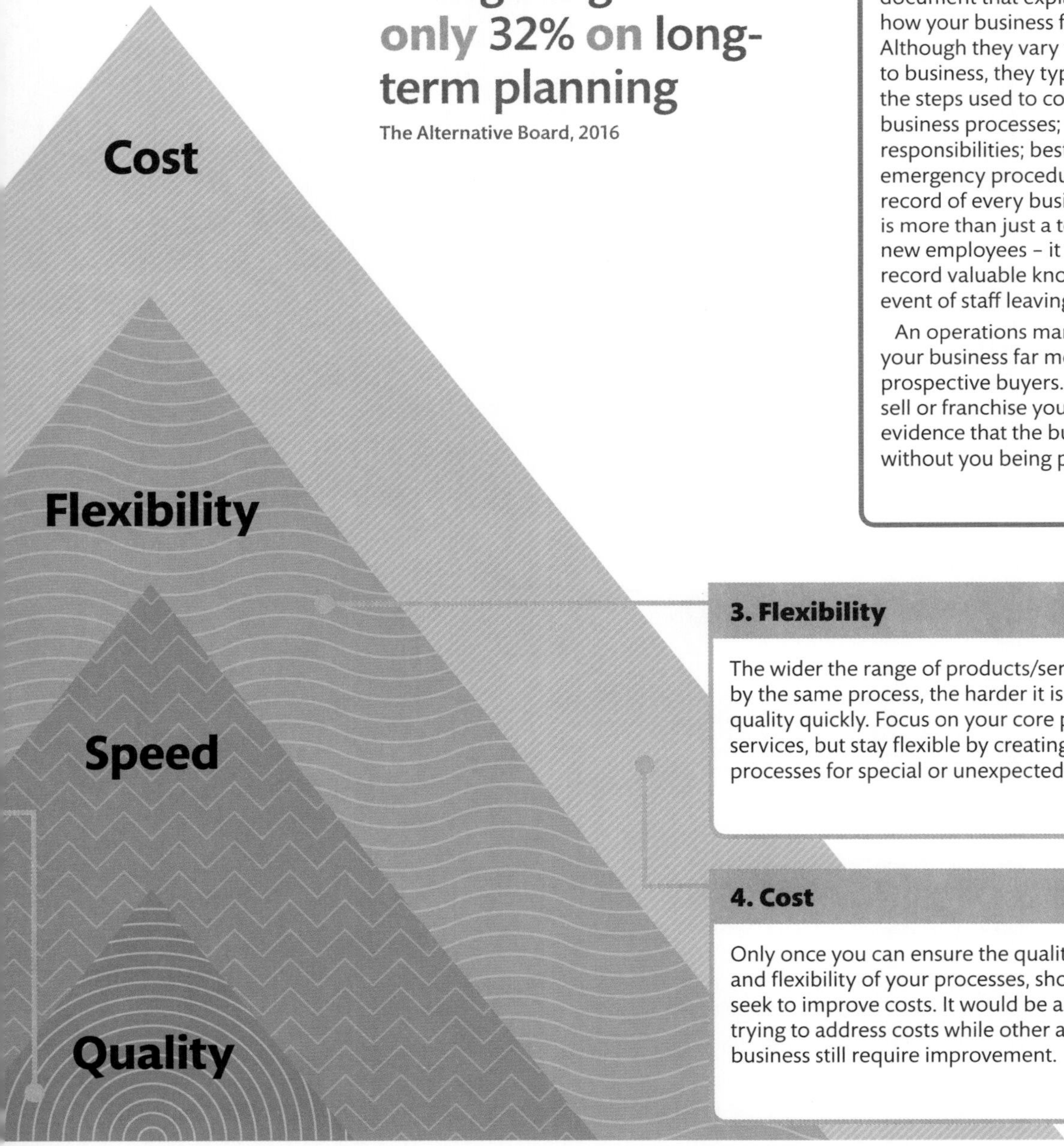

3. Flexibility

The wider the range of products/services delivered by the same process, the harder it is to deliver quality quickly. Focus on your core products/services, but stay flexible by creating alternative processes for special or unexpected orders.

4. Cost

Only once you can ensure the quality, speed, and flexibility of your processes, should you seek to improve costs. It would be a waste of time trying to address costs while other areas of your business still require improvement.

Preparing for a business crisis

You cannot predict exactly which crises will arise in the future. But when you prepare careful plans and processes, your business will be better equipped to handle unexpected events if they occur.

Planning ahead

Major incidents such as fire, flood, and IT failure happen rarely but can have a devastating impact on any small business. Create a plan for how to deal with such crises to save you time, reduce stress, and enable you to cope more easily. You can predict some of the impacts of a crisis, for example, being unable to communicate with your customers, and dealing with a lack of stock or damage to your premises. If you prepare in advance for these scenarios, it will make your business more resilient. You may also find that planning for one eventuality may prove useful in another unexpected crisis. Different kinds of crises can create similar constraints. For example, you might want to create a plan for people to work remotely and deliver customer services online in the event of a major flu epidemic. In the event of a natural disaster such as flooding or an earthquake, which could limit people's ability to travel, your plan for an epidemic could still be put to good use.

Making your plan

Assemble crisis control plans with the input of your colleagues and suppliers. Allocate responsibility for specific actions such as customer contact or dealing with emergency services. Write down the plan and ensure everyone is aware of it and understands their role. If possible, test your plan with a mock crisis, and review it regularly as situations change. Use the processes below to identify what should be in your plan.

Consider possible scenarios

Crises can be external, such as flood and fire, or internal, such as manufacturing a faulty product, or causing food poisoning through insufficient hygiene practices. Consider what would happen if any of these events occurred.

Assess the likelihood

Some businesses will naturally be more prone to specific problems. Food poisoning is more likely in a restaurant, for example, and businesses sited near rivers are more likely to flood. Focus on planning for situations most likely to occur in your business.

DEALING WITH A CRISIS

> ❯ **Keep a cool head** when you need to act quickly, and take a moment to think about what you are doing.

> ❯ **Establish your priorities** to ensure that your actions are likely to have the best impact on the situation.

> ❯ **Communicate clearly** with precise instructions, so that everyone understands exactly what is expected of them.

> ❯ **Manage people under pressure** by listening to their concerns, but remaining calm and reassuring to prevent any panic.

> ❯ **Stay positive** and be alert to the unexpected; sometimes a crisis can open up new opportunities.

£8.8bn
was spent by small businesses in the UK alone in 2018 to deal with crises

Gallagher, insurance brokers, 2019

Identify possible solutions

When working out solutions, think about ways of limiting the damage, and how you could prevent it from happening in the first place. For example, ensuring your data is backed up with adequate security is always a good idea.

Analyse the implications

Consider the consequences of your proposed actions. Additional cost is the most likely implication, but your plans could also affect your staff morale or your business reputation if you do not adequately take into account the needs of clients, colleagues, or suppliers.

Harnessing technology

Making effective use of technology will speed up communication, improve engagement with your customers, and enable you to work more efficiently.

Investing in technology

Even the smallest, one-person business faces a mind-boggling array of software, applications (apps), and other digital tools, all offering constantly changing features and benefits. Most will add purchasing and training costs to your business, so deciding how and when to invest in technology requires careful consideration.

Every business has specific technology needs, increasingly driven by the expectation of clients or customers, such as the ability to book services and pay for goods online. It is easy to overspend on hardware – such as computers or printers – and software that is not strictly necessary or offers only short-term benefits, so it can be worth paying for specialized advice.

A technology expert will consider your business activities and digital options, then make a plan for your immediate requirements, while also allowing for future capacity to be easily integrated. You cannot future-proof technology, but you can build some adaptability into your tech systems by choosing hardware and software that can easily be expanded and updated over time.

DATA SECURITY

As your business grows, it will hold increasing volumes of data, such as customer mobile phone numbers and email addresses, and lists of suppliers or investors. It is essential to keep this data safe to protect your business, and to ensure compliance with relevant local data regulations (see pp.212–215). Businesses are increasingly vulnerable to hackers, malware, and other forms of cyber attack, so it is vital to ensure the security of your systems. Even the smallest business should take at least some simple steps to protect valuable data (see pp.120–121).

Working smarter

As part of an integrated technology plan, the right computer systems, data and management software, and apps can help you and your business to work more efficiently, and improve your products and services.

Whatever tools you decide to use, you should make sure they are compatible with each other, both in terms of technology and in how they work together to develop the business. Here are some examples of how utilizing technology could help your business.

Portable hardware
Portable devices such as laptops and hard drives enable colleagues to work remotely. Ensure colleagues can access files from devices out of the office.

Free software
Commercial software can be costly. Consider starting with free-to-use software and apps, but check that they are compatible and secure.

Cloud services
Online cloud servers are a way of using someone else's computers to store data and run programs. Reduce your costs by moving business functions to the cloud.

Digital communication

Video calling apps and social media can connect people across the world. Collaborate more effectively with suppliers and colleagues.

Online support

Helpdesk applications and feedback apps put customers at the heart of technology solutions. Respond to customer's needs more efficiently using online support.

Digital marketing

Traditional marketing (see pp.64–65) is being overtaken by digital. Build a social media presence and identify online opportunities (see pp.140–141).

Mobile technology

Smartphone apps allow product browsing and instant purchases. Monitor customer habits and identify online buying and selling trends.

Data analytics

Online analytical tools capture and study data on customer behaviour and experiences. Improve your service or product with these essential insights.

✓ NEED TO KNOW

❯ **Algorithms** are sets of mathematical instructions fed into a computer, which can then process data to produce insights into a business and its customers.

❯ **Near-field communication (NFC)** enables two closely placed devices to exchange data, such as a chip and pin payment system.

❯ **Open-source software** is a usually free-to-use technology, although the source code is shared and open to modification.

"Once a new technology rolls over you, if you're not part of the steamroller, you're part of the road."

Stewart Brand, US author, 1987

GROWING YOUR BUSINESS

Growing your business

For your business to grow, you will need to sell more of what you are currently offering. There are many ways of doing this, from finding new customers to coaxing existing customers to spend more.

Developing a growth strategy

To give your business the best chance to grow you need to decide on a strategy for retaining buyers, winning repeat sales, and expanding your customer base. This may include offering enhanced customer care, better delivery options, improving existing products or services, and offering new ones – all of which should fuel growth and keep you ahead of your competitors. While lack of growth or slow growth is clearly undesirable, it is important to manage the growth process. Growing too fast can knock your business plan off course. Think ahead and ensure that you can increase financing, staffing, production capacity, and your supply of materials when needed.

Cultivating success

Increasing sales is challenging, but by applying simple strategies to your business, and developing your employees' capabilities, you can achieve growth.

MANAGING GROWTH
Pay attention to talented personnel who have the potential to grow your business. Maximize cash availability and borrowing power so you can fund growth strategies (see pp.196–197), and invest in systems and tools to help you.

PROMOTING GROWTH
Nurture existing customers and improve service to encourage loyalty. Reach out to new customers through social media and email, local networking, advertising, and marketing (see pp.198–199).

MAXIMIZING GROWTH

To maximize growth potential, keep in touch with – and be ready to exploit – changes in the world at large. Shifts in buying habits and new payment methods, technological developments, and social trends could open up fresh markets for your business, or expand existing ones.

! BE AWARE

It is vital to keep pace with demand, but not to grow your business too quickly. If demand grows too rapidly, you may not be able to fulfil orders or meet promised delivery times, and this can lead to customer and client disappointment. On the other hand, if growth is too rapid, you can run into cash-flow problems if revenues do not come in quickly enough to cover your rising expenses. Likewise, if staffing levels do not increase to match the extra workload, the burden on employees may result in personnel quitting. Such issues may put strain on your leadership and management abilities and divert you from your ideal business plan.

LEADING GROWTH

Since you are in charge, you will have to communicate clearly with your staff, and inspire them with your enthusiasm. If you feel unsure of yourself, consider undertaking training to improve your leadership skills, or working with a coach or mentor.

Expanding your business

As your business grows, you may be tempted to expand, but you need to recognize when the time is right. Consider different ways to expand, and decide which approach makes sense for you.

When should you expand?

Expanding a business is different from growing it. Growth would be selling more of your product, or providing more of your service. Expansion is a step further. It can include product diversification (see pp.194–195), which means adding new products or services alongside your original ones. Expansion could also involve moving into new lines of business and new markets. You may want to expand if your growth has slowed and efforts to increase sales have not worked. This can happen if your product or service becomes outmoded due to old technology or changing tastes, or if its value is under-appreciated in your current marketplace. For example, an ice-cream shop could decide to expand its original range of rich desserts by introducing fresh fruit sorbets to appeal to increasingly health-conscious customers. Or, a graphic design studio might expand into offering full-service website building to attract more clients. Keeping up-to-date with consumer news, and social and technology trends, as well as carefully tracking your earnings over time, will help you work out when the time is right to expand.

Expanding too fast

The main challenge when expanding your business will be managing your time, which will be stretched more thinly over both your original core business and

Ways to expand

There are various ways to expand your enterprise. As a small business owner, you may want to focus on offering a new product or service, while staying within your existing marketplace. Alternatively, you may be expanding beyond your current location, but with the original product or service, or perhaps combining both strategies. In all cases, you need to research your chosen path, cost it, create a schedule, and adjust your current business plan to ensure the expansion progresses smoothly. Here are a few options for expanding your business.

Products or services

Creating a complementary or "add-on" product or service to accompany what you already offer, or heading in a different direction with a brand new product or service are both effective ways to expand.

Acquisitions

Acquiring or investing in a related business may help you create new products or establish a new market more cost-effectively.

the new venture. To avoid losing touch with your customers, be prepared to recruit people to support your customer service. You will also need to manage increasing demands on existing staff. If they feel too much is being asked of them, they may quit, leaving you to hire and train new employees. Plan your rate of expansion carefully to avoid these problems.

> "Scale is important for a start-up. Think big, but take it one day at a time."
>
> Kunal Bahl, co-founder of Snapddeal

WHAT AN EXPANDING BUSINESS NEEDS

To meet the additional administration and service requirements that come with expansion, you need to take steps in advance to prepare and manage the process effectively.

> **Recordkeeping and infrastructure** Update your software and systems so that they can manage more products or markets when the demand for tracking business operations also increases.

> **Capital** Plan ahead to secure the extra financing that expansion often requires for new equipment, staff, or other needs. You can then show investors or lenders a business plan and projections based on current trading.

> **Personnel** Manage your existing staff, promoting where appropriate, and hire new members to fill key roles. Treat your personnel with sensitivity, so that you maintain a positive and engaged workforce.

> **Delegating** Be less hands-on. As your business expands, your role will demand more leadership and the delegation of day-to-day operations to others in your team. Review how your business is managed, (see pp.164–165).

Partnerships

Teaming up with a partner business could enable you to share resources or expertise. The business may be able to provide a specific service that your business needs in order to expand.

Global expansion

Crossing national borders (physically or online) can bring you rewards, but poses logistical challenges. To be successful, you may need to employ a mixture of strategies. Consider partnering with companies in the new region or seeking help from trade organizations.

Regional expansion

Establishing new locations, such as a branch office or store in another part of the country, or supplying your product to outlets in new regions can all help you to expand.

Growth strategies

There are a number of strategies you can use to help your business grow, depending on what you want to achieve. Once you have decided which option supports your objectives, you can start working towards it.

Planning to grow

Before committing to a growth strategy, first ensure there is sufficient demand to support your plans. If you are hoping to target similar customers as you do now, make sure your new plans will continue to meet their needs and expectations (see pp.40–41). Similarly, research the market thoroughly, as you did before starting your business (see pp.42–43), to ensure there is sufficient demand and to identify what competition you will face. Finally, be certain that the financial rewards of your intended strategy exceed the costs of implementing it (see pp.80–81). As part of this, also try to evaluate the disruption your plans may bring to your existing business – and to your personal life.

58%
of small UK businesses lack a plan to grow

smallbusiness.co.uk, 2015

CASE STUDY

Zomato

Founded in 2008 in Delhi, India, as a simple restaurant listing service, Zomato operates in 24 countries and 10,000 cities. Key to its growth is a willingness to diversify: as well as listings and reviews, it now offers delivery, a membership scheme, and the option to both book a table for, and a taxi to, the venue via its app. Zomato has reached out to eateries, too: it helps owners develop their own apps, provides consultancy advice based on data from users, and offers digitized management services. Acquisitions and forging alliances with other companies helped it to enter markets overseas.

Typical growth strategies

The four strategies shown here are based on a model proposed in 1957 by Igor Ansoff, a Russian–American mathematician and business manager. The Ansoff Matrix is still used to explain common growth and expansion tactics.

Market

New

Existing

Starting point
Your market stall sells organic tomatoes that you grow on your small farm. Every week you sell out of tomatoes and have to turn customers away.

Deciding your route

Once you understand your customers, the market, and the costs involved in growing your business, use this information to decide the best of four strategies (see below). Essentially, you can sell more of your offering to your existing market – sell the same offering to a new market – sell a new offering to your existing market – or sell a new offering to a new market.

Each option involves risk, which increases as your plan diverges from your existing business model. However, your research will help you choose the strategy most likely to lead to successful growth.

DECIDING NOT TO GROW

Although growth can potentially bring great rewards, it always entails some risk – many companies fail because they try to grow too soon, too quickly, or by too much. Ask yourself, do you even need to grow the business? For some businesses, staying the same size but improving how they operate can be more rewarding. Much will depend on why you started the business and what you want out of it. If your business is already successful, and allows you to maintain a healthy work–life balance, there may be little to gain by growing it further.

Market development

A few new restaurants open up nearby, prompting you to offer daily deliveries to them. This represents a new market, helping to balance out monthly revenues, since your stall trade slows down in cooler weather.

Diversification

Your local supermarket does not stock organic pasta sauce. You invest in more bottling equipment, buy up tomatoes from other local organic farms, and begin selling your sauce to the supermarket chain, which has 20 stores.

Market penetration

To meet excess customer demand, you will have to build a new greenhouse in order to grow more tomatoes. However, the increased revenue you gain from selling more tomatoes will justify the expense you incur.

Product development

You are selling as many market-quality tomatoes as you can produce, but you have to discard any that are misshapen. You decide to use these to produce organic pasta sauce, which you sell from your existing market stall.

Existing

New

Products

Financing business growth

Once your business has reached the point where it needs more money to grow, you will have to make decisions about how much additional finance you require and how to raise it.

Assessing your needs

If you have decided to take your business forward either by growing it or expanding it, your next step will be to plan a strategy to fund this phase. Start by listing the resources that your business requires in order to grow, and budget for each item. Over-budget slightly to allow for contingencies (unexpected costs that may suddenly arise and potentially derail your project). Having arrived at an overall figure, you should be able to calculate how much funding you need. Be prepared to justify how you will spend it. The next step is to find the right type of financing for your business.

Types of financing

The nature of your business will dictate the types of financing you might seek. For example, if you

Preparing your finances

When you approach potential lenders, investors, or grant-funding bodies, you need to be clear about what you are asking for and why. You must also be prepared to provide evidence of how far your business has come, how strong its finances are, and how promising its future is. To do this, make sure your finances are in order, and you have a well-thought-out plan for spending any money you borrow.

1 Compiling the information

Whatever the type of financing you apply for, you will need to produce the accounts for your trading history and revenue projections.

2 Improving your credit score

To ensure that you have a good credit score, pay business bills promptly, minimize debt levels, register your business with a credit reference agency, and optimize your personal credit score.

4 Planning how to use the money

Prioritize expenditure so that you do not run out of money before the key resources for growing your business have been acquired.

5 Calculate the impact on cash flow

Interest repayments on new loans will require you to have more cash available every month. Time your repayments carefully to ensure that funds are available.

are in manufacturing, you may decide that buying rather than renting premises will enable you to increase production capacity and add value to your business, in which case it may make sense for you to apply for a commercial mortgage. Also, think about whether your needs are short term or long term. If short term, investigate ways to help you manage cash flow during a growth period. If long term, your best options are to get a loan or a grant, or to find an investor.

FUNDING OPTIONS

Once your business has a track record, lenders (see pp.82–85) may be more open to you, and offer better interest rates. Venture capitalists will be most interested in your business during its high-growth phase, whereas grant-givers will be impressed if you are pioneering a new product or service.

〉 **Lenders** If you already have a loan, discuss consolidating this debt by taking out a new, larger loan that may offer more favourable rates of interest.

〉 **Investors** If your business is already showing promise, you will be in a stronger position to attract crowdfunding investors, venture capitalists, or a business angel (who will invest and take a share of the profits but not get involved in managing the business).

〉 **Grants** Funds are available through government (see pp.212–215), civic, university, corporate, and philanthropic bodies, especially for businesses making a positive impact on society.

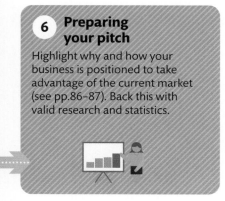

3 **Preparing a business plan**

Write a document that explains your business objectives, measures your progress, and projects how your business will fare in the future.

6 **Preparing your pitch**

Highlight why and how your business is positioned to take advantage of the current market (see pp.86–87). Back this with valid research and statistics.

$3.3bn
was invested in German start-ups alone in 2015

www.tatsachen-ueber-deutschland.de, 2020

Attracting new business

Gaining new customers or clients can help your start-up to grow. Conventional marketing may be costly, but you can achieve good results with smart ideas.

Analysing your customers

It is vital to focus your efforts on the customers who are more likely to give you repeat business and spend more on each purchase (see pp.152–153). Regularly examine your sales data, use free tools such as Google Analytics (see pp.212–215), and gather information on growth in your market to identify any changes in your customer base. Although your business may have appealed to a certain type of customer at first, you need to know whether that has changed, why those changes may have occurred, and which group is most valuable to your business. By always knowing who your potential customers are, and understanding their buying habits, you can target them.

Becoming more visible

Boost your presence in the places where your customers like to shop, whether virtually or face-to-face. Run a paid social media marketing campaign containing compelling or educational content, or an offer – starting small and analysing the response rate – and list your location on all popular and free online business directories and maps.

WORKING WITH INFLUENCERS

An influencer is an individual with a large social media following, sometimes with millions subscribing to their channels. They "influence" followers by posting paid-for content promoting a brand's product or service.

Partnering with influencers can be a valuable tool, enabling you to advertise your business to a particular target audience – the influencer's followers. For example, if you sell fitness equipment, you could sponsor an influencer known to be an exercise fanatic, whose followers would likely be interested in fitness and find your product appealing.

Ways to increase your customer appeal

Many of the methods for bringing new customers to your business will cost very little, other than your time. Brainstorm with staff, friends, and family to generate and improve ideas. Research what other successful businesses have done. Make the most of staff who understand and engage with social media, and sustain a genuine interest in your industry and customer communities.

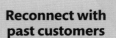

Offer promotions and discounts

For first-time buyers, offer discounts, free express delivery, a gift, or other incentive. Get the word out on paid-for social media, through your website, or with local flyers and marketing.

Reconnect with past customers

Give lapsed buyers an incentive to return by emailing a "we miss you" offer, with a discount or free gift on their next purchase.

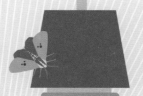

Find a partner

Collaborating with a complementary business enables you and your partner to market to one another's customers, and to benefit from each other's experience and expertise.

Increase referrals

Tap into your existing customer base by rewarding them when they refer their friends and make a purchase. Giving both parties a reward will build goodwill in your customer community.

Build a network

Consider joining trade bodies, chambers of commerce, and networking groups to gain ideas and win new clients. Sponsor activities for your customer or client community to make a direct connection.

Promote your website

Refine your SEO (see pp.118–119) thinking about the words customers might use to find you. Analyse social media content that gets the best response, and create similar material.

Target specific audiences

Reach your specific audience by tailoring targeted advertising campaigns (see pp.138–139). For example, sponsor a social media influencer to promote your brand (see box, left).

Monitor online feedback

Keep an eye on your online ratings and reviews. Deal with any complaints right away, and respond to positive comments. Link good reviews on external sites to your website and social media.

Retaining your customers

Surviving in your first year of business depends not only on building your customer base, but also on prioritizing customers who consistently spend the most, and ensuring they stay with you.

Know your customers

Establishing a loyal customer base can bring rewards to your business. Research by the Harvard Business School suggests that a 5 per cent increase in customer retention can increase profit by as much as 95 per cent. It can also be cheaper to keep existing customers than to acquire new ones, which may require considerable marketing effort and cost.

To retain your most valued customers, you need to engage with them and find out what interests them. Talk to your customers face-to-face, asking for honest feedback, and analyse customer interactions online (see pp.140–141). Armed with good information, you can tailor your product or service to meet specific needs of your customers, so they feel valued and value you in return.

How to keep your customers

There are two key ways of keeping your customers loyal. The first involves improving your relationship with customers by personalizing their experience and helping them to feel connected to your brand or business. The second involves maintaining the quality of your product or service. To do this, keep a keen eye on what goes on behind the scenes in your business. Regularly analyse your supply chain and look for ways of making it run as smoothly as possible (see pp.180–181).

Relating to your customers

❯ **Support a cause** your customers can relate to, such as sustainable sourcing of goods or community projects, and promote it so that customers always feel good about buying your goods or services.

❯ **Personalize communications** with your customers, using their preferred means of contact, such as email or Twitter.

❯ **Inform and entertain** customers with relevant additional content beyond your direct product offering, such as blogs, useful tips, quizzes, and competitions.

❯ **Be transparent** with customers, sharing the efforts that go on behind the scenes, to reinforce the integrity and quality of your product and the team behind it.

❯ **Reward customers** through loyalty bonuses and offers, refer-a-friend schemes, and personalized discounts.

Benefiting from loyalty

Loyal customers are more likely to buy higher-priced or additional products or services from you. For example, you could propose a more expensive product to them – known as "upselling" – such as a higher specification mobile phone. You could also entice a loyal customer with an additional product – known as "cross-selling" – such as a screensaver for a mobile phone. Making recommendations and suggestions throughout the buying experience, right up to checkout, are simple ways to upsell or cross-sell.

CALCULATING CUSTOMER RETENTION RATE

A simple equation can show you, as a percentage, how effective you are at keeping customers. It is known as the customer retention rate or CRR. If your CRR percentage goes down over a particular period, you may have a customer retention problem that will need fixing. If the percentage goes up, you are becoming more successful at retaining customers, and this should be reflected in increased sales.

Customer retention rate (CRR)
S = number of customers at the start of a specific period
E = number of customers at the end of that period
N = number of new customers acquired during that period

$$CRR = \left[\frac{E-N}{S} \right] \times 100$$

Optimizing your customer services

> **Prioritize customer service** and response times. Offer staff bonuses, tied to meeting customer service performance targets.

> **Respond immediately** when a customer makes contact. If something goes wrong, apologize straight away and rectify the problem as soon as possible.

> **Make it easy** for customers to buy from you, with a fast, secure, and flexible payment process. Always be available to answer queries.

> **Use analytics tools**, such as Google Analytics (see pp.212-215), to monitor website and social media interactions and continually learn about customer needs.

> **Set targets** for efficiency and speed in the flow of goods and services and their delivery. When targets are not met, investigate.

"It can cost five times more to attract a new customer, than it does to retain an existing one."

www.forbes.com, 2018

Changing your direction

When business conditions change, you may feel a sense of panic. However, you can use such times to reinvent yourself and to set off in a new, better, direction.

Changing circumstances

Staying alert to early signs of a change in business conditions enables you to take action before it is too late. Change may be dramatic and unexpected or the result of an evolving retail climate, new technology, regulatory updates, or increased competition. General Motors, which led the US auto industry for almost a century, collapsed because it ignored its customers' needs and failed to embrace new technologies and improve quality. As a small business, you may not have huge resources, but this can work to your advantage. You have the benefit of being lean, naturally agile, and able to adjust quickly in the face of change.

Ways of changing

To meet the challenge of a changing environment, you may decide to adapt, to pivot, or to diversify. Adapting means making small changes to your existing business strategy, continually refining your product and sales approach. Pivoting means adopting a new business model or strategy. Diversifying means broadening the scope of your business to offer different types of goods or services. In this example, the owner of a restaurant adapts, pivots, and diversifies in response to three different changes in her business environment.

ADAPT

Rowena adapts to her restaurant being closed during a pandemic by offering home delivery services to customers who cannot get to the restaurant to collect. To widen her customer base, she starts using a popular home-delivery app.

PIVOT

In response to competition from a new restaurant nearby, Rowena converts her restaurant into a cookery school offering classes in fine cuisine. She also posts how-to videos on social media.

TAKEAWAY

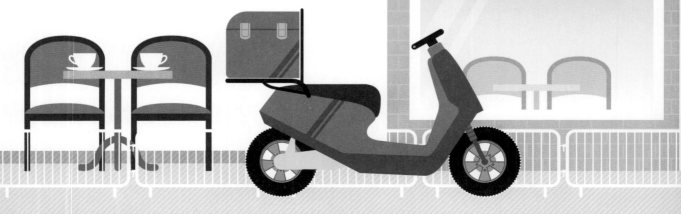

Considering your options

Whatever the cause of the change in the business climate, first address its effect on your business, and then identify any opportunities that it could create. Talk to staff or colleagues, collectively assess your resources, then brainstorm and research ideas to find a solution that is cost-efficient, timely, and meets clearly defined market needs. The solution may require adjustments to your product (adapting), taking a new direction (pivoting), or adding new products (diversifying). Aim to build on what you have already learned rather than starting over from scratch.

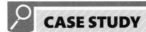

CASE STUDY

Stagekings

In the face of the 2020 coronavirus pandemic, specialist designers of theatre and movie sets, Stagekings, found themselves idle as the Australian entertainment industry closed down. The company responded to the unexpected circumstances by pivoting. They thought about the needs of the millions of office staff now working from home, and deployed their skills to create a range of work-from-home desks.

NEED TO KNOW

❯ **Black swan events** are unexpected changes that could not have been predicted.

❯ **Horizontal diversification** involves replicating your product, such as by opening more stores.

❯ **Vertical diversification** involves taking ownership of a part of your supply chain.

DIVERSIFY

To increase profits in the face of strong competition from other restaurants, Rowena begins to cook and package her delicious sauces, herbs, and flavoured oils. She uses social media to publicize the new range.

"All failure is failure to adapt."

The Art of Winning in an Age of Uncertainty, Max McKeown, 2012

Managing change

Anticipating change and managing it successfully are key to running a business. Take a methodical approach, with clear steps, and you can adapt successfully to new business conditions.

Reasons for change

When you start a business, making any significant changes in the short to medium term may be the last thing on your mind. But external and internal factors can affect what your business offers at any time, so being able to adjust is essential.

For example, new technology or shifting consumer trends could lead to significant rises or falls in demand for your products or services. Alternatively, you might have to comply with new regulations in your industry, set by the government. Or, even more

unexpectedly, an environmental crisis could throw the markets into total chaos.

Planning for change

If you prepare in advance to handle change and put a logical process in place, you will be ready to adapt

Managing the change process

When a business is faced with change, it needs the support and enthusiasm of everyone involved to guarantee a positive outcome. For this to happen, it is important that you, as leader of the business, are open and transparent about why change is happening. Engaging staff, important clients, and any affected business associates, such as suppliers or investors, is also critical. If you actively involve them in the steps you take, they are more likely to support the changes required and contribute to a smooth development of the business.

ASSESS THE CHANGE

Identify the business goals that the change should deliver. Consider how quickly you will need to implement change, whether it will be gradual or sudden, and who it will affect.

OUTLINE THE PLAN

Set out a course of action. List what changes need to occur at each level of the business. Think about what points staff may be resistant to, and how you will address these.

and move forward when the time comes. By providing a clear action plan, "change management" helps to minimize the risk of failure. The media giant Netflix is an example of a business transformed through careful change management. In 2007, after 10 years operating as a DVD rental service, the company moved to digital streaming in response to emerging technology. Netflix managed this change carefully from the outset, with clear communication to its whole workforce, so ensuring a highly successful and lucrative transition.

MAKING IT WORK

Before introducing changes to your business, develop a plan that acknowledges the practical and emotional implications.

Practical action

> **Schedule milestones** at which you can assess the impact of the change and spot potential problems.
> **Review progress** weekly, and keep staff and all stakeholders informed.
> **Remain calm** if change takes longer than expected. A longer wait with the support of employees might be more effective than rushed change.

Emotional awareness

> **Thank your staff** through regular emails and informal meetings.
> **Reinforce** the reasons for change regularly to remind your team why change will make working life better.
> **Reward colleagues** for their service if the change involves letting anyone go, and help them to find new jobs through networking or agencies.

"Where there are changes, there are always business opportunities."

Minoru Makihara, Japanese industrialist, 1996

COMMUNICATE AND ENGAGE

Explain clearly to staff and business associates why change is necessary, how it will affect them day-to-day, and how you will support them. Encourage feedback and answer any concerns.

IMPLEMENT AND EMBED

Introduce changes, following your formal plan. Make sure staff receive any new training or equipment they need. Encourage and motivate staff, giving them recognition for each step of the change achieved.

MONITOR

Set a good example as an engaged and decisive leader of the business and learn from any mistakes – made by you as well as staff. Continue to engage employees, not only during the change period but also in the long term.

Licensing

Once you are up and running, licensing is a way to grow your business. As a licensor, others pay to use your ideas, or as a licensee, you can pay to use other peoples' creative output.

Becoming a licensor

Some entrepreneurs do not sell a tangible product. Instead, they sell the use of their intellectual property (IP) to other parties. IP includes virtual creations, such as designs, music, photographs, illustrations, written text, software, and technical inventions. Under the licensing model, the licensor still owns their IP but allows someone else (the licensee) to use it under agreed terms, for a set period, and in return for a fee. For example, if you create a fictional character, you could sell a license allowing another business to use it, such as in their branding, or to produce merchandising products.

Being a licensee

Licensing gives licensees access to new ideas, concepts, and creations without needing to generate them.

How licensing works

Licensing is a legal agreement between the person who holds the IP (the licensor) and the person or business who uses or sells that intellectual property to a wider market (the licensee). The licensor assigns rights to the licensee for a particular purpose and specifies the territories they can sell in. In return, the licensee pays a fee or percentage of any profits made. A licensee can also use IP as the basis of another product. For example, an illustrator might create an image that they license to a clothing manufacturer who prints it on a T-shirt and sells it (see right).

WHAT CAN I LICENSE?

You can license a range of different kinds of IP, from virtual creations to physical products. For example you may be a software designer who licenses a new program out to universities. You might be a wildlife photographer who licenses your photo collection to a commercial picture agency. Or you may have invented a new gadget, then sell a license to an established company to distribute as part of their range.

STEPS FOR THE LICENSOR

1 Register your chosen product
Before registering your IP, ensure that existing patents and copyrights (see pp.96–97) do not prevent you from developing your ideas.

2 Develop your USP
The more innovative your idea, the more valuable it is to the licensee. Research the market to find out just how unique (see pp. 24–25) your offering is.

3 Identify potential licensees
Investigate who is selling or creating products in the same industry as yours. Visit the websites of trade shows for exhibitor lists to identify contacts to approach.

4 Approach and pitch
Make contact with the potential licensees you identify. Ask permission to send samples and let your idea sell itself.

However, they must have the skills and resources required to make use of the IP, and to fulfil the terms of the license. As such, licensors tend to choose established companies to license to, who are more likely to succeed and generate higher sales.

To be a licensee you generally have to be in a good financial position. You will also need a good track record in your industry, otherwise licensors may not be willing to license to you.

Getting the right licence

IP is protected by law (see pp.96–97) in order to stop others simply copying it without your permission. There are four main types of IP licence. Copyright applies to artistic works such as literature, music, photographs, and website designs; a patent applies to technology; a trademark protects brands, including the logo; whereas a registered design covers the look of a product.

NEED TO KNOW

❱ **Advance** is the payment made from the licensee to the licensor, usually when they sign the licensing agreement.

❱ **Infringement** refers to unauthorized use of someone else's IP, or the making of counterfeit products.

❱ **Licensing agreement** is the contract between licensor and licensee that becomes legally binding once both parties sign.

❱ **Sublicensee** is an extra (third party) licensee appointed by the main licensee. This may be for production or marketing purposes, for example.

❱ **Territories** are the countries or market region in which the licensee will use the licensor's IP.

❱ **Trade secrets** are another kind of IP, usually some type of commercially valuable "know-how" or formula.

STEPS FOR THE LICENSEE

1 Decide which product you want to license
If you lack the resources necessary to develop an idea from scratch, such as an artwork or logo, look for potential licensors in that field or industry.

2 Prepare a profile
Put together a detailed description of your company. Include current products, details about your market, and your manufacturing and production resources.

3 Secure funding
Calculate your expected profit, prepare your accounts, and approach lenders or investors, if needed.

4 Search sources
Look for potential licensors. Explore international licensing exhibitions, patent registers, and agents.

5 Contact preferred licence holder
Gather information from the licence holder to assess how their IP compares against the rest of the market.

6 Determine how successful the product will be
Assess any practical issues around introducing the product into your proposed market area. Prepare the relevant figures for negotiation.

7 Negotiate costs
Agree on an annual fees or royalties with the licensor. Decide who will benefit if you develop the original IP further.

Selling your business

There may come a time when you choose to sell your business. This is likely to be a difficult decision, but with careful planning and research, you can make the process as smooth – and as profitable – as possible.

Organizing the sale

Selling your business depends on you being able to convincingly state why you are selling. You may be retiring, taking up another opportunity, or perhaps splitting with partners and making a fresh start – all plausible reasons that are easy to convey. Be honest with all parties about your finances to encourage trust; if your business has not made a profit, call it a going-out-of-business sale to encourage a quick transaction.

A broker or agent can help to communicate with potential buyers, and identify those who are genuine, especially if your business is large or high value. Seek advice from several brokers, and choose one who gives a realistic valuation. Listen to their views, and consider the sales results of similar businesses that have recently sold, or the cost of those on the market currently, and any local factors that may impact price. For example, if your business is a burger bar and a new university is about to open in the neighbourhood, use this information to support your asking price.

Choosing when to sell

Industry estimates put the average selling time for a business at six months to a year, so it is not worth rushing – advance planning and patience will maximize your chances of success. If potential buyers feel you are desperate to sell you are unlikely to achieve a good price. Seasonal timing may also be important for introducing your listing to the market. For example, an ice-cream business will logically attract more attention in summer than in winter.

Preparing to sell

It is essential that you prepare thoroughly for a commercial sale. Think about how to improve sales revenue well in advance. Decide if you will manage the process yourself or engage a broker. Research your market, prepare financial figures, and develop a pitch. This will set you up with the best chance of attracting a committed buyer.

DUE DILIGENCE

In the world of commercial transactions, "due diligence" is the term used for a review of the financial records of a business. Carried out before a contract is signed, it helps the buyer identify any risks or problems.

> **Ask potential buyers** to sign a non-disclosure agreeement before allowing them access to your business data.

> **Approach the sale** from the buyer's perspective, and prepare an honest analysis of the business.

> **Put together a seller's pack** with all the financial details the buyer will need to make a decision.

> **Identify your business assets**, liabilities, sales, gross profits, rates of return, accounts receivable, and other key accounting measures.

> **Be ready** for any questions from the buyer, and do not attempt to conceal negative information.

50%
of agreed deals never close, as they do not make it through the due diligence stage

Benchmark International, 2020

FOR SALE

1 Valuing the business
> **Calculate the value** of your business. A rough estimate of this would be 3 x annual profit, but this will vary widely, and depend on market conditions and industry norms.
> **Research** the prospects of your market sector and take into account how this might affect your valuation.
> **Be honest about figures**, even if you are losing money.

2 Preparing documents and contracts
> **Compile records** documenting the financial history of the business, and seek advice regarding the tax implications of your sale.
> **List all of the assets** that will be included in the sale.
> **Include** any regulatory certificates and licences for your business premises.

3 Finding a buyer
> **Seek professional help** through a broker, who can provide advice and guide you through the selling process.
> **Continue your involvement** in the sale and actively promote it, even if you are using a broker.
> **Screen potential buyers** to ensure they are genuine.

4 Negotiating an agreement
> **Research your buyer**, and decide on the minimum figure you would accept from them.
> **Discuss the deal structure**, including the payout, and the shares or assets to be transferred.
> **Agree on a handover process**, including what will happen to existing staff.

5 Managing the profits
> **Take time to consider** what you will do with the sale proceeds, rather than spending them straightaway.
> **Set out your financial goals**, such as retirement or paying off debt, and plan for them.

Moving on

It can be difficult to give up a venture you have nurtured from the start, but eventually someone else may need to take over. Start succession planning early so that you are well prepared when you step away.

Choosing a successor

Preparing to hand over control is a challenging task for any business – whether you plan to sell your business, retain ownership but hire someone else to run the operation, or bring in a family member. There could be a number of reasons to seek a successor. You may be ready to retire or want to spend more time on personal projects, or you may have achieved all of your goals and decided to focus your attention on exciting new ventures. If your business is stagnating it could benefit from a transfer of power. Whether you have run out of steam, or are busy with other new projects, succession can provide a chance to find someone with different strengths ready to help expand the business and bring fresh energy and ideas.

Succession planning is not just a task for the end of your career. It should be considered well before retirement. An unexpected event could leave your business without clear leadership, so you need a back-up plan to keep the operation running in your absence, for the benefit of both your employees and family. Consider the shape you would like your business to take when you have moved on. To preserve the value of your business, it is vital that whoever

Handing over

Start the process of handing over control by reviewing your existing leadership practices. Assess the qualities and skills required in a leader for your business, and look within your workforce to see if an existing colleague would make a suitable candidate. Before you approach a potential successor, set a salary level and any benefits you are prepared to offer.

Review the existing leadership

❯ **Establish** who will most be affected by a leadership change.

❯ **Determine** which qualities staff would want to see in their new boss.

Construct a leadership profile

❯ **Reflect on** the attributes required to preserve and develop the business.

❯ **Compile** a profile of skills and experience your successor needs.

Consider the potential candidates

❯ **Consider** leadership potential of existing staff or family members.

❯ **Look beyond** the business if necessary, to find recruits with required skills.

takes over respects what it represents, and has the skills and drive to build on that. Identify staff or family members who show the potential to lead the business. If you feel none have the right abilities, be prepared to look for people beyond the business. Cultivating a successor should be part of the management process.

Stepping back

Ideally, your exit should be planned in stages, giving the new leader a chance to settle in and win the trust of staff and key customers. Step out of the picture gradually, reducing your days in the office, for example, but do not linger too long or your successor may feel hampered by your presence. The timing will depend on the identity of your successor – an existing member of staff who has worked closely with you may need far less time to get up to speed than an outside recruit.

PLANNING YOUR EXIT

An important part of your exit strategy is to plan for how your next venture or retirement will be funded.

> **Start planning** early, when you set up the business.
> **Have an idea** of the milestones you want to reach before you step away, or at what age you would like to retire, and how much capital you would need to fund your next project or desired lifestyle.
> **Get advice** on the tax advantages and rate of return for different types of pensions.
> **Build savings** into the business plan, so that money is regularly paid from the profits into a pension pot and savings accounts.
> **Make a will** to ensure your family are provided for.

42% of the UK's family-run businesses have a succession plan

smallbusiness.co.uk, 2018

Develop your successor's skills

> **Train your successor** in the new skills required, exposing them to all business areas.
> **Provide ongoing mentoring** to build their confidence.

Prepare for the final handover

> **Start to allow** your successor freedom to operate.
> **Phase your exit** if your successor expresses a need for ongoing support.

> **Review and assess** successors's performance before your final exit.
> **Avoid the temptation** to interfere once you have left – let your successor make the key decisions.

Resources

The laws and regulations around running a business are different from country to country. Always check government websites for the latest guidance, and stay informed by using websites and other online resources aimed at small businesses.

Choosing your business name
There are rules that all business names must follow. Make sure that your proposed name meets the requirements of the country you want to register your company in.
UK Outline of the different rules for sole traders and business partnerships
gov.uk/limited-company-formation/choose-company-name
Ireland Irish guidelines for naming a business with link to online service that reserves a proposed name for 28 days.
cro.ie/registration/company/incidental-obligations/company-name
EU Requirements for setting up a European company
europa.eu/youreurope/business/running-business/developing-business/setting-up-european-company
Australia Choosing a business name – what to consider and how to check availability
business.gov.au/planning/new-businesses/how-to-choose-a-business-name
New Zealand How to choose a company name and check its availability
business.govt.nz/getting-started/building-a-brand/choosing-a-business-name

Registering your business name
Check that your proposed name is not too similar to that of an existing business by searching company registers in the relevant country.
UK Company name availability checker
beta.companieshouse.gov.uk/company-name-availability
Digital services of Companies House
gov.uk/government/organisations/companies-house
Ireland Check if your name is available
cro.ie/Services/Company-Search
Companies Registration Office – business name registration
cro.ie/registration/business-name
Australia Check if your name is available
asic.gov.au/online-services/search-asics-registers/#companies
Apply for a business name and register
business.gov.au/registrations/register-your-business-name
New Zealand Reserve a company name and check availability
companies-register.companiesoffice.govt.nz/help-centre/starting-a-company/how-to-reserve-a-company-name
International registrees
gov.uk/government/publications/overseas-registries/overseas-registries

Registering your business
Look up the specific requirements for registering your company. These may differ depending on the structure of your business.
UK Setting up a business
gov.uk/set-up-business
Ireland Required steps to set up a company
cro.ie/registration/company/required-steps
Registering as a sole trader
citizensinformation.ie/en/employment/types_of_employment/self_employment/self_employment_as_an_individual.html
Registering as a limited partnership
cro.ie/registration/limited-partnership
Europe Running a business
europa.eu/youreurope/business/running-business
Australia Business registration service
register.business.gov.au
New Zealand Starting a company
companies-register.companiesoffice.govt.nz/help-centre/starting-a-company
Becoming a sole trader
business.govt.nz/getting-started/choosing-the-right-business-structure/becoming-a-sole-trader
Starting a limited partnership
lp-register.companiesoffice.govt.nz

Setting up non-profit organizations
Non-profit organization may have different set-up requirements to a conventional business, so be sure to research the process and relevant regulations in your country.
UK Setting up a social enterprise: limited companies, charities, cooperatives, community interest groups, sole trader, business partnerships
gov.uk/set-up-a-social-enterprise
Ireland Tax registration form for non-profit organizations
revenue.ie/en/starting-a-business/documents/reg-form-voluntary-non-profit-org.pdf
Australia Starting a not-for-profit organisation
ato.gov.au/non-profit/getting-started/starting-an-nfp
New Zealand Registering a new charity
charities.govt.nz/ready-to-register/starting-a-new-charity

Government finance
There are many grants and schemes available for small businesses. Your business may be eligible to apply for government funding programmes.
UK Finance and support for businesses
www.gov.uk/business-finance-support
Ireland Grants and financial support for small businesses
smallbusinessadvice.ie/government-grants-financial-support-small-business
Europe Funding programmes for businesses and projects
europa.eu/youreurope/business/finance-funding/getting-funding/eu-funding-programmes
Access to finance by country
europa.eu/youreurope/business/finance-funding/getting-funding/access-finance

Australia Grants and programs
business.gov.au/grants-and-programs
New Zealand Grants and help for new businesses
business.govt.nz/how-to-grow/getting-government-grants/grants-and-help-for-your-new-business

Business licences and permits

You may be required to hold a licence or permit to run certain types of business. Check whether you need to apply for one and be aware that licences may periodically need to be renewed.
UK Tool to find out what licences you will need
gov.uk/licence-finder
Directory of licences for events and businesses
gov.uk/browse/business/licences
Ireland List of excises and licenses
revenue.ie/en/companies-and-charities/excise-and-licences/index.aspx
Australia Guided search engine to find the licences needed for your business
ablis.business.gov.au
New Zealand Licences and certificates for businesses
justice.govt.nz/licences-certificates

Business insurance requirements

Insurance can help protect your business and customers. Make sure that you research which types of insurance you will need.
UK Insurance needed by small businesses
companieshouse.blog.gov.uk/2019/04/30/what-insurance-does-a-small-business-need
Ireland Only employer liability and motor vehicle liability is compulsory for businesses in Ireland
citizensinformation.ie/en/money_and_tax/personal_finance/insurance/
Australia Types of insurance to protect your business, customers, and income, including compulsory insurance
business.gov.au/risk-management/insurance/business-insurance
NZ Insuring business activities, types of risk and insurance
business.govt.nz/risks-and-operations/planning-for-the-unexpected-bcp/insurance

Corporation tax

In most countries, businesses are required to pay tax on profits. Be aware that tax laws and corporation tax rates can vary widely from country to country.
UK How to register for corporation tax and file a tax return
gov.uk/corporation-tax
Ireland Overview of corporation tax
revenue.ie/en/companies-and-charities/corporation-tax-for-companies/corporation-tax/index.aspx
EU Index of national rules for corporation tax
europa.eu/youreurope/business/taxation/business-tax/company-tax-eu
Australia List of company tax rates
ato.gov.au/Rates/Company-tax
New Zealand Overview of national tax rates
newzealandnow.govt.nz/living-in-nz/money-tax/nz-tax-system

Sales tax

Make sure that you understand how sales taxes, such as VAT (value-added tax) or GST (goods and services tax), are added to the prices of most goods and services.
UK Businesses and charging VAT
gov.uk/vat-rates
Ireland Index of VAT
revenue.ie/en/vat/index.aspx
EU VAT rules and rates
europa.eu/youreurope/business/taxation/vat/vat-rules-rates
Australia Overview of GST
ato.gov.au/business/gst
New Zealand Guide to GST
ird.govt.nz/gst

Importing and exporting

Familiarize yourself with the export and import laws of any country you wish to trade with.
UK Starting to import, EU and non-EU countries
gov.uk/starting-to-import/importing-from-noneu-countries
Exporting and doing business abroad
gov.uk/starting-to-export
Ireland Guide to importing and exporting
localenterprise.ie/fingal/start-or-grow-your-business/start-a-business/exporting-and-importing
EU Importing into the EU
ec.europa.eu/trade/import-and-export-rules/import-into-eu
Exporting from the EU
ec.europa.eu/trade/import-and-export-rules/export-from-eu
Australia How to import and export
abf.gov.au/importing-exporting-and-manufacturing/importing/how-to-import/requirements
New Zealand Importing and exporting laws
business.govt.nz/risks-and-operations/manufacturing/importing-and-exporting-laws

Intellectual property rights (IP)

Find out how to protect your ideas and innovations, and check that you are not infringing on the intellectual property of others.
UK Trademarks, copyright, design, patents
gov.uk/government/organisations/intellectual-property-office
Search for a trademark
gov.uk/search-for-trademark
Australia Understanding trademarks
ipaustralia.gov.au/trade-marks
Search for a trademark
search.ipaustralia.gov.au/trademarks/search/quick
New Zealand Guide to trademarks
iponz.govt.nz/about-ip/trade-marks
Search for a trademark
iponz.govt.nz/about-ip/trade-marks/search
International World intellectual property office provides a list of all national IP offices
wipo.int/directory/en/urls.jsp

Employment law

Before hiring staff, you must understand the legal implications of taking on employees or contracting freelancers.

UK AtoZ of employing people
gov.uk/browse/employing-people
Ireland Employers' obligations in Ireland
*citizensinformation.ie/en/employment/employment_rights_and_
conditions/employment_rights_and_duties/employer_obligations.html*
EU Labour law and rights at work
ec.europa.eu/social
Australia Fact sheets outlining workplace laws
fairwork.gov.au/how-we-will-help/templates-and-guides/fact-sheets
New Zealand Guide to employment rights
newzealandnow.govt.nz/work-in-nz/employment-rights

Avoiding discrimination in the workplace

As an employer, you have a duty to ensure that discrimination at work is prevented, or is tackled if it occurs.

UK Preventing discrimination
gov.uk/employer-preventing-discrimination
Ireland Overview of the legislation for equality in the workplace
*citizensinformation.ie/en/employment/equality_in_work/equality_in_
the_workplace.html*
EU Combating discrimination in the workplace
ec.europa.eu/social
Australia Guide to preventing discrimination in recruitment
*humanrights.gov.au/our-work/employers/step-step-guide-preventing-
discrimination-recruitment*
New Zealand Protecting people from discrimination
*employment.govt.nz/resolving-problems/types-of-problems/
bullying-harassment-and-discrimination/discrimination*

Health and safety

Ensure that your workplace meets the legal safety requirements set by your government and local authorities.

UK Information and services
hse.gov.uk
Ireland Overview of health and safety at work
*citizensinformation.ie/en/employment/employment_rights_and_
conditions/health_and_safety/health_safety_work.html*
EU Legal basis, legislation, legal policy frameworks
ec.europa.eu/social
Australia Requirements for employers and employees
*business.gov.au/risk-management/health-and-safety/work-health-
and-safety*
New Zealand Workplace safety
worksafe.govt.nz

Wellbeing at work

Check local laws and guidance for promoting wellbeing in your workplace.

UK Definitions, holistic approaches, surveys
cipd.co.uk/knowledge/culture/well-being/factsheet
Ireland Central resource to help businesses manage
health and safety
hsa.ie/eng/business_services_portal

EU Practical guide to wellbeing at work
*osha.europa.eu/en/publications/healthy-workers-thriving-companies-
practical-guide-wellbeing-work/view*
Australia Guide to promoting health and wellbeing
*headsup.org.au/docs/default-source/default-document-library/guide_
to_promoting_health_and_wellbeing_in_the_workplace*
New Zealand Wellbeing policy builder for businesses
business.govt.nz/news/workplace-wellbeing-policy-builder

Trading standards

Consumers and businesses are protected by laws that ensure fair trading. Make sure that you are aware of the regulations in your country, as they can differ greatly.

UK Directory of goods, services, and data protection regulations
gov.uk/browse/business/sale-goods-services-data
Ireland Trading standards information
nsai.ie/standards/about-standards
EU UK European Consumer Centre
ukecc.net
Australia Fair trading and consumer law
business.gov.au/products-and-services/fair-trading
New Zealand Government body for trading standards
tradingstandards.govt.nz

Consumer rights

Familiarize yourself with how national consumer law affects your business.

UK Consumer protection guidance
gov.uk/government/collections/cma-consumer-enforcement-guidance
Ireland How consumer protection laws apply to businesses
*ccpc.ie/business/help-for-business/consumer-protection-law-how-does-
it-apply-to-my-business*
EU Consumer rights directive and guidance on its application
*ec.europa.eu/info/law/law-topic/consumers/consumer-contract-law/
consumer-rights-directive_en*
Australia Guide to consumer laws and guarantees
*business.gov.au/products-and-services/fair-trading/australian-
consumer-law*
New Zealand What consumer law means for business
consumerprotection.govt.nz/guidance-for-businesses

Data protection

You must comply with local data regulations to keep personal data secure.

UK The Data Protection Act
gov.uk/data-protection
Ireland Responsibilities of organisations under data regulations
dataprotection.ie/en/organisations
EU General Data Protection Regulation
*europa.eu/youreurope/business/dealing-with-customers/data-
protection/data-protection-gdpr*
Australia The Privacy Act
oaic.gov.au/privacy/the-privacy-act
New Zealand Personal information and the Privacy Act
*data.govt.nz/manage-data/privacy-and-security/what-is-personal-
identifiable-information-and-the-privacy-act*

Cybersecurity

If your business handles personal data, you have a legal responsibility to protect that data from cyber attacks.

UK Cybersecurity guide for small businesses
ncsc.gov.uk/collection/small-business-guide
Ireland 12 steps to cybersecurity
ncsc.gov.ie/pdfs/Cybersecurity_12_steps.pdf
Europe Security guide for small and medium businesses
enisa.europa.eu/topics/cloud-and-big-data/cloud-security/security-for-smes
Australia How to protect your business from cyber attacks
business.gov.au/risk-management/cyber-security/how-to-protect-your-business-from-cyber-threats
New Zealand Protecting business data
business.govt.nz/risks-and-operations/it-risk-and-avoiding-scams/protecting-business-data

Corporate social responsibility (CSR)

Ensure your business takes responsibility for its impact on society by complying with ethical standards and guidelines.

UK Chartered Institute of Personnel and Development
cipd.co.uk/knowledge/strategy/corporate-responsibility/factsheet
Ireland Links, articles, and downloads relating to CSR
csrhub.ie/csr-resources
EU CSR policies, initiatives, resources
ec.europa.eu/info/business-economy-euro/doing-business-eu/corporate-social-responsibility-csr_en
Australia Corporate social responsibility and human rights
humanrights.gov.au/our-work/corporate-social-responsibility-human-rights

Environmental law

You must follow local environmental standards and laws.

UK Environmental management
www.gov.uk/topic/environmental-management
Ireland Legislation, policy, and funding programmes
citizensinformation.ie/en/environment/environmental_law/
EU Summary of environmental policy
eur-lex.europa.eu/summary/chapter/20.html
Australia Business and environment laws
austrade.gov.au/international/invest/guide-to-investing/running-a-business/understanding-australian-business-regulation/australian-business-and-environment-laws
New Zealand Outline of environmental legislation
mfe.govt.nz/publications/environmental-reporting/state-new-zealand's-environment-1997-chapter-four-environment-4

TEMPLATES AND TOOLS

When setting up your business make use of the numerous resources available online, many of which are free. Search for templates on offer – from business plans, action plans, bookkeeping, and budgeting to contracts and appraisals. Also investigate free software to streamline systems such as accounting or project management, and be aware of how various digital tools, some free, can help your online presence.

Marketing and social media marketing You will need to market your business by email, using a program that can collect opt-ins from your customers. ConvertKit, MailChimp, and Kartra are popular programs that maintain your lists and send emails. If you are selling to consumers, you will need to do social media marketing, too. The program you use for email marketing program may also be able to run social media campaigns, but you should research the benefits of dedicated social media programs such as Hootsuite, Later, or Tailwind.

Market research If you are doing market research, you can use survey programs such as Survey Monkey or Google Forms to collect and organize responses.

Search engine optimisation (SEO) There are many digital tools you can use to make the most of your website, assess its success, and increase its ranking by search engine listings, such as Google Search Console and Moz. Google Analytics is widely used for tracking and reporting on websites, but search online for the wide range of free software, with functions that include:

❯ Measuring traffic and checking if it is converting into action, such as clicks and shares

❯ Finding good keywords and variations of keywords to use on your site

❯ Looking up backlinks and keywords used on competitors' websites

❯ Conducting an SEO audit to see if potential issues are affecting search results for your site, such as broken links

❯ Creating visuals of the data about your website

Search engine advertising Google Ads is an online advertising platform developed by Google, where advertisers bid to display brief advertisements in the results of search engines like Google Search. It is a pay-per-click (PPC) system. Similar systems include Bing Ad or Amazon Ad.

Index

Acknowledgments

Dorling Kindersley would like to thank Fiona Plowman for proofreading; Vanessa Bird for the index; and Emma Kennett, James McAllister, Sally Newall, and Helen Poultney for technical content consultancy; DTP Designer, Rakesh Kumar; Jackets Editorial Coordinator, Priyanka Sharma; and Managing Jackets Editor, Saloni Singh.

Credits

p. 61 Developing your brand, *The Strategic Brand Management*, Jean-Noël Kapferer 1996; **pp.64–65 Marketing mix and 4Ps**, *Basic Marketing: A Managerial Approach*, E. Jerome McCarthy, 1960; 4Cs, "New Marketing Litany: 4Ps Passé C-Words Take Over", B. Lauternborn, 1990; **pp66–67 Sales funnel**, *Financial Advertising*, Elias St Elmo Lewis, 1907; **p.155 SWOT analysis**, *Business Policy, Text and Cases*, Edmund P. Learned, C. Roland Christiansen, Kenneth Andrews, and William D. Guth, 1969; **pp.174–175 TKI conflict model**, Thomas-Kilmann Instrument Conflict Model, Ken Thomas and Ralph Kilmann, 1974, **pp.166–167 SMART goals**, "There's a S.M.A.R.T. Way to Write Management's Goals and Objectives", George T. Doran, 1981; **pp.182–183 The Sand cone model**, "Lasting Improvements in Manufacturing Performance: In Search of a New Theory", Ferdows, K. & De Meyer, A, 1990; **pp.194–195 The Ansoff Matrix, Strategies for Diversification**, Igor Ansoff, 1957

Disclaimer

The information in this book has been compiled by way of general guidance in relation to the specific subjects addressed, but is not a substitute, and not to be relied on for legal, accounting, tax or other professional advice on specific circumstances, and in specific locations. So far as the authors are aware, the information given is correct at the time of going to press in 2020. Practice, laws, and regulations all change, and the reader should obtain up-to-date professional advice on any such issues. The authors and publishers disclaim, as far as the law allows, any liability arising directly or indirectly from the use, or misuse, of the information contained in this book.

Phillips & Leigh, Patent and Trade Mark Attorneys, have reviewed the IP sections of this book for accuracy, but readers should not take these sections as constituting legal advice.

The author and publishers welcome any comments, corrections, or other suggestions for subsequent editions of this work.